Cycling Past Pluto

Slowly Round Britain's Coastline

Cycling Past Pluto

Slowly Round Britain's Coastline

To Wendy, with best wishes
Robert Bluck

ROBERT BLUCK

Copyright © 2025 Robert Bluck

The moral right of the author has been asserted.

Apart from any fair dealing for the purposes of research or private study, or criticism or review, as permitted under the Copyright, Designs and Patents Act 1988, this publication may only be reproduced, stored or transmitted, in any form or by any means, with the prior permission in writing of the publishers, or in the case of reprographic reproduction in accordance with the terms of licences issued by the Copyright Licensing Agency. Enquiries concerning reproduction outside those terms should be sent to the publishers.

Troubador Publishing Ltd
Unit E2 Airfield Business Park
Harrison Road, Market Harborough
Leicestershire LE16 7UL
Tel: 0116 279 2299
Email: books@troubador.co.uk
Web: www.troubador.co.uk

ISBN 978 1 83628 111 5

British Library Cataloguing in Publication Data.
A catalogue record for this book is available from the British Library.

Printed and bound by CPI Group (UK) Ltd, Croydon, CR0 4YY
Typeset in 11pt Minion Pro by Troubador Publishing Ltd, Leicester, UK

In memory of Bernard – who got me started

CONTENTS

	Introduction	ix
1	Gretna to the Grampians – Carlisle to Fort William	1
2	Winterval One: Ravens and Repairs	37
3	The North-West Highlands – Fort William to Thurso	45
4	Winterval Two: Service and Surgery	76
5	Eastern Scotland and Northumberland – Thurso to Sunderland	81
6	Wearside to Humberside – Sunderland to Hull	114
7	Humber, Thames, Dover, Wight – Hull to Southampton	127
8	Summerval: Hill Training	164
9	Solent to Severn – Cycling Past Pluto	169
10	Winterval Three: The Long Delay	203
11	Wales and Lancashire – Cardiff to Lancaster	215
12	The Last Lap – Lancaster to Carlisle	245
	Appendix: Helpful Rules for Coastal Cycling	262
	Acknowledgements and Bibliography	267
	About the Author	271

INTRODUCTION

In the island we call Britain, almost two-thirds of us live less than ten miles from the sea. Could you cycle all the way round this coastline? How far would that be? How long would it take? Could you do it all at once? Or maybe a bit at a time?

This is the story of an epic journey in sections. Two otherwise fairly sensible men – my cycling pal Steve and I – pedalled round the entire coastline of mainland Britain. Unlike younger and fitter cyclists, we're too old to do it all at once. Instead our wives waved us off each June for a fortnight or so. We tried to persuade them to follow us with a campervan to save money, but for some reason they declined.

We began cycling together in 2012, inspired by the London Olympics to get back on our bikes. We rode from Land's End to John O'Groats to raise money for our local hospice, and had a marvellous time. Wherever we stopped, strangers saw the pennants mounted on our bikes, and generously donated money to a charity they had never heard of. After completing LEJOG (that's what cyclists call the end-to-end ride), we set off cycle-camping on the Hebridean Trail from Barra to the tip of Lewis. The extra weight of tents and sleeping bags and camping kit in our panniers slowed us down and wore us out. But we loved cycling in Scotland and vowed to come back. That's when we got the idea of riding right round the coast.

At first it was only going to be cycling round Scotland's coast, from Gretna Green to Berwick. This was much further than we thought. It took three trips to cover the wiggly coastline, with train journeys to and from Carlisle, Fort William and Thurso. (We live in the Tyne valley, so Carlisle and Gretna aren't far away.) When we arrived back in Northumberland, we weren't far short of half-way round the whole mainland coastline! That's when Steve had the mad idea of cycling round England and Wales as well. With two trips in England and one in Wales, we'd only have Lancashire and Cumbria left.

These trips began with detailed planning which didn't always work out in practice. There was some imperfect map-reading and confused route-finding. The carefully-chosen kit felt heavy on the hills. Cycling clockwise meant westerly winds behind us in the north, but in our faces along the south coast. We tried to keep close to the sea, but had to miss out headlands and peninsulas to keep the daily mileage manageable. Our Three Simple Rules of Coastal Cycling soon became ten, and points were awarded (almost always to Steve) for lowering the tone of the conversation.

The variety of the landscape kept surprising us – wild country and urban jungles, deep forests and industrial wasteland, flat farmland and Scottish mountains. We found Britain's bumpiest road and hills so steep we had to walk, riding through places we'd never heard of, with extremes of poverty and wealth. We met unusual people, stayed in wonderful guest houses and Scotland's worst hotel. There was a long-running competition for the perfect cheese scone and the best carrot cake.

Britain's coastal history has many memories of heroism and tragedy at sea. Once-prosperous fishing villages and tourist resorts have declined through overfishing and railway closures. The coast itself is always changing: silt deposits leave ancient ports high and dry, and erosion topples houses over cliff edges. Mainland Britain has more coastline than you think. The shortest LEJOG route is 840 miles, but by the time we arrived back in Carlisle we had completed almost 5,000 miles – mostly on minor roads and traffic-free cycle tracks. As the crow flies, this is almost as far as London to Los Angeles – or like cycling from Madrid to Moscow *and back again*. Ours is the ninth largest island in the world, and probably has the wiggliest coastline.

As well as the invaluable Rules for Coastal Cycling, you'll find helpful information scattered through the book about the perfect touring bike, how to dry your kit in a B&B, what to take on tour, and how to lose weight. The importance of winter training and regular bike servicing is underlined, and the whereabouts of Britain's most spectacular hill climb and Britain's worst road are revealed. (It's good to know in advance about both of these.)

There were several earlier titles for this book. It started as *The End of Every Road*, but this would double the distance. *Britain's Longest Bike Ride* seemed too daunting.

What made it possible for us was riding *Two Weeks at a Time* – but you might want to tackle the coastline differently. And you probably won't be riding *Clockwise from Carlisle* as we were. As for *Cycling Past Pluto*, which might seem a bit obscure – you'll have to read the book to find out.

Two earlier books about cycling round Britain gave me helpful tips. Mike Carter (*One Man and His Bike*) and Anna Hughes (*Eat Sleep Cycle*) both began in London, cycling round *anti*-clockwise on their own, in a single journey taking a whole summer. They both got exhausted and their bikes needed serious repairs. Anna often cycled 75 miles or more in a day – once over 100 – which was way beyond us. They took too much kit and too few maps – and they both missed out big sections of the fantastic Scottish coastline.

Mike was 45 when he cycled round Britain, and Anna a mere 28. By the time we finished, I was as old as both of them put together! If I can do it, anyone can – given reasonable fitness, a decent bike, and some free time. You can start at any railway station. You can do it one week at a time, though this will double your rail fares, unless you have a patient partner with a campervan. You don't have to be young and fit: you can be older and a little overweight and *still cycle round Britain*. Why not follow in our tyre tracks and ride your own journey round part of our wonderful coastline – or even all of it?

1

GRETNA TO THE GRAMPIANS – CARLISLE TO FORT WILLIAM

DAY 1   HOME TO CASTLE DOUGLAS   (68 MILES)

'You've cycled from *where*? From *Carlisle*? That's *miles* away!'

The café owner brings us coffee and cake. She can hardly believe that people our age could pedal forty miles before lunch. Steve tells her this is normal for us and her eyebrows shoot up again. She looks genuinely astonished.

We can't help feeling a little intrepid. Sitting in the Caerlaverock Castle tea room, looking out at the triangular red-sandstone ruins, it feels like a bit of an adventure already. We hopped onto an early train to Carlisle, hoping this time we wouldn't get lost. We've had difficulties finding our way out of this small, well-signposted city, which has a series of underpasses to confuse cyclists. But today we were soon over the bridge across the River Eden, and heading north-west towards the Solway Firth on a bright spring morning.

A newish section of National Cycle Network (NCN 7) on a minor road alongside the M6 saved us a winding detour via Longtown, and brought us to Gretna, twelve miles from Carlisle – where we got lost. Gretna Green is not in Gretna, but a little way to the north. The famous blacksmith's shop – where young lovers could run away to get married in Scotland – must have been close by, but we didn't see it.

After a confused meander, we re-joined NCN 7 and headed off west, passing a garage with a tartan microbus. Bonnie Scotland! The weather was cool but sunny, and we paused for coffee at the Devil's Porridge Museum at Eastriggs, where there was a huge munitions factory during the First World War. We were tempted to look round, but thought we'd better press on.

Cycling through Annan, Steve reminded me that until 1935 there was a railway bridge running south across the Solway Firth from here to Bowness. Both ends of this dismantled line are marked on the map, only a mile or so apart, but the bridge has gone. There'll be 5,000 miles of cycling before we can look across from Bowness to Annan. Let's not think about that on Day One.

Our first close-up view of the sea at Powfoot was very pretty – the village was created as an eighteenth-century sea-bathing resort. Today's holiday camp road looked like a dead end, but NCN 7 emerged at the other end and back onto a minor road. Sustrans signs are excellent – as long as you look out for them.

The tiny village of Ruthwell boasts the world's first savings bank, created in 1810 by local minister Dr Henry

Duncan, and celebrated by the Savings Bank Museum in a cottage next door. It was closed this morning – perhaps for stocktaking – so we rode on to Caerlaverock, past a nature reserve and bird sanctuary, and turned off for the castle and tea room. Excellent scones!

Is that admiration or pity on the woman's surprised face? We have to get going again. A couple of miles further on, dark clouds appear on our right. A sudden deluge sweeps across the road in front of us, and we dive under the trees on a side track. No time to look for our waterproof kit – we're soaked to the skin in seconds. All we can do is stand here, as the trackside gutter turns into a little brown river. Passing cars throw sheets of water up from the road, turning the B725 into what looks more like a tidal estuary.

It's half an hour before the rain begins to ease off and we decide to press on, plodding back to the road with heavy waterlogged socks. Back on the bike, water splashes up from the road to replace that squeezing out of my shoes. Each car throws a little bow-wave across at us. But you can only get so wet and no wetter.

Everything is still very damp as we arrive in Dumfries. We hide under a bridge, miss the NCN turn, and cycle back in the rain to find it again. (Gretna and Dumfries – shall we get lost twice each day?) Then we're off the main road onto a disused railway line, beautifully tarmacked by Sustrans. The coast road here is the A710 which looks busy, so we feel justified in popping inland for a while.

This brings up the question of The Rules. Who needs rules? It's simple on an island. Going clockwise, keep turning left towards the sea. All we need is **Rule One: Keep to the Coast**. Hang on, that means some dangerous trunk roads. A week after Steve and I finished LEJOG, two lads were killed by a lorry on the A30 in Cornwall. Let's avoid the dual carriageways, even if it means coming inland. So we can add **Rule Two: Avoid Major Roads**. This overrides Rule One, unless a short bit of main road saves a huge detour. What about those tiny roads which only lead to a farm? Cycling down each of these (and back again) would add hundreds of miles to the route. So we arrived at **Rule Three: Ignore Dead-end Roads**. There you have it, the three rules. Keep to the coast where you can, avoiding major roads and roads that lead you nowhere. If only it were that simple.

Another fifteen miles on gently undulating minor roads brings us into Castle Douglas, via the oddly-named Haugh of Urr. Haugh of Urr wants to go cycling, but the other Haugh just wants to get warm and dry.

Apart from the deluge, this isn't a bad first day. I planned 65 miles, but we've done 68, so Steve is teasing me. On LEJOG there were a few navigational alternatives – I hesitate to call them mistakes or map-reading errors – which added a mile or two here and there. Steve christened these 'Bluck Miles'. I said getting lost was surely a joint effort, but he replied: 'You've got the maps, not me.' He carries the bike tools and I take the maps. Unless something goes wrong with the bikes – which it almost never does – he can't lose any points. But I'm exposed to ridicule every time I fail to find the exact route. It's so unfair.

Vegetarian food in Scotland is not always the most original, so I was pleased to be offered a choice at the pub. Sadly their idea of vegetable curry was vegetables with a sachet of warm curry sauce poured over them. It wasn't as bad as it sounds.

DAY 2   CASTLE DOUGLAS TO WIGTOWN   (55 MILES)

Porridge for breakfast! Served with fruit – bananas, strawberries and blueberries – delicious! Slow-release carbohydrates – better for the digestion than any fried food.

We set out in good sunshine, a little hazy but with no threat of rain. (That's what we thought yesterday.) It's only eleven miles into Kirkcudbright, but we find an early coffee there anyway. You never quite know when the next café will turn up. The excellent NCN 7 leads south again, with the Dee estuary on our left, then inland for a few miles, through Borgue and back down to the coast at Kirkandrews. A roe deer leaps up and bounds away across a field of long grass.

There are little islands ahead of us in Wigtown Bay. As we draw level with Barlocco Isle, peculiar buildings appear on our right. This looks like a ruined church, with crosses in the stone work and a huge square tower. Roof slates are missing, timbers rotten or askew. It's an odd mixture of Victorian gothic and Scottish baronial, almost like a little monastery. There's no signal here on Steve's phone, so we're left with a mystery to sort out later.

Another few miles brings us into Gatehouse of Fleet – an eighteenth-century town divided in two by the Water of Fleet – for a delicious lunch in the new deli on the main street, with a dozen swifts wheeling noisily round the town centre rooftops.

The A75 coast road to Creetown is a major trunk route, so we apply Rule Two and head out north on NCN 7 along the B796. A gentle climb up into the Fleet Valley is the best part of the day, seven miles through woodland and moorland, with the Water of Fleet on our right. We pass Nether Rusko, Upper Rusko and New Rusko – little more than single dwellings – before passing Gatehouse Station, home to a now-dismantled railway. After traversing a long flat area, we descend alongside the Moneypool Burn towards Creetown, a thriving port in the nineteenth century. Rusko Road becomes much steeper, and we flash past the Gem Rock Museum in the Old School, too quickly to stop and examine its collection of 'rose quartz, amethyst… and other gems from around the world'. Perhaps I'll make a list of interesting places we almost visited.

After a long climb on the NCN7, partly on the disused railway, we're relieved to drop down again into Newton Stewart. We walk into a time-warp café with 1950s crooners on the juke box. Nat King Cole serenades *Mona Lisa* and Andy Williams glides down *Moon River*.

One of the three elderly men at the next table turns towards us.

'Where are you off to, lads?'

'Wigtown.'

'You'll not get to Wigtown tonight…somebody's pinched your bikes!'

The other two roar with laughter. We finish our coffees as Perry Como launches into *Magic Moments*.

Steve is amused by the music, but I remember it from the fifties – I'm nine years older than him – and I didn't like it even then.

We're reluctant to leave NCN 7, which we've followed for 108 miles from Carlisle, but it turns inland here and we need to head south along the coast. The last nine miles, on flattish country to the west of the widening River Cree, seem endless. We're not tired and it's only 55 miles today, but the last hour stretches on and on. This sets off a rambling discussion about whether time is relative, and what would happen if we cycled round the equator in different directions (if there weren't oceans to cross). By the time this peters out we are almost in Wigtown.

Our B&B is a substantial Victorian house. The owner appears in a T-shirt bearing the single word *Yorkshire*.

Steve: Yorkshire! Where in Yorkshire are you from?

Owner: Redcar.

Steve: Redcar! Me too!

They are of similar age, and plunge into their joint memories of growing up in Redcar and going to the same school. I tell them I spent fifteen years in Leeds, and they look at me as if I'm from Norway.

Steve googles the strange building we passed this morning. Not a monastery, but an Edwardian dairy known as Corseyard Farm. The original owner was James Brown – no, not the godfather of soul – who must have been a wealthy eccentric. The locals teased him and called it the Coo Palace. There are plans to restore the buildings as luxury apartments, but nothing is happening yet. Steve wants to buy it when he wins the lottery – when the cows fly past to their palace. (We later discover that restoration is in progress – and it becomes a posh holiday complex with 26 apartments and an indoor swimming pool.)

We eat at Craft, a burger and real ale bar, with the best veggie-burger I have ever tasted. Yummy! Near the harbour a signboard reveals that Wigtown was not always friendly and tolerant. In 1685 two women Covenanters who refused to change their religious allegiance were tied to stakes in the salt marshes in front of us, and left to drown in the rising tide. On the quayside we find an oystercatcher's nest, which reminds me about today's birdlife. We've seen swifts and swallows, house martins and sand martins, wheeling round above the water. The messengers of summer.

Our 55 miles today is exactly as planned. Shouldn't this be credited in some way? A mile or two in the bank for each day I get right? Steve will have none of this.

Tone-Lowering Points have been particularly prolific today. It started on the very first day we went out cycling together. We were pedalling along and discussing how to make the world a better place, promoting peace between nations, developing renewable energy, and radiating compassion and goodwill towards politicians and all other living beings. A few miles along the road we passed a young woman, and Steve made a comment which lowered the tone of the conversation. I won't repeat what he said – mercifully out of earshot of the young woman – to the effect that he would welcome a chance to get to know her better. I promptly awarded him the very first Tone-Lowering Point (TLP). Since then I monitor his comments for unsuitable remarks which might be considered sexist, offensive to the Scots or Welsh, randomly obscene, or otherwise inappropriate.

In the early days I awarded Steve several TLPs on each ride, even in rural areas. Now we can have a whole morning with none – though he sometimes makes up for this at lunchtime. Perhaps my restraining influence has improved his vocabulary and choice of topics for discussion. Or he only *thinks* the comments now. Or maybe my hearing is going.

Very occasionally, Steve will attempt to award *me* a TLP. This is only when he leads me astray and I make some unguarded and wholly innocent comment which he twists into another meaning entirely, perhaps when we are passing a field of sheep. By now you will understand why I considered calling this book *He's Not with Me*. Today I had to award a dozen TLPs. He kept on and on about…. no, I'd better not go into details.

DAY 3   WIGTOWN TO STRANRAER   (60 MILES)

Today is overcast, and we begin with a gentle ride into Garleston, whose harbour fails to impress Steve. Soon we reach Isle of Whithorn – a village rather than an island – at the end of the Machars peninsula. The community-run café and shop is a fine example of how to do things – light and airy, friendly staff, good coffee and scones. And Steve likes the harbour, which looks exactly like the other one.

Steve is a keen and very experienced sailor, who teaches people to sail, and trains instructors to teach other people to sail. Just looking at choppy water make me feel queasy. He and I come from different backgrounds. Steve's a gritty northerner from Redcar, with a degree in maths and computing, and after a long career in IT he now works as a freelance web designer. I'm a soft southerner from Hertfordshire, with degrees in English and Religious Studies, now retired from work in academic libraries and Open University teaching. I can just about make calls on my mobile phone.

As an avowed atheist, Steve finds it hard to think of any good that religion has ever done. (Setting aside a spiritual life, I have reminded him about religion's pivotal role in centuries of education and charitable work across the world, and the wonders of religious architecture, painting, sculpture and music. All to no avail.) He's a Sci-Fi addict who can't stand Shakespeare and thinks poetry is a waste of time. Steve and his wife Julie are Dog People with a succession of border collies. I've been a Buddhist for many years. (Most Buddhists are also atheists, but let's not dwell on that for too long in a book about cycling round Britain.) I can't stand Sci-Fi, but love Shakespeare and have been known to write and publish poems. My wife Caroline and I are Cat People.

There are things Steve and I have in common (apart from being atheists). We both went to grammar school and then to northern redbrick universities. We're both married, neither couple has children, and we're both left of centre politically. And our homes are a mile and a half apart, which is convenient for days out cycling.

Out of Whithorn, we take a signposted left turn out of the village, up a steep hill, and ride for a couple of miles with the road surface getting worse. Suddenly we're in a large holiday camp. The road goes round in a loop and brings us back to the entrance. Ten minutes later we're back in

Isle of Whithorn, staring at the same signpost. Four miles wasted! The signpost was poorly aligned, turned round by a local wit, or just possibly misunderstood by both of us. How many extra miles will we have to cycle if we do four more than planned every day?

The sun comes out, brightening the day and our mood. We take off long-sleeved tops, but then re-enter the same coastal mist we left an hour ago. We glide down towards Port William, which looks less active and alive than I remember, perhaps because the tide is right out. (Mike Carter's rear wheel gave way in Port William for the *third* time, but he had ridden anti-clockwise from London. We're completely free of mechanical problems so far – but it's only Day Three.)

Now we fly along the A747. *I'm cy-cling, on a jet plane.* Did Mr Boeing come from round here and name the plane after the road? The scenery is pleasant enough – bushes and rocky shoreline on one side, bushes and sloping woodland on the other – but it doesn't change much for about an hour. Perhaps we're in a kind of time-loop. If I see that big rock again I'll start worrying.

We drift into the village of Glenluce, hoping for a café, but the place is dead or dying, with boarded-up hotels and shuttered shops for sale. Instead of riding up the valley to Glenluce Abbey to avoid a stretch of the A75, we find a brand-new bike route alongside the trunk road. Safe but noisy. When it peters out we find our own way along minor roads into Stranraer, the railhead for the ferry to Larne in Northern Ireland.

We're booked for two nights into a former manse, huge and impressive, and we have a room each. Sharing is OK – we're used to it by now and there are few singles to be had – but privacy is also good. Today's mileage is 60 from an estimated 58, generously within Steve's limits.

DAY 4   MULL OF GALLOWAY   (70 MILES)

There's been overnight rain and more forecast, so we set off in our wet kit. It's quite chilly, so waterproof jackets and overshoes are a good idea anyway. We leave our panniers and luggage in the B&B, and the bike feels a good bit lighter.

After an easy ride through Sandhead, we continue along the almost deserted A716 down the east coast, which for tourists promises 'sandy beaches and a softer landscape'. Softer than what? We reach Drummore – Scotland's most southerly village, whose isolation once encouraged smuggling – and turn inland for the last five miles to the Mull of Galloway, on an increasingly narrow road. At the very end, near the lighthouse, we park the bikes next to a turf-roof building which looks familiar. Caroline and I came here some years ago and weren't impressed with the café or its tartan-related souvenirs. It feels a lot more welcome after two hours cycling!

The building has a spectacular location on the edge of the cliffs, and a massive pair of chained binoculars invite you to survey Ireland. Sadly it's misty and there is no view of Ireland or anything else out at sea.

We head back through a rolling agricultural landscape to find Port Logan, on the west coast of this narrow peninsula. On a brighter day it would look more attractive. Nearby is Logan Botanic Garden, 'packed with exotic trees and flowering plants' from all over the world. We add this to the list of places we almost visited. Another hour and a half brings us into Port Patrick for a late lunch with superb sandwiches – hummus and chargrilled vegetables, very Mediterranean.

A long afternoon on the B738, winding round above the coast. Several dead-end roads may lead down to wonderful coves or sandy beaches, but we remember Rule Three and ignore them. A signpost reads 'Corsewall Lighthouse 3' but three miles later the turn is marked 'Lighthouse 2'. That's close enough. We turn back towards what passes for the main road.

The ride into Stranraer along the main A718 is not very exciting, but the tide is in, and we see a pair of shelduck, several cormorants, and a group of seven male eiders with a couple of swans. Our 70 miles today was almost exactly nine to five, including two stops, so we are feeling pleased with ourselves, though we both felt tired during the last hour, even without panniers. This could be age-related. I estimated 72 so should be able to claim two Bluck Miles back. No chance.

DAY 5 STRANRAER TO AYR (65 MILES)

Today's forecast is rain, but the morning looks fine. We have an easy start along a footpath beside the busy A75. At Castle Kennedy we turn off on a minor road following the Southern Upland Way to New Luce. This is a lovely ride up into the hills beside the Cross Water of Luce, and the railway from Stranraer to Girvan, with fine open country and big hills in the distance. We pass Glenkitten Fell and

Miltonise, which might mean turning a narrative into high-sounding blank verse.

Gliding down through nondescript forestry, we follow Cross Water (a different one) to Barrhill and the A714. After Pinwherry we turn off right to avoid Girvan, though it's on the coast. Soon we're following the fragrant River Stinchar on a beautiful run up the valley into Barr, where the community café and shop is happily open on Sunday for a sandwich and coffee.

Higher up we reach tiny South Balloch and North Balloch, on opposite sides of the infant River Stinchar. Here we re-join NCN 7, which has cut across from Newton Stewart through the Glentrool Forest. We considered coming all the way on this route, but it would have been cheating to miss out Stranraer and the Mull of Galloway.

The road winds up steeply to over a thousand feet, in and out of more forestry, before descending towards Maybole, which has boarded-up shops and houses and a gloomy air about it. (The Scottish government has its work cut out here.) The next half-dozen miles are very hilly, almost as if put there deliberately as some kind of test. The drizzle turns into proper rain, another steep uphill pull comes into view, and we're both feeling weary by mid-afternoon.

Slower and slower we go, until we crest the ridge of Brown Carrick Hill, just over six hundred feet, and plunge down alarmingly towards the A719. I'm not usually scared on descents, but this one is narrow and twisting, with gravel on the road. Slow down, you imbecile! The busy main road leads us into Ayr, birthplace of John Macadam, he of tarmac fame. Ayr was once western Scotland's main port, but has now turned into a large and active marina, with miles of sandy beaches and the inevitable 'seaside amusements.'

It's extremely wet as we find our way through the town to the guest house, where we are made very welcome, and the owner recommends where to eat. Soon the rain stops, we are showered and dry, and we can wander a little way into town for an excellent meal at a new Thai restaurant.

DAY 6   AYR TO GREENOCK   (60 MILES)

Our day begins with an easy run up the coast from Ayr through Prestwick and into Troon, where posh Victorian houses look out over *five* golf courses, including the Royal Troon, which has often hosted the Open Championship. I can't help thinking golf courses would make wonderful parklands for their local communities.

A few miles on we pass through Irvine, and ride past the Scottish Maritime Museum, which 'traces shipbuilding history from the driftwood craft of the Isles to the steamships of the Clyde', and is almost certainly fascinating. I'm losing track of the museums we failed to visit.

At Kilwinning we wave goodbye to NCN 7 and head west on the short NCN 73 to Ardrossan, where we caught the ferry to Arran last year, en route to the Hebrides. Ardrossan still looks half asleep. There's a path along the main road to West Kilbride, but we're going slowly after yesterday's hilly exertions, and feeling apprehensive about the rest of the day. It looks like twenty miles on the A78 trunk road. However, there's either a wide tarmac footpath or a diversion along minor roads for most of the way into Largs. We resort to the main carriageway for some of the time, but the traffic isn't too bad. It's overcast, with only occasional views across to the two Cumbrae Islands, known locally as Big Cumbrae and Wee Cumbrae.

Beyond Largs we find minor roads leading to Wemyss Bay and then to Inverkip, a village with a history of witchcraft and smuggling, and more recently a vast power station – now demolished – and a large marina. Beyond Inverkip NCN 75 takes over again, with views across the Firth of Clyde to Dunoon, only two miles away. We won't get there until the day after tomorrow, due to the wiggliness of the Scottish coastline.

The cycle route brings us safely into Greenock. The town was once famous for the herring trade and shipbuilding, with extensive docks, and is the birthplace of James Watt, who patented the steam engine as early as 1769. There's a James Watt dock, lecture hall and library. No, we didn't see any of them.

It's still overcast, with a couple of sharpish showers. We've cycled through some tired-looking coastal towns not looking their best today, with listless people hanging around. Riding through some of these places makes me want to get out the other side as soon as possible.

At the Holiday Inn in Greenock our bikes get their own meeting room to stay in overnight. Steve and I discuss our bikes quite a bit on our rides. Maybe they'll talk about us while we're having a meal.

Red bike: That Steve, he's so good to me, keeps me nice and clean, does the service himself, looks after me properly.

Black bike: Robert knows nothing about bikes, he can barely fix a puncture. My chain's always filthy. I don't mind the bike shop for my service, at least they know what they're doing. But it's not so personal is it?

We order a meal in the bar, which is a big mistake. Despite several reminders it is *one hour* before my fish and chips arrive – and the fish has not been fully warmed up from frozen. Where is Steve's meal? Fifteen minutes later both meals are finally served with a series of excuses. There's a queue, they're busy, there's only Helen on in the kitchen. If any of this is true, why not tell us earlier? We could have been out and fed and back again by now. This is a real low point, and we're struggling to see the funny side. I email a complaint to Holiday Inn Customer Service, but get no reply.

DAY 7   GREENOCK TO STRACHUR   (70 MILES)

An early start with a long day in prospect, and a surprisingly hilly ride through Greenock and Port Glasgow, with an odd mixture of surroundings. One minute we're crawling up a steep road in a housing estate, then we're out into farmland, with cows grazing and a good view across the Clyde in the sunshine.

We leave NCN 75 and find minor roads leading through Bishopton towards the Erskine Bridge. Suddenly we're 180 feet above the Clyde river, with a grand view in all directions. Although the bridge is made from 30,000 tons of concrete and steel, including a safe cycle track, it's scary to have motorway traffic roaring past a few feet away. A couple of miles upriver on our right is Clydebank, site of the famous John Brown shipyard, where the great Cunard ships were built – *Lusitania* and *Mauritania*, and then in the 1930s *Queen Mary* and *Queen Elizabeth*. In their heyday Clyde shipyards built one-fifth of world shipping, but the last one closed in 1971. The magnificent Titan crane remains as a reminder of an industry destroyed.

On the far side of the Erskine Bridge we re-join NCN 7 for a quiet run along the north bank of the Clyde, close to the busy main Dumbarton Road, but on a super route in a convenient strip of woodland, alongside the road but sheltered from it.

Dumbarton goes way back. St Patrick, who introduced Christianity into Ireland, was born here in 373, and in the sixth century this was the capital of the Kingdom of Strathclyde, which stretched from Lancashire right up to Loch Lomond. We think of England and Scotland as separate countries, and it is odd to learn that Dumbarton and Lancaster were part of the same kingdom a thousand years before the 1707 Act of Union. Nationalists please note!

Turning inland, we follow the River Leven north on a winding off-road path. I know we should continue along the coast to Helensburgh and Garelochhead and cycle round the Roseneath peninsula, but this would mean a long ride on main roads, so we take the Loch Lomond route instead. The map shows a local bike route along the A82 to Tarbert, but it's mostly on the pavement right beside the trunk road. Safe enough, but neither quiet nor relaxing. Cars and lorries roar past us, but there are spectacular views of Ben Lomond across the loch.

At Tarbert we take the A83 for Arrochar, with quite a bit of traffic, and a fine hard ride up Glen Croe to the aptly-named Rest and Be Thankful. I like this idea of helpful names. Several Scottish towns could be called Don't Bother to Stop Here. (There's also a village in Perthshire called Dull, which has been twinned with Boring, Oregon. I'm not making this up.) We notice the old military road below us on the left, which would have been a much quieter route, if only we had spotted the turn. Steve promised a fast descent on the other side, freewheeling downhill for miles, but it's windy today, and we have to pedal to keep going. Pedalling downhill is against the laws of nature.

At the bottom a much quieter A815 hugs the coast of Loch Fyne towards Clachan Strachur, where we ride back and forth a bit to find the farmhouse B&B. Eventually we realise we've cycled past it, turn around and see a large sign on the side of the house. I'm sure that wasn't there half an hour ago.

It's too far to walk to the Creggan Inn, so we jump on the bikes in our 'evening clothes' – a T-shirt and lightweight walking trousers for me – and have an excellent meal accompanied by pints of Jarl, Scotland's prize-winning real ale. Sampling local beers is one of our ride's highlights, and there's a wobbly return along the path to the B&B. A long day with an extra four miles on the 66-mile estimate, and some further teasing about Bluck Miles.

DAY 8   STRACHUR TO TIGHNABRUAICH   (61 MILES)

'Where are you off to today?' asks the friendly woman serving us breakfast.

'Tighnabruaich.'

'Tighnabruaich? What? Over the mountain?' She rolls her eyes and returns to the kitchen. Surely it can't be that bad.

It's wet as we set off, following the A815 through the Glenbranter Forest and half way along Loch Eck, which sounds like a Yorkshire exclamation. *Loch Eck, it's steep up there, lad.* And so it was, uphill through the drab forestry, but only five hundred feet or so – not much of a mountain – and then down to sea level and Ardentinny, on the west side of Loch Long. Are the inhabitants called Ardentinnians? Don't talk about the Falklands War.

It's good weather for ducks today, with plenty of eiders on the rocky shoreline, one pair with half a dozen fluffy eiderlings swimming around. Further on an oystercatcher sits on a wall by the road and gawps at us cycling past three feet away from him, while another pecks and screams.

We round Strone Point and turn west into Holy Loch, named either as ancient sacred site, or when a ship sank here with its cargo of earth from the Holy Land, intended as a foundation for Glasgow Cathedral. More recently it became the base for American Polaris submarines – a friend has been arrested here several times during anti-nuclear protests – but it was closed in 1992.

Dunoon, a resort for over two hundred years, now

offers 'every conceivable amusement, entertainment and shop to the visitor', and we find a good café for a stop. The owner repeats the breakfast questions in the same tone of voice.

'Tighnabruaich? Over the mountain?'

Ah, the mountain is still in front of us. I know we should cycle south from Dunoon, along the Firth of Clyde, round the corner opposite Rothsay and up the east side of Loch Scriven, where the road ends and you have to ride the same fifteen miles back into Dunoon. But Rule Three says we don't have to. Life's too short.

Instead we ride back north and take the NCN 75, leading west on the B836 along the Little Eachaig River and into Glen Lean. There are some steep pulls up through the forestry, but where's this mountain? Past Loch Tarsuin we glide down to sea level again at the head of Loch Striven – and the road disappears into the sky. An eight-hundred-foot ascent in only a mile or so, an average gradient of 1 in 7. It may not be a mountain, but it certainly takes the wind out of us.

Eventually we're down at sea level again, skirting round the head of Loch Riddon or Loch Ruel – don't they know what to call it? After more hilly NCN 75 riding on the A8003 through fine natural woodland, we find ourselves in Tighnabruaich. It's only 49 miles from Clachan Strachur and we are both whacked. The mountain was on the edge of the map, which I think was deliberately confusing.

Despite being tired, we cycle another twelve miles round the southerly loop towards Ardlamont Point, past the sailing centre and campsite which Steve and Julie often visit. This loop only takes an hour, probably because it's flat and we know there's no more to come.

Five people are chatting in the pub when we order a meal. One woman is clearly drunk and very loud. She and her husband – also a bit the worse for wear – sit up at the bar, while the other three (two giggly women and a quiet man) are on bench seats next to us. They really are noisy, shouting across the bar to each other. We look at each other, roll our eyes and tuck into our fish and chips.

Then all five of them stand up and walk out, one woman leaning on her husband. The barman explains – they're all from the Isle of Man, and have come here to scatter their mother's ashes. Suddenly they're changed from loud-mouthed drunken tourists to grieving brothers and sisters drowning their sorrows. We feel ashamed to have thought ill of them.

My back tyre has been slowly subsiding. I pumped it up twice yesterday and four times today. This fills me with gloom – I hate bike repairs. It's probably a leaky valve rather than a puncture, but that's no consolation, it still needs fixing. Outside the B&B it's swarming with midges as I upend the bike and wrestle with the rear wheel. Why is it always the complicated one? Eventually I swap the inner tube over, prise the tyre back on, and fit the bloody wheel back onto the bloody bike. Steve points out that the back of my shirt is covered in midges, so I rip it off and run around shaking it and shouting obscenities. Regaining a little composure, I put the shirt back on, hoping that nobody has witnessed my half-naked anti-midge rant, apart from Steve, who is grinning inanely at me.

DAY 9   TIGHNABRUAICH TO LOCHGILPHEAD (73 MILES)

The B&B is advertised as Janet and Ronald MacDonald (names are changed to protect the innocent and the guilty), but only himself is in evidence, offering us packets of obscure health food to augment our breakfast cereal.

'They're the wife's stuff', he explains mysteriously.

We stick to Alpen and Corn Flakes. Who has she run off with? Is she buried under the patio? Perhaps she is with her dying mother in Glasgow. We don't like to ask.

In a midge-infested garage, Steve kindly adjusts my brakes. I'm a useless mechanic. Then we're away. I offer a silent prayer to the patron saint of incompetent cyclists, if there is one, hoping the back tyre is now properly fixed.

We set off in the drizzle on the B8000, heading north towards Clachan Strachur again. Uphill into forestry drizzle, downhill to Otter Ferry and coastal drizzle, along the east shore of Loch Fyne – hilly drizzle on the right and lochy drizzle on the left, but intermittent rather than continuous. We take almost three hours to reach Strachur in a long stint of 28 miles. This is less fun than I imagined.

After a welcome coffee stop, Steve is off like a rabbit, and I follow as best I can. There was a time when he couldn't keep up with me, despite being nine years younger. But things are changing. Eighteen miles in an hour and a half, pushing solidly along the A83. As we cross the River Aray on a little humpback bridge with stone balusters, there on the right is the magnificent

Scots-baronial frontage of Inveraray Castle, all towers and turrets and castellations. We pull into Inverary for a late lunch, after some hard work along the main road. At least it's at sea level and flat.

Then we continue along the west shore of Loch Fyne, which is sometimes obscured by forestry and mist, passing the Auchindrain open air museum of Scotland's rural history – another one missed – and after another 24 miles on the dreaded A83 we arrive in Lochgilphead. The B&B is pretty basic, but after 73 miles we're both done in and we don't care.

With quite a lot of traffic to contend with today, and a poor road surface for much of the way, we've been paying attention to the tarmac and the preservation of life, and so had less time to admire the views of Bonnie Scotland. I'm sure they were there as usual, though often hidden in the drizzle, particularly this morning. But we did see some nice coastline, and more eiders, including another group with their delightful tiny eiderlings. Aaah....

Lochgilphead was not our favourite destination last year on our way to the Hebrides. We had a soaking wet couple of nights in the waterlogged campsite, and could cheerfully never set foot here again. The town seems to have gone a little downhill. We had a good meal in the Argyll last time, but now it's closed, and the ST_G Hotel still has the A missing. At least it's not raining, and we find a restaurant offering an odd combination of Indian and Chinese food on the same menu. Steve has Chinese, I choose Indian, and they are both good.

DAY 10   LOCHGILPHEAD TO CAMPBELTOWN
(53 MILES)

Blue skies at last! We put away our waterproof jackets and overshoes. Our lurid yellow helmet covers made us look complete prats, but make good wet-weather saddle covers. There's nothing worse than getting onto a wet saddle.

We head off south along the Crinan Canal towpath, to its southern end at Ardrishaig, which has a tiny harbour and a lighthouse. The nine-mile canal dates back to 1794 and links Loch Fyne to the Sound of Jura, allowing boats to avoid the 120-mile journey round the coast of Kintyre. Even when we re-join the A83 the road surface is good and there's not too much traffic. The sun's shining and yesterday is forgotten. After a level lochside run along to Tarbert, Steve – who knows the area from his sailing holidays – finds the best coffee shop.

Tarbert was once the main port of the local herring industry, and the Fish Quay is still sometimes busy, though most of the boats moored here now are for sailing rather than fishing. Prising ourselves away from carrot cake and scones, we head across the isthmus between Loch Fyne and West Loch Tarbert, and fairly soon turn left to head for the east side of the Kintyre peninsula. There's a long pull up to Spion Kop, but no sign of Liverpool fans.

It's warming up nicely now and we stop for what we call sun-cream-gate. This is not a scandal involving Ambre Solaire, but the first gate we notice after the bright sunshine starts. We prop the bikes up against the gate, lather ourselves in sun cream and pedal off again. The highland cattle are mystified by this bizarre ritual.

After the watershed there's a steep descent to Claonaig, with a vicious S-bend in the middle. I see the edge of the road getting suddenly much closer, but scrape round, narrowly missing a crash into some prickly bushes. There was a sign Robert, you could have slowed down *before* the bend, instead of locking your back wheel up and drifting towards the foliage. Use your brains, you idiot.

(Mike Carter and Anna Hughes took the Claonaig ferry across to Arran. So they both missed all of the Mull of Kintyre, and most of our last five days of cycling – well over 300 miles in all. I'm just saying.)

From Claonaig to Carradale along the B842 really is a *long and winding road* as we ride through more hilly forestry towards the *Mull of Kintyre, oh mist rolling in from the sea*. Each time I start singing Steve tries to push me into a ditch. At Carradale we find an excellent lunch stop, where you can have delicious veggie rice salad, and also hire a bike. This is our second bicycle café. We found one in Inverness on LEJOG and intend to go back there on our way from Thurso to Berwick. How many miles further on will this be? (Answer: a hell of a long way.)

Campbeltown does not hold happy memories. When we were marooned by rain in Lochgilphead, Steve stayed put in his tent, but I took a bus ride down the aforementioned *Mull of Kintyre, oh mist...* Shut up Robert. I spent a couple of hours in a soaking wet Campbeltown and caught a bus back again. Even the guide book admits that with harbour buildings 'dwarfed by the high, bare hills behind, there is something grim about Campbeltown'. Once prominent as a whaling and herring port, with coal and distilling industries, it is now trying to recover as a sailing and holiday destination. It still has some way to go.

Today Campbeltown is bathed in sunshine and we have a superb B&B on the seafront road, in a large south-facing Victorian house. The kindly woman owner offers to put our cycle kit through the wash and recommends the best bar meals. Steve plunges into the bath and then we wander off in search of food, in glorious early evening sun. There are great views of Arran, which looks huge – I can't believe we once cycled round it in a day. Campbeltown Loch is a picture as we wander back from the pub. All our freshly-laundered kit is neatly folded in a large blue plastic basket, ready for tomorrow. What an angel!

When you're tired you can make mistakes. My toothpaste and my skin cream for nether regions are in similar white tubes. (If you've seen the film *Amelie*, you'll understand.) I just caught sight of the label in time. Steve admitted starting to brush his teeth with Savlon once, and wishing he had applied the toothpaste to his backside instead.

DAY 11   CAMPBELTOWN TO TARBERT   (67 MILES)

In the morning we leave the panniers at the B&B and set off round the 26-mile loop to Southend and back. No, not that Southend, obviously, though this one is also on the sea. It's a lovely sunny day, but the road round the eastern coast is full of steep little hills. The map shows four of them at 14% to 20% (1 in 7 to 1 in 5 in old money) and three which are even steeper. This means some hard climbing and a few scary descents. Halfway round we pass a hill labelled

The Bastard on the map. Perhaps someone overheard a cyclist shouting his displeasure at the gradient. Round a bend, there's a hare in the middle of the road, who just stares as us. Whose road is it anyway? After a few seconds he lollops off into a field.

This northern Southend is only fifteen miles from Ireland, and is said to be St Columba's first landing place in Scotland. The café is slightly eccentric, with an odd collection of clocks and antiques around a massive brick fireplace. At long last we have views of Northern Ireland, though there's not very much to see.

Turning back towards Campbeltown, we pass the road to the lighthouse, but it's seven miles each way, with four more hills of 1 in 7 or worse, so a long view of the famous *Mull of Kintyre*…. will have to suffice.

We're back in Campbeltown in time to pick up our bags and head off for lunch. Now we have a long fast ride going north along the A83 to Tarbert. I wasn't looking forward to this, but there's not too much traffic. Perhaps people have better things to do on a Saturday afternoon. Most drivers are considerate, and my fears of main road cycling have partly evaporated.

Half-way along we stop at Big Jessie's Tearoom at Tayinloan, close to the ferry across to the Isle of Gigha. What would it be like living on a small island with half a dozen farms? Lonely I guess, unlike the excellent café, which is packed, though there is no sign of Big Jessie. We get chatting to a couple of other cyclists, comparing stories about rain and hills.

Then we bat on and do *twenty* miles in an hour and a half – almost unheard of for us mature cyclists. A buzzard drifts across from the hill on the right, circles round and lands on top of a telegraph pole as I whizz past, ignoring both me and the traffic.

The Tarbert B&B overlooks the scenic harbour, as does our restaurant. My delicious mushroom burger is laden with tomatoes and mozzarella, and Steve tucks into an enormous plate of fish and chips. We gawp across at the boats and yachts, while sipping delicious pints of local beer. My estimate of 64 miles today was actually 67 but Steve doesn't even mention this. A good day after all.

DAY 12 TARBERT TO OBAN (56 MILES)

We should be cycling on the Kilberry loop today, but we pedalled round it two years ago, on our way out to the Hebrides. Why should we do it again? Our plan instead was to turn inland at Inverneill, cycle over the hill to Achahoish, and follow the public right of way to Kilmory, where a road leads up the side of Loch Sween to Bellanoch. The map and the weather both suggest this isn't a smart move. The hill is over six hundred feet, and we came down it last year in pouring rain, which is forecast for today. (We saw a fantastic triple rainbow, but it was still bloody wet.) Steve has no desire to go up it again, and I only pretend to be keen. Instead of a hard 71 miles, we are looking at a relatively easy 56 miles. It's a no-brainer.

Breakfast brings a familiar exchange of pleasantries. Steve and I appear in black lycra shorts and bright yellow tops, and a couple turn to me with a smile.

Wife: Good morning.
Robert: Good morning.

Husband: Going cycling then?

Robert: Mmm…. Of course we are, you daft person. What does it look like?

(No, I didn't say that out loud.)

We follow the main A83 back up to Ardrishaig, then ride on the towpath for the full length of the wonderful Crinan Canal. At Crinan there are locks and quays and basins, with a variety of boats moored up, from small fishing vessels to a large and expensive yacht. We wave at the paunchy man in a dark-blue blazer and white trousers, but he ignores us.

The Crinan café is well worth the extra two miles beyond our turn for a good coffee and a cheese scone. Retracing our path to Bellanoch reminds us that it's *four* extra miles for the coffee stop, but the towpath is a fine route and worth doing in either direction. We have broken Rule Three, so we immediately invent **Rule Four: Visit Interesting Places** (even if they are sometimes down dead-end roads).

Turning left, we head north on the straightest road I have ever seen, for most of three miles across the boggy-looking Moine Mhor towards Kilmartin. This area is full of prehistoric monuments. We walk round the two stone circles at Temple Wood, wondering when and why they were constructed, then ignore the museum at Kilmartin, which probably explains everything.

There's drizzle coming on during the afternoon, as we hit the main A816 leading towards Oban, but we're going well with the wind more or less behind us. We pull in for a late lunch at the Loch Melford Hotel, which is quite posh, but we're past caring about our sweaty lycra-clad appearance. Excellent sandwiches in the Bistro and a lovely sea view of the rain coming in hard, with yachts running for shelter. The couple at the next table – let's call them Gordon and Deirdre – look across at us and we smile.

Deidre: Hello.

Robert: Hello.

Gordon: You're cycling then?

Steve: No, we're mime artists.

Where did that come from? Steve can't see the bewildered look on Gordon's face. Gordon doesn't do irony. He launches into a description of an accident they saw last week involving two motorcyclists.

Gordon: One of them had a… you know… (strokes chin) facial stuff… like him (points at me). He looked like a Taliban. Maybe he was a terrorist.

Robert and Steve: Mmm.

Gordon: When I see someone cycling uphill, I think they must be doing some kind of penance. They must be suffering or something, they've done wrong.

Robert and Steve: Mmm.

I suddenly feel the need to leave, before Gordon gets on to hill walkers and immigrants. Back out on the bikes, their conversation continues in my imagination.

Gordon: You know Deirdre, I think those two may have been terrorists as well. One of them had… you know (strokes chin) facial stuff.

Deirdre: No Gordon, they're mime artists. Why don't you listen to people?

When we find our B&B in Oban we're wet through and still need our kit for one more day to get to Fort William.

If your kit is wet – after rain or after washing – how do you get it dry? Hang it in the shower on coat hangers from the wardrobe. But first, try the Towel Trick. After you've had a shower and dried yourself, roll your wet kit up in the largest towel provided, and twist the ends in opposite directions. Kneeling on the towel helps. This may leave the B&B owners bemused. How did they get all the towels so wet? But you'll be away by then.

Original joke for today: What's the difference between Superman's magic power and this evening's television viewing? One of them is Kryptonite, and the other one is Kraptonite. All my own work.

DAY 13   OBAN TO FORT WILLIAM   (48 MILES)

Making decisions is much harder when you're really tired. The B&B owner emerges from her kitchen with a smile and asks a simple question: *What would you like for breakfast?* This poses an intellectual challenge. *I'll have what he's having* is no good, as Steve has the full English and I'm a vegetarian. Surely my brain will click into gear soon. *Scrambled eggs on toast, please.* There, that wasn't too difficult was it?

At least we start with an easy ride out of Oban, except for a very steep hill on the start of this section of the Sustrans route NCN 78. This will stretch right up to Inverness when the Fort William section is sorted out. It's a lovely ride round the coast to the Connel Bridge and the famous Falls of Lora. There's often a massive tidal race here at the narrow mouth of Loch Etive, and we pause to take a look. Even at mid-tide, as we are now, there is swirling water below us which would gobble up a swimmer in no time.

A heavy shower sends us scuttling into a bus shelter. The rain eases off and we sneak out, but a few miles further on the same thing happens again. And again – this is a three-bus-stop day. Or is it a time-warp? It's frustrating to be held up, but we have plenty of time – and at least we're on a bus route. I suggest a bus shelter on wheels you can tow round with you, so it's always there when you need it. Steve says it's called a waterproof jacket and trousers.

Later the weather brightens up a little, though it's windy for a while. NCN 78 follows the main A828 but keeps us off the road itself for most of the way, using the track-bed of the dismantled railway along the Strath of Appin, and then round the coast towards Ballachulish. By the time we reach the bridge across the mouth of Loch Leven the wind is so strong we can barely cycle in a straight line. A girl on a bike hurtles towards us with the wind behind her.

The Sustrans route eventually gives out at Corran Ferry with eight miles to go to Fort William, and we're left with the A82 trunk road – winding, narrow and very scary. The sensible thing would be to catch the ferry across to Corran, cycle up the minor road on the west side of Loch Linne, and catch a ferry back across to Fort William. We both decide this would be cheating, and so invent **Rule Five: No Ferries.** Obviously. We should have thought of it before. It's only eight miles, we'll be fine. (This rule, like most of the others, does not last the journey.) Lorries and buses belt past us, and we take cover in a lay-by to let the traffic thin out a bit. Then we race to the next parking place before more lorries zoom up behind us.

After a few miles there's a footpath on the left. We shouldn't really – but nobody else is using it and it's a great deal safer. A mile further on the traffic starts to back up, and soon there's a long queue with everything almost at a standstill. Except on the footpath. Steve and I glide past every single car, van, lorry and coach which roared past us in the last half hour. We're tempted to thumb our noses at each of them, but instead we just grin inanely. It's quicker by bike.

Fort William is exactly as I remember it – swarms of foreign visitors looking at pictures of Ben Nevis, and outdoor shops with expensive boots. It's the tartan-shortbread-whisky cliché, Scottish tourism at full throttle.

Bank Street Lodge is basic but perfectly adequate. After showering and changing into our barely-respectable evening clothes, we're ready to head off for a meal. Steve picks the wrong door and walks into the wardrobe. This is straight out of Laurel and Hardy. It's a mistake anyone could make – if they weren't looking where they were going. My map-reading and mileage estimates may not be perfect, but at least I can find my way out of a bedroom.

The Grog and Gruel serve us an excellent meal, with another outstanding veggie burger for me. Instead of 'wine-bollocks' on their menus, they have 'beer-bollocks'. Steve learned that his beer was 'ripe and fruity with slightly vinous esters, married to interesting hop notes', while mine had a 'floral peaty aroma, full malt character, a spicy herbal flavour and dry wine-like finish.' *Another pint of your floral peaty aroma, please.*

We return to the lodge tired but happy, and I glance at Steve's copy of The Times. (He's a news junkie. Early morning TV, newspaper during lunch, updates on the smartphone all day. Obsessional or what?) Oh, Scotrail are on strike tomorrow, that's interesting. *What?*

Let's just amble back down to the station to check. That's right sir, no trains tomorrow, we can put you on the sleeper in half an hour. Can we get packed in time? Do we fancy arriving in Glasgow at midnight? We decide against this and wander back to the lodge.

HOME BY TRAIN

We're due to get the 1140 train – or rather the replacement bus service to Glasgow, from where trains should run south as normal. Steve suggests that we turn up for the 0740 instead, which may be less crowded, with a better chance of getting bikes on board. It turns out to be a master-stroke. We're packed and down to the station by 0715 – and the café is open!

When the bus arrives we're ushered forward before everyone else to put our bikes into the cavernous hold. By 0800 we're off on a direct route to Glasgow, with the bonus of a scenic trip up Glencoe and across Rannoch Moor. At 1030 we reach Queen Street Station, and as soon as we walk across to Glasgow Central, there's a train for Carlisle. We arrive home five hours early – because of the rail strike!

My bike computer measures Trip One as 806 miles, to the nearest whole mile each day. Cycling round the coast to Fort William is four times further than driving there! (Steve's GPS gives it as 802.65 miles, but I don't trust a satellite to tell me how far round Scotland I'm cycling. There's only 0.5% difference, and anyway I'm writing the book.) 806 miles in 13 days makes exactly 62 miles per day on average. It has sometimes felt a bit much, with three 70-mile days, and more ascent than I had reckoned with. My memo for Trip Two is to keep it to about 60 miles a day, and to check the ascents. A 60-mile day looks fine until you have to climb a thousand feet a couple of times!

2

WINTERVAL ONE: RAVENS AND REPAIRS

It's not just the summer. We needed to keep cycling all year round. It's so easy to knock off for a few months and put on weight over the festive season. Suddenly March arrives, the next trip is in sight and we're out of condition. Our plan is to go out once a week throughout the winter, a forty-mile run out to Brampton with a café stop in the middle. I found I weighed as much as Steve, who is taller than me. He had started going to a weekly keep-fit class, and could now keep up with me on the hills.

This year the winter never seemed to arrive. There's no snow, and it's not nearly as wet as previous years. The bikes we rode on LEJOG have been relegated to winter cycling, and we pedalled through rain and snow on them last winter. This winter we don't need them at all.

Steve and I started out with very different bikes, but ended up with almost identical ones. We had old machines we pottered around on, but neither of them was good enough for Land's End to John O'Groats. I bought a Thorn Nomad from St John Street Cycles in Bridgewater – a specialised touring bike, not lightweight but perfect for long distances, with wide-range gears to get up all those hills. Steve consulted our local bike shop and was soon equipped with a new Ridley, a beefed-up road bike with wider gears and fatter tyres.

Three days into LEJOG, we stopped for a rest day with my friends Chris and Hilary near Taunton, and went over to Bridgewater to visit St John Street Cycles. Their showroom was full of Thorn bikes, some with derailleurs, and their Raven model with Rohloff hub gears. All the wide-range gears you could want, fourteen in a single evenly-spaced sequence, with a twist-grip gear changer on the handlebar.

I was apprehensive at first. If a derailleur fails, a bike shop can fix it. A Rohloff has to go back to Germany! But examples of Rohloffs going wrong are extremely rare, and usually due to mistreatment by the owner. I got measured up for my Raven – and Steve did too, just in case.

Ordering the Raven was fun – you can pick exactly which components you want. (Please ignore the following details if you're not into this kind of stuff.) Mine has a matt black frame, flat bars with Ergon anatomic bar-end grips, hand-built 26-inch wheels with Rigida Grizzly rims and 1.75-inch Panaracer Pasela Tourguard tyres, Shimano XT V-brakes and levers, and a Brooks B17 leather saddle. (I had a Brooks on the Nomad, but found it unbearable and swapped it for a gel saddle for LEJOG. This became less and less comfortable, and I put the Brooks back on when we returned. It was perfect! It's not just the saddle that needs breaking in, it's your backside as well.) The Rohloff hub on the Raven – with a 40-tooth chainwheel and 17-tooth rear sprocket – gives me all the wide-range gears on the Nomad, apart from the very top. I can still pedal up to about thirty mph, when I'm whizzing downhill anyway.

The Raven was a complete delight to ride from the very beginning, and after several thousand miles it's even better. Young men glide past me on road bikes with pencil-thin tyres, stretched forward onto their drop handlebars. I don't care – my back and my backside are more comfortable than theirs!

A year later Steve bought his own Thorn Raven. It's a little larger since he's taller than me – and it's red. Cyclists know red bikes go faster. But do they? When we crest a hill and freewheel down the other side, my Raven will edge slowly ahead of Steve's, much to my delight. I think it's his extra wind resistance. Maybe I have smoother tyres – his are Schwalbe Marathon. Or is my Raven just a tiny bit better than his?

So this winter we've ridden our black and red Ravens right through from November onwards, which has been great – no derailleurs to fret about, and the bikes fit us so much better. (Steve also joined a running group to get fit, which I consider cheating.)

By March we can set out on what we call the Big Loop, which is 70 quite hilly miles. On the way up from Alston to Hartside Top the wind is strongly against us and we are down to five miles an hour. There's a real gale on top and we have to pedal *downhill*, against the laws of the universe.

At Melmerby our route is blocked by road works and we reluctantly cycle back up Hartside again. At least the wind is behind us, and we have a fast descent back down into Alston. We arrive home after 60 miles and over 1100 metres (3600 feet) of ascent. My knee hurts.

It's April before we can tackle the Big Loop again. Twenty miles up to Alston for a coffee stop, then a five-mile ascent of Hartside, which is 1900 feet at the top. We plunge down into Melmerby and into the café, and then it's round to Brampton, where we pause for further refreshment. Even with three café stops, we came home completely exhausted. Whose idea was this? Why haven't I lost any weight? What do you mean, grumpy old man?

We're off round the Big Loop again the following week, on a lovely spring day with neither gales nor road works to hold us up. The fields are full of young lambs, curlews call out as they drift above us, and a hare stares hard as we glide past. A grey bird floats along the hedgerow, ducks through a gate into the field and stops only a few yards away – a male sparrowhawk. You see a lot more from the bike, moving faster and more quietly than any walkers. Pausing in Brampton for a coffee, Steve is feeling tired, and I tease him about his keep-fit class and running. Did I mention he's nine years younger than me? At a fortnight each year, we'll need seven years to ride round the whole coastline. I'll be 74 to Steve's 65. Let's see who's tired then!

It doesn't always go according to plan. There's another loop we've done a couple of times, a hilly fifty miles over to Blanchland and Allenheads – where there's another good café. We've set out twice on this route, only to find the wind too strong for us. We head back down into the

Tyne valley, cursing each other, it must have been his idea, not mine. We shouldn't have started out up Moralee Bank. It's lung-bursting steep going up, and scary coming down on a terrible road surface. Northumberland roads are *full* of potholes!

If we stay in the Tyne valley and head off to Corbridge and Wylam – both of which also have good cafés – there's the problem of getting back again. We usually cycle up the Stanegate, a good minor road through Fourstones and Newbrough – and then five miles uphill, grinding out the ascent to the highest point on Hadrian's Cycleway. This is a wonderful Sustrans route, running from Ravenglass to Tynemouth, partly along Hadrian's Wall. *Hadrian's Cycleway*? I imagine a figure slogging up here in his armour. Hello your Emperorship, bit breezy today? Your bike looks interesting, did you know they haven't been invented yet? *Hadrian's Chariotway* more like. Cycling up long hills is doing something to my brain.

In April I try the Blanchland and Allenheads loop on my own, on a cold but sunny spring day with no wind. I meet three much faster cyclists. The first one walks into the Blanchland café, looking very young and very fit. His bike has hardly any spokes. I look around before surreptitiously lifting it up. It weighs nothing. It's made of space dust.

A few miles out of Blanchland – where the road surface suddenly improves as I leave Northumberland for County Durham – I'm struggling uphill when a cyclist about my age drifts past me with a wave. He's not making much effort, and is up the road and away. Either he's a super-fit athlete or it's an electric bike. A small rust-coloured bird flashes across the moorland in front of me, and the only one I can think of is a male crossbill. Perhaps the hill-climbing is bringing on hallucinations.

After a steep descent there's a four-mile climb up to the county boundary. A young woman on a bright yellow bike overtakes me, and I push hard to try to keep up. But she might not like being chased by a panting pensioner, so I change down into gear eight and she disappears. A few minutes later she hurtles past in the other direction. She's been to the top, turned round and set off down again. I try to work out how far behind I am, and why everyone is cycling much faster than me.

Gear eight is one of my favourites. (What sad person has favourite gears?) The Rohloff hub has two ranges of gears, low and high, a wee bit like a Landrover. Gears eight to fourteen are silent, but the seven lower gears make a slight whirring noise. I do like a bit of quiet, so I stay in gear eight as much as I can, until it gets steep and I have to change down. When I get home, Caroline tells me that friends above Blanchland have seen crossbills near their house. Maybe I'm not going mad after all.

A few weeks later, Steve and I head off for Innerleithen and an overnight stop at our favourite B&B from LEJOG. After Longtown and Langholm we are back on the wonderful A709 to Eskdalemuir, with a brief stop at Samye Ling Buddhist Centre for a calming cuppa in the Tibetan Tea Rooms.

The road gets steeper and the breeze stronger. As we climb up onto isolated moorland, there's a squishy feeling from the back wheel. Puncture! I jump off and swear profusely, stamping my foot on the road in frustration. Steve's face says it all – *you've lost it, pal.* It's only a puncture. No, it's much worse – the back tyre is badly worn. I do have a new tyre – but I've left it at home. At least there's a spare inner tube, so we cobble together temporary repairs – some sandpaper inside the worn tyre, and puncture repair pads glued on the outside. Not recommended! Off we go, fingers crossed, and the repair lasts another two hours until we get to the B&B.

In the morning my rear tyre is strangely distorted – the inner tube has tried to escape during the night! But Innerleithen has a bike shop, half a mile from the B&B. The owner comes in early to open up, and he has the same tyre as the one I left behind. By 9.30 we're off again, an hour later than yesterday, so we might be late back to Carlisle. No, we won't have a puncture to deal with, and the wind will be behind us all the way.

Slogging up the first couple of hills, the wind isn't behind us, and my legs have turned to rubber. We cycle past Samye Ling and on into Eskdalemuir, where there's a community-run café. A really good lunch stop, and we reckon all the climbing is now behind us. Not so, there are several little hills before we get to the watershed. Then down into Langholm, and off onto minor roads to avoid the A7 – and they are far from flat. But we're making good time, and arrive in Carlisle by five, having taken two hours less than yesterday to do the same 70 miles. 140 miles in two days, we must be fairly fit.

I've spent a good bit of time planning Trip Two. Cycling round Scotland in one go would take us six weeks and cost a fortune. Steve wouldn't have that much time free – and forty days cycling in a row was too much for us. So we broke it up into three fortnights in June, so it will only cost a third of a fortune each year.

Steve is always busy, designing websites or sailing or running courses. I'm the fully retired one. So I did the planning for the three trips round Scotland, starting and finishing in the bottom corner at Gretna, near Carlisle, not far from home. I'm sure it was Steve who suggested cycling round England and Wales as well. Three trips became seven trips, though this seemed too much, and we had lengthy discussions on how to reduce the time it would take to get round to Carlisle again.

I bought more coastal Ordnance Survey maps, though we may not need that much detail, and the Sustrans maps have all the cycle routes marked. Anyway, planning should be dead easy, with only two things remember – stick to the coast and choose a B&B every sixty miles.

Unfortunately neither of these guidelines work in Scotland. The roads often don't follow the wiggly coastline, and there are big gaps between towns. It took ages to plan a good day's ride which ended with somewhere to stay. Perhaps we could go cycle-camping again? There are campsites everywhere, and we could pitch up in a field if need be. Hang on, I remember slogging up the hills in Harris, and struggling into the wind up the west coast of Lewis, always lugging an extra 15 or 20 pounds of camping kit. Let's stick to B&B.

Are we ready for Trip Two, from Fort William to Thurso? I seem to remember the west coast of Scotland is a wee bit hilly in places....

3

THE NORTH-WEST HIGHLANDS – FORT WILLIAM TO THURSO

We begin with a wet train journey back to Fort William. In Glasgow we have to change stations to get further north, walking the bikes from Central to Queen Street in the rain. I'm rewarded for lunch with a delicious falafel and salad wrap – some places in Scotland *can* cope with vegetarians! I've at last joined Steve with technology, a new mini iPad, so I can check my emails and find out how much it's going to rain. I also have eleven OS maps – extra weight, but at least we can see where the hills are.

DAY 14 FORT WILLIAM TO LOCHALINE (66 MILES)

Today is overcast but dry. We set off early, after scrambled eggs on toast in the station café. NCN 78 runs out of Fort William to Corpach, with tantalizing views of the lower slopes of Ben Nevis and a patch of snow higher up, coming and going in the cloud. Then an hour along the north side of Loch Eil on the A830, with not too much traffic.

After Kinlocheil we turn left onto the A861, running back along the south side of the loch. A level road for most of the way, with steep woods above us on the right. It's odd to see Fort William again after two hours cycling, a kilometre away across the loch. We could have caught the Camusnagaul ferry, but that would have been cheating, and we would have missed all the flora and fauna. A buzzard drifts across the road in front of us, Canada geese swim along the loch with four goslings, a pair of bullfinches shoot out of a bush beside the road. The verge is sprinkled with heath-spotted orchids. I pick a few bog myrtle leaves and crush them between my fingers, releasing the smell which always reminds me of the highlands – and is also said to repel midges.

By 11.30 we're in Corran after an easy morning, with 34 miles behind us and the sun breaking through the clouds. We lounge outside the pub until opening time, watching the Corran ferry sail back and forth across the loch. An SNP campaigner is putting up posters for Ian Blackford – MP for Ross, Skye and Lochaber – and tells us the constituency is half the size of Belgium. This fails to impress us, due to our ignorance of European geography.

When the pub opens we order sandwiches and have a game of darts (Steve 1, Robert 0). The afternoon is another scenic ride, along Loch Linne on the B8043 to Kingairloch, then inland up the valley, and a steady run down Gleann Geal into Lochaline. We're a bit whacked after two stints of over thirty miles, with only a single stop for lunch. The Lochaline Dive Centre is closing, but the friendly owners are happy to provide coffee and cake. An excellent day with few hills, cycling through gorgeous woodland with dappled sunlight and flowers – a few bluebells still in flower, a single primrose, and common sundew and butterwort in the drainage channel by the roadside.

DAY 15   LOCHALINE TO SALEN   (51 MILES)

Election Day! Steve and I have postal votes, but we're in a safe Tory seat. It's overcast. We consider rushing for the 0845 ferry over the Sound of Mull to Fishnish, but decide to linger for the 0940 crossing. This breaks Rule Five (No Ferries), so we invent further rules to justify our onward progress. **Rule Six: Avoid Detours Inland**. It would take forever to get round here without a ferry. **Rule Seven: Visit Islands as Appropriate**. I know they're not part of the mainland, but a brief trip to Mull avoids a massive inland detour, which would break Rule One (Keep to the Coast). Isn't coastal cycling complicated?

An hour and a half along a twisty road, with a good bit of traffic, brings us into Tobermory, with its colour-washed houses and hotels, three large buildings in a row painted bright red, yellow and blue. There's said to be a sunken galleon in the bay, laden with treasure, but nobody's found it yet. The café in an old church serves milk in little school milk bottles, bringing back distant memories.

Steve decides (after four years cycling) his rack-top bag is surplus to requirements. He rearranges his kit and sends the bag back home in a posting box, minus the toilet roll he's carried on all previous trips. Don't ask. He tips it into a waste bin – posting it home might look a bit weird – then realises we could have left it at the B&B. Too late, resources squandered. After all this excitement, we catch the ferry back to the mainland at Kilchoan.

It's only six or seven hilly miles from Kilchoan to Ardnamurchan lighthouse, the most westerly point on the mainland (beating Land's End by 23 miles), where there's a welcome café. It's a dead-end road, but we're breaking rules everywhere today. From the lighthouse you can see Barra and South Uist, or you could if it was clear. The bag-posting adventure has drained our energy, so we need another injection of caffeine and buns.

Retracing our route to Kilchoan, we then find bigger hills along the Ardnamurchan peninsula towards Salen. We're beginning to feel tired. After a sweeping descent back to the coast, we pause at Glenmore's Natural History Centre, which has another café. The last few miles seem like really hard work, with frequent stops on narrow roads to let cars through.

In the middle of a long pull uphill I suddenly feel faint. *Oh no, I've got a bug, I'm going to be ill.* I take a long swig of water, and a minute later I'm fine, just a little dehydrated. Keep taking the water. Whooshing down the next hill on a twisty single-track road, trees on either side masking the view, I glance at the bike computer. 35 mph. A big van might be round that bend, I'll slow down a bit. There was no van, but there could have been.

In Salen we reach a great B&B, run by a German couple, and have a good meal at the nearby hotel. Then we watch the general election coverage on TV. Can the exit poll be true? Has Theresa May shot herself in the foot?

DAY 16 SALEN TO BROADFORD (57 MILES)

Yes, she has! We wake up to find there's a hung parliament. Theresa May's gamble on a snap election has backfired spectacularly. Will she still be PM by the end of our ride?

It's been pouring down for most of the night, and our bikes are dripping at the back of the house. The mist starts to lift as we set off, but my saddle is wet, and my bottom is soon damp as well. (Memo: ask for somewhere safe and dry for the bikes.) Streams pour off the hill and rush into churning peaty rivers, down to the loch at the roadside. We head north on the A861 to Lochailort, where it joins the much busier A830 – though a couple of feet between the white line and the edge make it safer for cyclists. Suddenly there's a cycle track, which conveniently runs most of the way to Arisaig.

An ugly concrete bridge crosses the road above us and disappears into a cutting. We hear a steam train and see its white smoke. At the top of the hill we can *smell* the smoke, but there's no train to be seen. Maybe the line goes further away from the road, or perhaps it's a trick, luring steam enthusiasts to their doom with audio recordings and mobile bonfires. Why do I only get these ideas when I'm cycling uphill?

Arisaig has been called a wooded paradise where you can watch the sunset over a mass of tiny islands. Sadly we don't have time to test this out. Café Rhu gives us an excellent lunch and an earful of loud Scottish folk-rock. We stumble out into bright sunshine, take off the overshoes, apply sun cream and glide away on a minor road towards Mallaig, again with a cycle track for part of the way. Things are looking up!

Mallaig is as uninteresting as ever. We board the Armadale ferry, avoiding a 130-mile detour inland and away from the coast. (Anna Hughes and Mike Carter both took this route, and for once I agree with them.) On the ferry Steve bumps into his former colleague Mark and his friends, who are also cycling onto Skye. They're on road bikes with no panniers and hardly any kit at all. How do they do that?

At Armadale we ride past the Museum of the Isles. I've lost count of missed museums by now. The last seventeen miles across Skye are on the main road, but again with a couple of feet beyond the white line. Mark's group overtake us, but a couple of them are slower on hills. We catch them up and ride past feeling smug. Road bikes, who needs them? Then a cycle track leads away from the traffic and onto the old road, overgrown but still well-surfaced.

In the B&B we get chatting with a portly man in highland dress, hosting a whisky tour for an American group, driving from one distillery to another, a refined and expensive pub crawl. There's good food at the hotel, with delicious Corncrake bitter, brewed in Orkney.

DAY 17   BROADFORD TO SHIELDAIG   (48 MILES)

We're reluctant to get going this morning, due to the weather rather than last night's beer. It's pretty murky outside. Cycling over the bridge connecting Skye to the mainland, it's cold and windy, with nothing to see. Kyle of Lochalsh is aptly described as a town of 'provision stores, souvenir shops and abusive seagulls'. Hiding in a bus shelter, we meet a Dutch couple who like us want

Britain to stay in the EU. Scots voted 62/38 to remain. UK under-25s and graduates both voted even more strongly to remain, but older and less qualified voters swung it the other way. I'm just saying…

The rain eases off as we ride into Plockton, where you might almost be in the Mediterranean, with palm trees along the shoreline gardens. We search in vain for a coffee shop to celebrate completing the first thousand miles on our coastal circuit. Unrefreshed, we take a lovely wooded road – whose sharp inclines take your breath away – up to Stromeferry,

A pine martin ambles onto the road, chocolate brown fur and a white front, only a few metres away. After a few seconds he sees us and scoots off into the undergrowth. The silence of cycles! He would have vanished much earlier hearing walkers or a vehicle.

There are even more hills before we regain the lochside, stopping for lunch at a restaurant whose place mats have Simon Drew's cartoon riddles. First it's countries, *Braseal* and *Pear-egg-Y*. Then it's Beatles songs, with *Pole-mow-cart-knee* singing about *L-hen-gnaw-wig-bee* until the food arrives.

We ride round the head of Loch Carron to the linear village imaginatively called Lochcarron. Then there is a drag up the last big hill for today, and past the end of the Applecross Road. After a heavy downpour we arrive bedraggled in Shieldaig, which of course is soon bathed in sunshine.

Shieldaig has an odd history. The loch was famous for herring even when Norsemen ruled the area, but the village was only built in 1800 by the Admiralty, when the navy were short of trained seamen. Could they not have trained somewhere more convenient? The friendly woman at the B&B helps us to dry out a bit, and we potter along to the Coastal Kitchen for a good meal, with a fine evening view across to Shieldaig Island and Loch Shieldaig beyond.

DAY 18   APPLECROSS LOOP   (46 MILES)

Today is the biggest challenge of our entire coastal trip, the fearsome Applecross Pass – sea level to two thousand feet in six lung-bursting miles. We set off in a fierce shower, straight into the wind and rain for three miles, almost all uphill. I'm not looking forward to this. The rain eases off a little as we ride over the watershed and down to sea level again, with a right turn marking the start of the Applecross road.

There's a huge noticeboard here, with dire warnings for learner drivers, caravans and the faint-hearted: 'This road rises to a height of 2053 feet with gradients of 1 in 5 and hairpin bends.' As we cross the River Kishorn the road bends left, and a powerful headwind hits us, with driving rain in our faces. We've picked the wrong day.

I've been up here twice before. The first time took 75 minutes, and the second ride an infuriating 61 minutes. I was keen to get under an hour this time, but there's no chance. We're thinking seriously about turning round. The guidebook claims this old drovers' road 'shoots up in a series of dizzying hairpins', passing close to several 'dreadful precipices', and finally reaching 'a flattened moonscape of shattered rock before swooping down to

Applecross.' This sounds exaggerated, but it's entirely accurate.

We force our way on and up into the rain, with visibility closing in and mist all around. Steve pulls away, but my legs are made of lead this morning. However hard I try, I can't catch him. We struggle round the first bends and the gap widens. Steve jokingly promised to save me with CPR if I had a heart attack today. He won't hear my pathetic cries for help while he's in front. Maybe I'd better take it easy.

The straight section in the middle seems endless. The road suddenly kicks up into 1 in 5 as promised, and I have to walk for a hundred yards or so. I can't see where I'm going. Cars loom out of the mist a few yards in front of me. At last I see a bend in the road and realise I must be near the hairpins, close to the top.

Jumping onto the bike in bottom gear on a 1 in 5 hill is fraught with danger. The first push makes such little progress that you can't get the other foot on the pedal in time to keep going. But unlike derailleurs, Rohloff hubs give you instant gear-changes, even when the bike is static. Set off in fourth and change down into first while you're still moving forwards. German engineering!

Beyond the zigzag hairpins, the road levels off towards the summit, the *Bealach na Ba*, the Pass of the Cattle. On the misty plateau a chilly figure stands by his bike, waiting for me. I've never been so glad to catch up with Steve.

The descent is decidedly scary, braking hard in strong wind and poor visibility on a damp road. A few yards in front, Steve suddenly swerves right across the road. *What?* A second later the wind hits me side-on and

I do the same. We both struggle to keep our bikes on the tarmac, with a big drop on the left, squeezing the brakes to get the speed down. Soon we're out of the mist, but still buffeted by sudden gusts of wind, threatening to push us off the road.

Half-way down we pause to let another car past, and without realising it I'm moving off again. The hill is not too steep just here – the wind itself has set me going, like a bird lifting its feet up and gliding away. But the bird doesn't have to worry about the bends in the road, as we hurtle down two thousand feet to sea level at Applecross.

We ride along to the Applecross Walled Garden, and the excellent Potting Shed Café and Restaurant. The waitress asks sensible questions. *Do you want to see the lunch menu? What kind of coffee would you like?* Freezing wet and exhausted, I'm still focused on sitting down without tipping the chair over. We order soup and coffee, which are both so good that we order them all over again, so as to warm up and not have to go back outside.

While we're slurping our soup, I tell Steve about the magic shoes I'm inventing, which detect whatever terrain you're in. When it rains they turn into wellies, if it's hot they become sandals, and on rough ground they transform into boots. Steve listens carefully and says he'll phone the doctor when we get home.

We planned an excursion along the flat coast road running south to Toscaig, five miles out and five miles back. The end of every road? Forget it, we need to set out for Shieldaig before the weather closes in again. The road round the Applecross peninsula was only built in the 1970s. Before then the terrifying pass was the only land access to the village. Applecross was one of the most remote and inaccessible places on the mainland.

At first we head north with the wind behind us, zooming along the coast with views of Raasay and Rona, islands to the west. But when we turn the corner at Fearnmore and head east, the wind and rain hit us again. This seems peculiarly unfair, since it was a *westward* turn which brought us head-on to the foul weather this morning. The ride back along the shore of Loch Torridon is increasingly hard work, with a succession of little hills and not-so-little hills, ten of those 'one in seven or steeper' arrows on the OS map. If we'd ridden this circular route in reverse, as Anna Hughes did, we might have been exhausted before we even started on the Applecross Pass, and would have missed the classic hairpin-bend ascent. There's as much ascent on this coastal route as on the pass itself. We've climbed well over 4000 feet (1200 metres) today – it's like cycling up Ben Nevis!

At least I'm now in front for most of the way, so I can collapse in safety and wait for Steve and the CPR, though it would be nice to get back in one piece. We're riding directly into the wind and rain for most of the way, and arrive in Shieldaig completely exhausted. But the kind B&B woman offers us a clothes horse to hang up our wet kit, and after a hot shower we repair to the Coastal Kitchen for another good meal.

DAY 19 SHIELDAIG TO GAIRLOCH (46 MILES)

Today it's not raining. Hooray! Overcast but dry is a massive improvement. It would have to be the worst weather on the most spectacular day's cycling. I'm keen to come back and tackle Applecross again, but Steve is not so daft.

We have a good run along the south shore of Upper Loch Torridon and into the Torridon Glen, which reminds me of my father. He was a keen cyclist and hillwalker, and told me as a child about cycling along this wonderful glen. There are three great mountains above the road, Beinn Alligin and Beinn Eighe, and between them the one which looms above us now, the fearsome Liathach, the Grey One (pronounced *Lee-aghach* – does that help?). Today it is greyer than we would like. The mist comes down as we gain height and ride into gentle rain. Bracken and heather all around, with only occasional glimpses of huge walls of rock above us to our left. These mountains are 750 million years old, formed of some of the oldest rock on the planet. Where was the rock before then? Hiding away, waiting for the right time to become mountains? I think of Slarty Bartfast from *The Hitchhikers' Guide to the Galaxy*, who was proud of his award for designing the Norwegian fiords. (Other creation myths are also available.)

Over the watershed the rain eases off, as we pass Loch Clair on the right with its fine wooded surround, and Beinn Eighe's long ridge and scree slopes above us on the left. Caroline and I spent a whole day walking along this massive ridge, with its peculiar trees – matted areas of prostrate juniper, a metre or so across, but only an inch or two high.

My spellcheck turns this into *prostate* juniper, an interesting Freudian slip, which reminds me of a delicate matter, increasingly part of our daily routine. If you are male and of a certain age, you begin to be more conscious of the… plumbing. Without going into detail (no, please don't)… think of turning taps on and off. One of us sometimes has a little trouble turning the tap on, and the other one sometimes needs to turn the tap on quite urgently. So when one of us stops at a gap in the hedge and shouts, 'I'll catch you up!', the other will slacken his pace until this BRI (Bladder Related Incident) is complete. Enough said?

The Whistle Stop Café in Kinlochewe is a good stop with a most amusing Gents. (The Ladies may be equally amusing.) The afternoon is spent riding steadily along the beautiful Loch Maree, my father's favourite, though there are one or two long hills to slog up on the main road. Hills on a lochside road? Why isn't the road level like the water? I should have paid more attention in the geography lessons. The weather has cleared and there are good views of the islands on the loch, and the more rugged far shore, with Letterewe Lodge, a little stately home accessible only by boat, which you can rent from £4,000 a week. Maybe we'll stick to bed and breakfast.

I remember Gairloch from years ago, not much more than a grocers and a heritage museum. Now it's a bit more alternative, with a wonderful shop called *Buddha by the Sea* – an oriental Aladdin's cave – and further on *Hillbillies*, an excellent independent bookshop with a café attached. Along the shoreline road is yet another SNP poster for Ian Blackford, six days after the first one at the Corran ferry. Now we know what half the size of Belgium looks like – Ross, Skye and Lochaber is a huge area.

Of course we pause for coffee and a look round the bookshop. On a short day with plenty of time, we ride past the B&B to Big Sand, where there's a holiday centre. Ravens drift above us as we pass the Youth Hostel, and sitting on a fence post close to the road, aware of us but undisturbed – a barn owl. Five minutes later, riding along the River Sand (how can you have a river of sand?), we come to a hill and decide to turn round. As we approach the barn owl again he glides across the road, lands on the top of a red triangle road sign and sits looking at us, swivelling his head round as we drift by, only twenty feet away.

The B&B is good, though the pub's vegetarian option is a runny risotto. I prefer the soup to be liquid and the main course to be solid. Like the curry in Castle Douglas, it wasn't unpleasant – but I wouldn't order it again.

After completing Day 20, we're a quarter of the way round mainland Britain! We didn't realise this at the time, as I was planning on only doing Scotland, and Steve hadn't begun to persuade me that riding round England and Wales would be a good idea. So I was thinking we were half way round. Oh well.

DAY 20   GAIRLOCH TO ULLAPOOL   (60 MILES)

With heavy overnight rain, we're in no hurry to set off. After a steep pull up from Gairloch, we drop down to sea level again at Poolewe. If we had more time, it would be interesting to stop and look at Inverewe Gardens, described as 'a riot of subtropical colour' due to its sheltered position, with magnolias and rhododendrons and 'exotic shrubs from all over the world.' We'll just have to resign ourselves to missing out on the most northerly eucalyptus.

There's a long stretch of fairly isolated road past Aultbea and Laide and not much else. This is a good place to fret about whether we should have gone to the end of every road. The B8021 runs for six miles beyond Big Sand up to Melvaig, the B8057 goes nine miles along the east shore of Loch Ewe to Cove and beyond, and minor roads stretch out past Aultbea (four miles to Mellon Charles) and Laide (five miles to Opinan). Adding these dead-end roads together and doubling the total to get back again adds 48 miles, most of a day's cycling. They're probably all nice roads leading past lochside beauty spots to deserted beaches, and we are the poorer for not cycling down each and every one of them.

Soon we're passing Gruinard Island, where anthrax was released during the Second World War as a chemical weapons test, poisoning the sheep and contaminating the land. I'm trying to imagine the thinking behind this experiment. *They won't mind, it's the middle of nowhere, it's for the greater good. What do you mean it's against the international conventions of warfare?* The island was quarantined for decades and only decontaminated in 1990 after a lengthy campaign by microbiologists and local people.

I'm still pondering the evils of chemical warfare and being unfair to the Scots, when we glide down the shoreline of Little Loch Broom into Maggie's Tea Room at Dundonnell. Some places are just perfect, with friendly staff and super coffee and cake. It is full of people sheltering from the rain, and we again get chatting to a couple of cyclists who are as usual younger and fitter than us. We're getting used to this.

From Dundonnell there's a lengthy slope up the glen, following the river a thousand feet and more above sea level. The rain gradually moves away, and we look back at the fabulous summit ridge of An Teallach. The cloud lifts to reveal the whole of the range. As we approach Fain Bridge, an unusual machine hurtles towards us, like a motorbike with the pillion rider standing up. It's actually a semi-recumbent tandem packed with camping gear. He's lying down in front, and she's sitting up behind, as on a conventional bike. Unlike conventional tandems, both riders have a good view of what's going on. But recumbents cost a fortune!

Eventually we descend to the main A835 close to the Corrieshalloch Gorge, and turn left for Ullapool. I'm just thinking I could do with a cuppa, when there's a sign for a tea room and art gallery. We turn off and find a lovely couple running an unusual little gallery and serving excellent coffee and cake.

Six miles further on we reach Ullapool, and a good meal at the Ceilidh Place, which has a fine little bookshop. Tempting, but we don't fancy carrying bulky volumes home. Ullapool's grid pattern of streets, dating from the 1780s, shows it was a planned village – almost a small town – which began when a fishing station was set up to service the herring industry. Today its harbour has a large ferry terminal, and the town relies more on tourism. (Mike Carter took the ferry to Stornoway, returning to mainland cycling much further south at Fort William – after his second broken wheel – missing out both Applecross and Ardnamurchan.) I hesitate to mention that the old herring-curing factory has been turned into a small museum.

It was here that Steve first mentioned cycling round England and Wales as well. I'm sure it was only going to be Scotland at first. Anyway three trips round Scotland somehow turned into seven trips round mainland Britain. This would take seven years at our current rate! To get round the whole of the mainland while I can still ride a bike, we may need another plan.

DAY 21   ULLAPOOL TO LOCHINVER   (54 MILES)

It's overcast but dry this morning, with some wind, which may be the best we can hope for. There's a long drag out of Ullapool, a couple of hundred feet of ascent, but then we glide back down to sea level at Ardmair Bay.

With some relief we turn off the busy A835 onto a delightful minor road leading to Achiltibuie and Lochinver. The next ten miles are just wonderful, riding along a gently undulating road beside a succession of big lochs, with mountains on either side – Ben More Coigach and Sgurr an Fhidhleir across Loch Lurgainn on our left and Cul Beag and Stac Pollaidh above us on the right. Caroline and I have climbed all of these on our Scottish holidays. Everyone's favourite is Stac Pollaidh (or simply Stack Polly), a short steep ascent onto a spectacular ridge of sandstone pinnacles. A perfect mountain in miniature, with its own special car park. We ride past a dozen people putting their boots on to tackle the climb.

This area known as Assynt was visited by the explorer Thomas Pennant in 1772. He described 'a most tremendous view of mountains of stupendous height', although none of them even reach 3000 feet. Soon we're drifting past Loch Bad a' Ghaill and Loch Osgaig, and the trees and bushes and bracken give way to a barren heather-clad wilderness, which looks natural but was once covered with forest. Pennant complained about 'the blackness of the moors', which he found gloomy and oppressive. Perhaps he was having a bad day. A bird flashes across the road, close enough to show itself as a snipe.

A left turn takes us past two smaller lochs and on towards Achiltibuie, opposite the Summer Isles, where we stop for lunch at the Piping School Café, mercifully free from piping. I cannot bear the wailing of the bagpipes, but I'll keep this to myself in Scotland. Driving through Glencoe once, I saw there was a piper in highland dress in every car park, each playing *Scotland the Brave* in a slightly different key. Even after walking into the hills for an hour I could still hear them. It was a nightmare.

We cycle on for a few miles of this lovely road (even though it's a dead-end), past a series of scattered cottages. Some roads are just too good to miss, and there's a grand view of the gentler side of Ben More Coigach. Caroline and I were up here thirty years ago, and surprised a golden eagle on the summit of Sgurr an Fhidhleir. He took off from a rock only twenty feet below us, gliding away and disappearing in a few magical seconds.

It's damp in the afternoon, cycling round a loop to Altandhu and back along the moorland plateau to the turn for Lochinver. Sandstone moorland gives way to rocky outcrops, and then back into ancient woodland. I'd forgotten how hilly this road is, winding down to Inverkirkaig, where the bookshop and café provides a welcome break.

The Inverpolly National Nature Reserve, second only to the Cairngorms in size, is a largely uninhabited wilderness, with a wide range of habitats, including 'lochs, streams, bogs, scree, barren mountain tops and a scattering of birch, hazel and rowan woodlands.' The base rock is Lewisian gneiss, said to be 'between 1,400 and 2,800 million years old – the oldest British rock.' Hello Torridon, our rock's much older than your rock.

We've crossed into Sutherland, Britain's most north-westerly county. For the Vikings this was the 'South Land', across the sea from Scandinavia. The winding and hilly road continues to Lochinver, where the B&B is pretty basic. The restaurant and the pub are fully booked, so we try the Lochinver Larder, a pie shop and restaurant. But what pies! There are *twenty* different fillings, with three veggie choices for me, and fruit pies for afters. We are well filled by the time we leave.

DAY 22   LOCHINVER TO DURNESS   (62 MILES)

There's a pleasant surprise as we leave Lochniver – sunshine! We work our way round towards Clachtoll and Clashnessie on a road Caroline and I know well. Then the lovely scenery turns dull, with a spit of light rain for a while. The road is a good bit steeper on the bike than in the car! It's a hard ride to Drumbeg, where we find the Little Soap and Candle Company (Assynt

Aromas) with its excellent secret garden café, much to be recommended.

Between here and the main road leading down to Kylesku, there are *ten* steep-hill-arrows on the map, some of them worse than 1 in 5, and they may have missed a few. Just past Nedd there are three 1 in 4 hills. Mercifully we go *down* two of them, with brakes full on, and we only have to get off and push on the very steepest uphill. We usually pride ourselves on not pushing, but even with very low gears we have no choice when fully-loaded and faced with a 1 in 4 – and us not getting any younger. We both come to a halt and step off. I remember when Steve couldn't keep up with me on the hills. Either he's getter fitter or I'm getting slower. Of course I could lose a stone and transform my power-weight ratio.

With a steep pull from sea level up to four hundred feet, for the second or third time, we ride round the northern end of Quinag, with magnificent views of the undulating ridge and its separate tops, which Caroline and I have climbed. Joining the main A894 we glide down and almost miss the Geopark café at Unapool. There's no prominent sign, but we're always on the lookout for coffee and cake. I feel another rule coming on: don't pass a café unless you know where the next one is.

Just beyond here is Kylesku. When I first came here forty years ago, you had to wait for the ferry across the loch. I remember missing the last boat and spending an uncomfortable night dozing in my minivan. Since 1984 there's been a gracefully arched bridge, designed by Ove Arup, stretching across to Kylestrome. The main road beyond Kylesku has some long hills, but nothing as steep as the Drumbeg road, so we make good progress to Scourie and beyond. There are fine views of Ben Stack, Arkle and my favourite mountain, the great undulating ridge of Foinavon – Fionn Beinn, the white mountain, with its quartzite slopes shining in the sun.

Laxford Bridge sounds like a Derbyshire town where you can have a meal in one of several restaurants. Actually it's no more than a bridge over the River Laxford, and a road junction where we join the A838, which runs from Lairg up to Durness. We ascend a mere two hundred feet before dropping down into Rhiconich, where there's another road we don't take – five miles to Kinlochbervie, and another five to the road-end beyond Oldshoremore, where a rough path leads on to the wonderful Sandwood Bay. Another twenty miles saved.

Beyond Rhiconich there's a steady pull up five hundred feet to Gualin House, where the owner has persuaded the council to re-route the road behind (rather than in front of) his property, at his own expense. A house with a by-pass! Money talks. A fantastic long final descent, six or seven miles bowling down gently to sea level at the Kyle of Durness.

Driving round Britain for *The Road to Little Dribbling*, Bill Bryson was particularly impressed with the landscape between Ullapool and Durness. He described it as 'pure grandeur', with mountains and glens, streams and lochs and open sea 'all continually reshuffled into new combinations of unsurpassable majesty.' Four centuries earlier, William Camden's *Britannia* (1586) fed the legend of this area as a fabulous wilderness, rich in minerals. He told his readers that Sutherland had coal, iron ore and limestone to be mined or quarried, and also pearls, silver and 'it is supposed there is *Gold in Duriness*'. You can see why people might fall in love with the far north-west.

A smiling woman greets us at the B&B. 'Hello, you're the friends of Mike and Jean, aren't you?' Everyone knows everyone in Durness. A wonderful day's cycling, sixty miles with some fierce hills – but the sun makes all the difference.

DAY 23   CAPE WRATH   (30 MILES)

This is the second day to be intrepid. Cape Wrath is the most north-westerly point on the mainland, and it takes some getting to. We ride down to the ferry against the wind. Twenty people are already here, and it's not yet nine o'clock. We get the second crossing, hugging our bikes on a small boat as we slurp over the Kyle at £9 each return fare for bike and rider. On the far side, everyone else boards the minibus, looking at us with bewildered pity.

As soon as we start away from the jetty we realise this is a horrible, horrible road. It snakes across the largest area of uninhabited land in Britain, a hundred square miles of 'peat-bog, heather, scrub and rock' – but that's not the problem. This is the public road U70, whose surfacing dates from 1956 and is now more potholes than tarmac. The holes are so big that loose stone has been used to fill them, giving an incredibly bumpy ride. It was recently described as 'the worst-maintained road in Britain'. We wobble from side to side trying to find the least dangerous line. Hill after hill and into the wind, these eleven miles take us fully two hours. It's hard going on the uphill sections, the rear wheel spinning on the loose surface, slowing us down and risking a sudden fall with feet still in cleated pedals. Downhill is just as dodgy, braking hard to avoid building up speed and hitting an even worse patch too fast. Or will our bikes simply fall apart?

The Ozone Café at Cape Wrath brings a welcome coffee-and-cake reward for our struggles. It's run by John Ure, the only inhabitant on the peninsula's hundred square miles. He claims the café is open '365 days a year, 24 hours a day', but how many people turn up at midnight in winter to see? (None, the ferry and minibus don't run in winter.) We get chatting to a couple who have cycled there with a large maritime buoy on one of their bikes. They are sea kayakers, doing the journey in memory of a friend who has recently died. Guess what? They have mutual sailing club friends with Steve! Is there anywhere he doesn't know people?

The wind is behind us on the way back, but because of the dreadful road it still takes almost another two hours. There's a long wait in the drizzle for the minibus and ferry, sitting on a log and gazing out at the choppy water. The ferryman finally appears in a *much* smaller boat, a RIB (rigid inflatable boat) rather than the solid ferry which brought us across. The minibus driver is squeezed in between us, and Steve and I cling onto our bikes, perched precariously on the inflated tubes on either side. The tiny craft feels very low in the water. It's choppy as we plough across the Kyle, a distinctly up-and-down crossing. I can see myself swimming for it, my lovely bike drifting down into the sea, covered by sand before the tide recedes. Steve has grave doubts about the boat's seaworthiness, but he keeps this to himself until we are back on dry land, saying he didn't want me to panic.

We shower and change and head off in driving rain to meet friends Mike and Jean at the craft village at Balnakeil. This was once an early warning station, but when it became obsolete the buildings were rented and then sold off to jewellers, artists, weavers and potters. I first came here forty years ago and made friends with Alan Herman, a skilled woodworker, and he's been down to stay with us a couple of times. Sadly Alan died a few years ago, and we've not been back here since. Mike and Jean were also friends of Alan, and it's good to see them after a long gap. Mike's a keen birdwatcher, and often finds unusual birds blown in from all corners by the wind – which has been known to shred sheets on the washing line. The four of us go up the Whale Tale Restaurant for a good meal and a chat.

DAY 24   DURNESS TO TONGUE   (40 MILES)

This morning brings a stiff breeze and light rain, with forty-mile-an-hour gales forecast. The first hour is hard going into the fierce wind, on the west side of Loch Eriboll, until we find an unexpected café stop at Laid. Usually we know where cafés are going to be, so it's a bonus to sit in the warm, out of the wind for a few minutes. Next we pass Lotte Glob's pottery, and find we both remember when she was working at Balnakeil. Neither of us knew the other one had visited the craft village.

Soon we hit a real *wall* of wind, and it's hard to keep moving forwards. Round the head of the loch there's a crosswind for half a mile, so strong that it threatens to push us across the road into the reeds and grass – a bit like Applecross, but at sea level rather than 2,000 feet. I see why soldiers and sailors who were stationed here in wartime called it *Loch 'Orrible*. North Atlantic convoys were often assembled here, and Eilean Choraidh, the poor little island in the middle, was used in 1944 as target practice for bombers preparing to attack the German battleship *Turpitz* in a Norwegian fiord. It was here that German U-boats finally surrendered to the British navy.

We come round to the east side of the loch and suddenly a strong tailwind blows us along at fifteen miles an hour, with no effort at all. We glide past Ard Neakie, almost an island but connected to the mainland by a thin isthmus. (There's a word for this not-quite-island, and later I discover it's a *tombolo*.)

Many years ago I was driving along this single-track road in my minivan, when a black limousine appeared from the other direction. The chauffeur drove past the only passing place and we were soon bumper to bumper. A female hand from the back waved me out of the way. I pointed to the passing place, and the hand waved more vigorously. I switched off the engine and waited. After an exchange of views inside the limo, it reversed very slowly into the passing place and I drove by with a friendly wave. Underpaid Schoolteachers 1, Landed Gentry 0.

Steve and I climb away from Loch Eriboll and across to Hope Bridge, crossing the river Hope, the outflow of Loch Hope, under the massive Ben Hope, the most northerly Munro. (Mountains over three thousand feet, and yes, I have been up it.) With the positive energy of all this Hope behind us, we planned to turn south and make a loop inland to Altnaharra. But it's far too windy today, and we stay on what passes for the main road, up those steep-hill-arrows again for almost eight hundred feet, over the Moine, a wild and barren landscape. Then we're treated to a wonderful three-mile descent to sea level, hurtling along at forty miles an hour, and over the causeway across the Kyle of Tongue. Sadly fast descending doesn't last very long and you can't see much of the landscape, you have to keep your eyes on the road. Nothing's perfect.

The first building we pass is an hotel. We stop for coffee in a big lounge and play chess with posh pieces set out on a table. (Robert 1, Steve 0.) Steve calls this a draw, as he beat me at darts in the pub at Corran. I claim chess is more intellectual than darts, and Steve tells me where I can put the chess pieces. Yet another TLP is awarded.

It's still only two o'clock so we tackle the twelve-mile Kyle of Tongue loop. How difficult can it be? Turning back into the strong wind to re-cross the causeway, I'm riding with the bike leaning over, to keep myself upright. It's a hard five miles going south. Our Sustrans map doesn't show the arrows for steep hills, but they're there on the road itself – the hills, not the arrows, that would be silly. Then we pass into stunted woodland and a more sheltered ride back into Tongue. H.V.Morton drove round the Kyle of Tongue in the 1930s, before the causeway was built, describing it as 'the world of loch and yellow weed, of high, impregnable hill and dark gorge, of brown moor and wild forest'. He's overdoing it a bit.

The B&B is a good one and the bikes are safely stored in the garage. We've parked our bikes overnight in some odd places in Scotland. We usually get the garage or a shed, but they've also spent a night in a workshop, a corridor, the dining room – and a couple of nights outside, which seems ungrateful. They deserve a place in the dry.

DAY 25   TONGUE TO THURSO   (51 MILES)

Steve puts his cycling shorts on inside out, and only discovers this after breakfast. I suppose I could have told him. Today – again – it is sunny! We start out uphill out of Tongue with good views back over Ben Loyal, though the cloud is still on Ben Hope. I try to work out how high the cloud is, looking back over my shoulder and wobbling across the road. Subtract the height of one mountain from the other, estimate the proportion of Ben Hope in cloud – or get on with the rest of my life.

Again we forgo the trip to Altnaharra. Seventy miles seems too much for today – or any other day, the way we're feeling. Instead we make a minor diversion to the coast at Skerray, with a little loop and a nod to our rules. If not the end of every road, you should really go round a loop. We'll probably break this rule as well.

Another long pull up to five hundred feet, then a fine descent into Bettyhill, a place with a terrible history. Its economy now is crofting and tourism, but two centuries ago it was a refugee camp. In 1814 the Countess of Sutherland began evicting her tenants from Strathnaver, the long glen running north to the coast, and over 500 families were moved here before being shipped to America. Her plan was to 'improve' the land (i.e. to make more profit) by removing people and importing sheep. Many Scottish landowners did the same in the forcible depopulation known as the Highland Clearances, but Countess Elizabeth was the only one vain enough to give her name to the refugee camp she created. Thanks Betty.

It's Sunday, but the hotel looks open. I feel awkward turning up bedraggled and sweaty in a posh place, but we're welcomed and served excellent coffee and scones. Our money is as good as anyone else's. Below us is a series of half-built roads, laid out for housing which hasn't happened. A bankrupt builder or a failed EU grant? Bettyhill doesn't seem a likely place to need a holiday village.

Another drag up to five hundred feet, and then onwards over the wild moorland again to Strathay and Melvich, which have dead-end roads leading off to Strathy Point and a tiny place called Bighouse. We save another ten miles by ignoring them.

Walking into a pub for a coffee, we realise we've been here before, on the last day of LEJOG. Steve recognised a man from last time, propping up the bar with his pint and whisky chaser, at 11.30am. It wasn't his first. On our previous visit here we ended up weeping with laughter. Steve saw a map of the British Isles on the wall, which made him think of sailing, a gormless member of his sailing club, and other people he knew to be gormless. Soon he was saying how useless the English were compared to other Europeans, who were much more efficient and generally on the ball.

I saw what was coming and tried to signal, but he carried on towards the Fawlty Towers punch line: *How ever did we win the war?* Then he saw me pointing and turned round. I don't think the two hefty German bikers at the table behind him heard what he said, but when he turned back and caught my eye we were both giggling. Somehow we got out of the pub and back on our bikes. We could hardly cycle in a straight line, and I had to stop and wipe my eyes. We really did laugh till we cried. (If any German bikers are reading this, I'm truly sorry, but it was all Steve's fault.)

At Reay we turn off the main A836 onto NCN 1 for the last few miles into Thurso, a gentle run to finish off. It also keeps us a little further away from the massive Dounreay Nuclear Power Station, now undergoing a very lengthy and unbelievably expensive decommissioning project – measured not in years and millions, but in decades and billions. Don't get me started on the economics of nuclear energy.

Our B&B in Thurso is a bit scruffy, but we are past caring. I don't name the places we stay at, to avoid embarrassment and libel and disappointment – they may have closed before you get there. We've had a variety this year, ranging from basic to luxurious, and the price often doesn't match the standard. We've slept in an immaculate guest house with a good hotel next door for a meal; a run-down hotel with a slightly grumpy owner, drinking in the bar rather than looking after guests; a perfectly adequate room-only bunkhouse; and eight other bed and breakfast places, again varying from shared loo and shower to posh en-suite facilities. We've stayed in bungalows, cottages and town houses, and in someone's spare room, very informal. (I was also called 'sir' once or twice, which felt awkward.) In Shieldaig, for example, we were in a lovely cottage on the seafront, close to the hotel and bar, with its excellent restaurant. You never quite know how it's going to turn out.

Thurso is the most northerly town on the mainland, and the population has trebled since Dounreay started up in the 1950s. It had earlier been a centre for exporting flagstones, which seems like hard work. It also has a Folk Museum.... In the pub Steve says he's had a flash of genius, so I remind him about walking into the wardrobe in Fort William. This time he's onto something. Instead of five more fortnightly chunks, maybe we could do England and Wales bit by bit, to reduce the number of years we need? Worth pondering...

After the scenic journey down from Thurso, we change trains at Inverness. There's a large empty buggy in front of the bike racks, and we ask the owner politely if she could move it so we can load our bikes. She isn't happy. 'What is a bicycle compared to a child's life?' she asks loudly. There's plenty of room for both bikes and buggies, and I don't see how we're threatening the life of her toddler, smiling on the seat beside her. But something tells us not to argue with this woman. We turn our bikes round, wheel them along the platform to the next carriage, squeeze them onto the rack with another bike, and chat happily with its owner, all the way to Edinburgh. I'm still trying to think of a smart reply to her question.

For the return journey, each of us has a receipt ticket, a travel ticket, three seat-reservation tickets – and six cycle reservations! Each leg of the journey needs two bike tickets, one for the bike, and one to show we have a reservation. At Edinburgh Waverley the ticket man tells Steve to take the ticket *off* his bike, to prevent someone stealing it and putting it onto *their* bike. Hide your cycle reservation tickets! Steve and I look at each other, bewildered by this bizarre instruction. But something tells us not to argue with this man either, and we let the moment pass.

Trip Two seems to have been a mere 611 miles, with an average of 51 miles each day, though some of them were very hilly. Adding these first two trips together means we've done 1417 miles in cycling two-thirds of the way round Scotland. I'm thinking about Steve's idea to ride round England and Wales in fewer years. We don't fancy cycling through London with a loaded bike, but trains run direct to Newcastle from Southampton. I started working east and west from there. How far could you get in a fortnight? A long and short trip each year might bring us back from seven years to five years. Would it really work out that way?

4

WINTERVAL TWO: SERVICE AND SURGERY

Our training has been pathetic. The weather was unhelpful, with another wet winter, and heavy snow later on, just when it should be starting to get warmer. Steve and I made our way up to the Stanegate, our local Roman road, and found it covered in snow with ice underneath. Undeterred, we rode on, picking up speed as the road goes downhill. Any braking would lock up the wheels and we'd slide over. That's when the big tractor appeared. We couldn't slow down or steer out of the rutted ice, and could see ourselves being flattened. Luckily the farmer saw the problem in time and swung his machine into the verge. He waved and shouted as we went past, not in a friendly way. Let's not go out in the snow.

Steve's had a bronchial infection which was slow to clear up, and put him out of action for several weeks. When we got going again, I was pushing too hard on a ride back from Carlisle, and pulled my left hamstring. A visit to the sports physio gave me some exercises to do, but it was slow to heal (especially as I kept forgetting to do them), and I had to go gently for another month.

We resolved to take it easier this year, with our lack of winter training, the illness and injury, and the advancing years. Steve is still a mere 61, but I turned 70 in December and was beginning to think maybe this wasn't for me any more. Having said that, there's a cyclist called John in our local café who's seven years older than me and seems to go out every day. He's also very skinny and used to race when he was younger, which I consider cheating.

It seemed harder to book B&B this time. A hotel owner in Crail, near St Andrews, insisted on taking a hefty deposit, which sounded a warning bell. Another guest house cancelled our reservation after several weeks with no explanation. I was looking forward to staying at the post-hippy Findhorn Community, but nobody replied to my emails. Are they too laid-back to do business?

To make things worse, Scotrail's summer timetable was badly delayed. You can usually book tickets twelve weeks in advance to get the cheapest fares, though bike reservations often can't be made until late on. Why not? Without the complete rail and bike bookings, the trip would just fall apart, and I was starting to fret. Steve likes to have a Plan B and he suggested Julie could drive us up to Thurso – though I don't think he told her. With only five weeks to go, the timetable finally emerged and bookings could be made.

Our bikes are booked in for their annual service in Carlisle, which we combine with a much-needed training ride. We take the early train to Dumfries, and set off for an easy ride on a glorious sunny day at long last, with another good café stop at Caerlaverock Castle for coffee, cheese scone and carrot cake – reminding us of our first day out of Carlisle.

Along a narrow country road, a vehicle behind starts hooting for no reason. Steve looks back and sees his yellow top has fallen out of the webbing on his rear rack. A smiling postman drives past with a wave as Steve returns to pick up his kit. A happy coincidence – or maybe there are guardian angels after all.

As we turn off the minor road beside the M6 south of Gretna, a couple flag us down. 'Are you going to Rockcliffe? Could you take this back to the school?' They give Steve an exercise book which a boy dropped beside the road – accidentally or on purpose – and we promise to return it. Riding on, we consider how to approach the school. Lycra-clad men of mature years waving exercise books at young children may not be welcome. Fortunately a young teacher is on the pavement as we approach, so Steve hands the book over to her. She reads the boy's name and rolls her eyes. Perfect – except for Steve's comment about the teacher's attractive appearance after we pedal away. Even in the winter I have to award TLPs.

The bikes are wheeled into Palace Cycles, and we catch the train home. A group of elderly tourists are visiting Hadrian's Wall country, so it's unusually full for mid-afternoon. I feel slightly foolish in yellow and lycra with no bike, and imagine people are looking at us. What do you mean, paranoid?

The next day brings bad news. After several thousand miles, my chainring needs replacing. More seriously, the rear rim is badly worn with heavy braking. With derailleurs you just cough up for a new rear wheel, but I need a new wheel built onto the Rohloff hub. Fortunately this is all in a day's work for Joe at Palace Cycles, it just takes a wee bit longer. A couple of days later we have both our Ravens back, looking good and riding very smoothly. Mine looks different with black spokes on the rear wheel – the only ones available – but I'll get used to it. This rear-wheel surgery could have been needed in the middle of a long ride, as Mike and Anna both found to their cost. Another reason for cycling in stages, with regular servicing in between.

With two weeks to go, Steve and I have one last ride together, and opt for the Big Loop, the 70-mile run which we haven't done for a whole year now. Three coffee stops! Sadly no longer at the lovely Hartside Café, which was completely burnt out in the winter. We take it fairly steadily, and are pleased to get round in reasonable time. We've both been conscious of taking on another long Scotland trip with little winter training, but this ride has given us confidence. We'll be OK.

I cycle round the Big Loop again the next week on my own, just to make sure. Steve prefers to cycle in company, but he's busier than I am, and I'm always happy to go out alone. On the long and twisting descent into Melmerby, I see two young men ahead on road bikes with pencil-thin tyres. They are surprised when I sweep past them – I don't need to brake on the corners with my wider tyres. They make up ground on the straight, but I'm in Melmerby before they can catch me. It's not every day I overtake someone.

After a coffee stop, feeling childishly pleased with myself, I catch up with a couple on a tandem as we come into Renwick, and we get chatting for a while. Unlike the semi-recumbent in Scotland, the woman's main view is her husband's back. They're a wee bit slower than me, so I push on towards Brampton. I'm feeling good about overtaking *four* cyclists today! Bowling along towards Lambley, two more young guys on road bikes come past with a friendly wave. I push for fifty yards or so to keep up with them, before realising how much faster they're going, seemingly with little effort. I'm old enough to be their grandfather. Let's not get too ambitious.

5

EASTERN SCOTLAND AND NORTHUMBERLAND – THURSO TO SUNDERLAND

DAY 26   TRAIN TO THURSO

It's an early drive to Carlisle for the train to Glasgow, after a sleepless night, due to my silly anxiousness about the trip. As we pull away from the Gibbon's house, with Julie in the back to drive the car home, Steve turns to me and asks: *Have you remembered the condoms?* That's the quickest TLP ever. He has no shame.

All trains are on time. We walk across Glasgow to change stations, and take three-and-a-half hours winding our way up to Inverness, the morning dullness giving way to a lovely sunny day. This brings memories of LEJOG, cycling for two days beside the A9 on the excellent NCN 7, from Perth to Blair Atholl. Over the Drumochter Pass and down to Kingussie, gradually up towards Slocht

Summit before descending towards the Beauly Firth and Inverness.

The train from Inverness takes another four hours to Thurso, with good views of the shoreline after Golspie – seals, lots of eiders, the males looking fine in their breeding plumage, plus the usual gulls and oystercatchers. After Helmsdale we turn inland and pull gently uphill along the Strath of Kildonan, a lovely valley which we will cycle back down in a couple of days.

Instead of last year's OS maps, I have four Sustrans maps with me. These should take us all the way from Thurso to Inverness, Aberdeen, Edinburgh and Berwick, then down the Northumberland coast to Newcastle. They have less detail, but route-finding shouldn't be a problem this time. I've found a better B&B in Thurso than last time, since we'll be here for two nights. We have a good meal at Red Pepper, but both eat too much. Pigs! Only two more TLPs for Steve today. He promises to try harder. I think he means trying to earn them rather than avoiding them.

DAY 27   THURSO TO THURSO   (59 MILES)

At breakfast this morning we get chatting with a fellow guest called Ian, who's in Thurso for a Highland Railway conference. We arrange to meet up for a meal this evening. Steve decides he's not comfy on his bike, and needs to adjust the handlebars. He unbolts them, twists them round a bit and bolts them up again. We ride off and he is now super-comfy on the bike. During the day he goes on about it a bit. He's complained on previous rides about a sore shoulder, and it's taken him four years to sort this out. Still, if he's comfy at last, that's good.

I've been fretting as well, making sure everything is safely in the panniers. On LEJOG one of us often imagined we'd left something behind. Each time we set off from the B&B or a coffee stop, or even a direction-finding pause, there would be that nagging doubt. After a few yards, or half a mile, one of us would glide to a halt, swivel round and unzip the top of the rear bag, to make sure that his wallet (or his phone or bike lock or today's map) hadn't opened the zip by itself and forced its way out. This became known as a Paranoid Check. It was repeated each time the bag was opened. It's not just me who's paranoid, though Steve does call me The Worrier – not always without cause.

Now we both have front bags mounted on the handlebars, to keep everything we need during the day – wallet, B&B details, phone, bike lock, maps, spare glasses and emergency crunchy bars. They close with an audible click and are lockable. It's impossible to set off with the bag open. You would notice straight away. So we don't need any more Paranoid Checks.

Hang on, is my wallet still *inside* the bag? Did I *see* it when the bag was open? Where's my phone? Did I leave the bike lock on that windowsill? Let's just stop to make sure. No, here it is, Paranoid Check complete. But I may need another one soon. What do you mean, insecure? I'm just being careful.

There's a sea mist along the coast as we leave Thurso, but no hint of rain. The A836 takes us through Castleton, which used to export paving stones to Australia and New Zealand. Do they have no stone of their own? Local fields here in Caithness often have flagstones instead of fences or walls round them. Stone is easier to find than timber in this mainly treeless country. (My notes say '*manly* treeless country' – a wasteland where lumberjacks have chain-sawed everything.)

The road curves round the beach of Dunnet Bay, and we turn north for Dunnet Head, an increasingly deserted landscape. When we reach the lighthouse there are twenty people equally determined to visit the most northerly point on the mainland. The water below is calm today, but the Pentland Firth can be a fierce stretch of ocean. Winter storms can throw stones up 300-foot cliffs and smash lighthouse windows.

I was hoping for a good view of Orkney, six or seven miles away, but it's hidden in the sea fret. Our landlady kindly told us where to see puffins, so we nip down to the cliff edge below the wall in front of the lighthouse, and are rewarded with a fabulous view. Below us is a turquoise sea with birds everywhere – kittiwakes, guillemots, razorbills, and a few puffins as well, with their red-and-yellow striped bills and comical waddling. Fulmars glide round on stiff wings, staring at us. A couple of great skuas – known as bonxies – drift past, hoping to bully smaller birds into giving up their catch as they fly in from the sea.

We cycle back to the main road, past the Castle of Mey – formerly owned by the Queen Mother – along to the famous John O'Groats. Did you know it was named after Jan de Groot, who began a ferry service to Orkney in 1496, after James IV won the islands from Norway? No, neither did I. Stopping at the café where we celebrated finishing LEJOG, I order a large coffee which arrives in a porcelain bucket. A group of overweight visitors waddle in, making us feel relatively slim.

Hoping to look at Duncansby Head's famous sea stacks, we cycle a couple of miles further east on a dead-end road to the most north-easterly point on the mainland.

The stacks are a mile away across fields, and we don't fancy a wet walk in our bike shoes. But we do visit the world's smallest roundabout, ten feet across and completely useless, as if someone has laid the tarmac out for fun. It doesn't go anywhere, but we cycle round it twice anti-clockwise, just for devilment. We know how to enjoy ourselves. Perhaps we should notify the Roundabout Appreciation Society. (It does exist, but they've probably visited already.)

From John O'Groats we get back onto NCN 1, which leads from here to Dover, almost 1,700 miles, though this includes Orkney and Shetland as well. How far from here to Dover? I don't want to think about it. We decide on **Rule Eight: Keep to the Sustrans Routes**, which only lasts a few miles. With plenty of time, we turn off for the Lyth Loop, a detour in pleasant sunshine. The miles slip away, it's fairly flat and we're travelling light, with our panniers and overnight kit at the B&B. Our projected 50 miles has become 59, but these don't count as Bluck miles as they were cycled by mutual agreement rather than gormless planning. This leads us to **Rule Ten: Rules are Made to Be Broken**. (Don't hold your breath, Rule Nine comes a little later on.) We're back in Thurso before 4.00 and still feeling fine and pleased with ourselves. How long will this last?

Showered and changed, I wander off for a walk along the banks of the River Thurso, watching common terns dive into the water for fish. I meet a couple of tourists from Switzerland. We get chatting about their trip to Scotland, and spend several minutes commiserating about Brexit.

We head off with Ian from the B&B to the Pentland Hotel, where the bar's full on a Friday night. Ian's a retired viola player as well as a railway enthusiast, and a convivial evening ensues, with decent food, several pints of delicious Corncrake Ale, and uplifting conversation on music and railways, as well as life, the universe and everything.

DAY 28   *THURSO TO HELMSDALE*   *(57 MILES)*

Today's question is how to get to Inverness without being flattened by a lorry on the A9. (Mike Carter and Anna Hughes both cycled along the coast from Inverness to John O'Groats, surviving a hundred miles and more on busy trunk roads, but we want to avoid them wherever possible.) Meanwhile, we can add Thurso to the list of places where we got lost. That Co-op's in a completely different place today. Could this have to do with the Corncrake Ale and the convivial evening?

We both feel sluggish as we pull out of Thurso going west, with our full kit again and hills, albeit gentle ones, to contend with today. The weather's overcast but mercifully dry, and we make steady progress past Dounreay and Reay village on the A836 again. Before Melvich we turn south along Strath Halladale towards Forsinard on the A897, which has hardly any traffic. We overtake four cyclists, one of whom is pulling a trailer carrying a large white guitar case. He's giving a series of concerts and cycling between them. Why not? The sun shines brightly now, skylarks sing above us and there's a cuckoo calling. It's just perfect.

The musical cyclists catch up with us at Forsinard's unusual tea room – a shed in the owner's garden. Coffee and cake and cycling talk is enjoyed by all. Forsinard marks another milestone in our coastal cycling – 1500 miles completed, and we're nothing like half-way round! Steve and I wander over to the old station's RSPB exhibition, and out to the observation tower, where we see no birds except swallows. The exhibition is staffed by an attractive young woman, and Steve receives yet another TLP. At least she didn't hear him.

The train arrives from Wick and Thurso and we wave to Ian, who has wangled himself a ride in the cab. Waiting for this train was a mistake. As we set off down the valley for a twenty-mile glide into Helmsdale, black clouds bring heavy rain. We shelter at Kinbrace station and ride on when the rain seems to have passed. A sudden shower brings us to a halt, diving into the panniers for waterproof tops and overshoes, but the thunder and lightning we can see and hear doesn't quite reach us. It's an odd experience to ride *through* a band of weather and out the other side.

A strong breeze off the coast slows us down a bit. There are red deer on the hillside, close to the road, not at all concerned by the cars whizzing past. Are they half-tame, or perhaps farmed for venison? We have a good B&B in the village. The River Helmsdale is said to be the best salmon river in Scotland, but Helmsdale has relatively little to offer vegetarians.

DAY 29   HELMSDALE TO DINGWALL   (74 MILES!)

On LEJOG we avoided the whole of the A9 north of Inverness by riding inland to Lairg and up to Tongue. This would definitely be cheating on our coastal trip. We've already missed 37 miles between Wick and Helmsdale, by cycling up Strath Halladale and down the Strath of Kildonan, but now there's no alternative. We pedal out of Helmsdale for our tussle with this scary road, planned for a Sunday morning to reduce the risk of being flattened. The first vehicle is a massive articulated lorry, and there's more traffic than I had hoped for, but it's quieter than a weekday, so we shouldn't complain. With the wind behind us, progress is quite speedy, and there are few hills. This is just as well, since a heavy sea fret engulfs us for several miles.

We keep wiping our glasses to see where we're going, and discuss the prospect of making our fortunes by inventing miniature windscreen wipers for cyclists' spectacles. The mechanics would be straightforward, but powering them might be tricky. Glasses with batteries strapped to them would look odd, and dangling wires could be a problem. Soon we give up. It's a bit of a niche market.

An hour and a half later we're coming into Golspie, with eighteen miles done already, feeling very pleased with ourselves. Better still, there's a café open at 10.30 on Sunday, with superb warm cheese scones. Steve orders apple pie with both cream *and* ice cream. Maybe we won't lose any weight on this trip.

Golspie has a large statue of the first Duke of

Sutherland on the summit of Ben Bhraggie above the town, to remind everyone that he and his wife (Elizabeth of Bettyhill fame) cleared people from the highlands in favour of sheep-farming. The inscription describes how 'a mourning and grateful tenantry' erected the statue to remember 'a judicious, kind and liberal landlord' who would generously 'open his hands to the distress of the widow, the sick and the traveller'. There have been several attempts to tear the statue down. His grandson the third duke had a private train, and built his own station at Dunrobin Castle, a rustic hunting lodge we passed through on the train to Thurso. But the seventh duke has had to sell several of his Titians to balance the books. It's tough at the top.

After another five miles on the A9 we turn onto a side road round the shore of Loch Fleet. Two hundred years ago there was a ferry across the mouth of the loch, and Thomas Telford built a causeway across, but both are long gone. The tide's out and seals lounge on the sandbanks. Soon we're in Dornoch and stop for a coffee near the cathedral. Now Presbyterians don't have bishops, so the Church of Scotland has no cathedrals. But nine churches (including Dornoch) are older than Presbyterianism and still *called* cathedrals, even though they're not. I do hope that's clear. Dornoch also has a stone marking where one of the last witches was burned, for turning her daughter into a pony. Presbyterians frowned on that sort of thing.

The sea fret is gone and sun cream is liberally applied before we set off again. A minor road around the Dornoch Firth leads us back onto the feared A9 for the last few miles into Tain. The bridge across the Dornoch Firth has a narrow footpath, and care is needed to avoid veering onto the road and the fast-moving traffic a few feet away. It's only one o'clock and we've done 38 miles. On the A9, fear makes us faster. Tain is called after the Viking word *thing*, which means *council* rather than… thing. There's a small local history museum, but we rode past it. One more on the list.

Having decided the Nigg ferry route is too long, we change our minds in Tain, while taking in further sugar-laden refreshments. So we head off on NCN 1 for Balintore and Nigg. I'm on form today and pull ahead, feeling really fit for once, and clock up almost fourteen miles in the next hour. When Steve catches me up, he demands a drug test, but I'm fuelled only by shortbread.

The Nigg ferry is the smallest car ferry I've ever seen. One at a time please! We glide across the mouth of the Cromarty Firth with a grand view of the massive cranes, rigs, towers and oilfield platforms. Quite a tide is running, and the ferry comes in at an angle, working hard to get square-on to the jetty. This has a lovely amateur feel to it, like the old Kylesku ferry before the bridge was built. It's skilled work, and I'm filled with admiration for the medieval ferrymen who *rowed* local people across this stretch of water.

Cromarty is a fine little town of fishermen's cottages, though a previous village here was swept into the sea during storms. It is the birthplace of Hugh Miller, an amateur geologist who worked on sandstone fossils, controversial in the nineteenth century. His cottage has been turned into a small museum….

By three o'clock we've done 54 miles and set off on the

B9163 round the north coast of the Black Isle, going fast with the wind behind us, not sure of how much further there is to go. Five miles in the next twenty minutes must be a record for us. Then there's a pull up into the breeze, and a long straight run with the Cromarty Firth on our right. I hear a couple of yellowhammers but can't see them. Steve is largely ignorant about birds, but happy to challenge my identification. 'Are you sure it wasn't the lesser-spotted wongle-warbler?'

Finally there is a fast glide down to sea level – and the busy A9 again. There's a wide footpath on the long bridge leading us over the Cromarty Firth, with a strong wind in our faces. Dingwall brings a pleasant surprise – separate rooms in the guest house. A guest has been taken ill and cannot vacate the room we booked. I'm so pleased with my en-suite double room that I don't even give Steve a TLP when he suggests I could bring a woman back from the pub. We've done 74 miles before five o'clock and I don't feel completely exhausted. We must be getting fitter.

DAY 30 *DINGWALL TO FORRES* *(56 MILES)*

It's overcast but dry this morning, with an easy run down to Inverness on NCN 1, beside the A835 and then on a minor road avoiding the A9, apart from crossing the spectacular Kessock Bridge over the Beauly Firth, and even there we have a cycle lane. I remember when you drove all the way round the Beauly Firth, though there was a foot ferry for centuries until 1982 when the bridge was opened.

There's some confusion – not what you'd call getting lost – before we find the Velocity Café again for a refreshment stop. Coffee and cake and a chat with the mechanic in the back-room bicycle workshop. Wardrobe malfunction! One of the fingers on my track mitts is unravelling. I'll just have to cope.

Inverness is known as the capital of the highlands, and is a fine city, though any city is a bit of a shock after our rural rides. We ponder about **Rule Nine: Avoid Big Places**. (I told you it was coming.) Now we have all of them, the Ten Rules of Coastal Cycling – except for the other six that come later on and need these ten to be re-numbered. (See Appendix: it's too complicated to explain here.) As regards Inverness, relics of the 1745 Jacobite Uprising are housed in a museum in Castle Wynd – and we didn't go in.

Cycling out of Inverness seems complicated, as we're both feeling sluggish after our long ride yesterday. Pulling up at a red light, my left foot is still clipped into the pedal cleat… *crash!* Elbow, knee and helmet all hit the pavement at the same moment, with little damage to any of them. Only my pride is hurt – a grown man falling off a bike, what a complete prat. As the first-aider, Steve is full of concern, but admits that it looks *very* funny. I agree – he did the same thing on a training ride a few weeks ago. It's not quite so hilarious when you're the one falling over. Mercifully it only happens if you're going slowly, with your bike in gear but your brain in neutral.

There are long hills up to Culloden battlefield, and we decide not to visit the place where 'the brave highland army was killed'. It's all farmland and forest now, rather than the open moor of 1746, when the Duke of Cumberland's men butchered Bonnie Prince Charlie's troops in less than an hour, in the last pitched battle in Britain. (We do need to remember that the prince – a Catholic in Protestant Scotland – wasn't fighting to liberate the Scots, but to take over the British throne for himself.) There's a National Trust for Scotland Visitor Centre, offering a '360-degree battlefield immersion theatre' a museum displaying contemporary artefacts, and guided tours of the battlefield. The shop has 'enticing Scottish products', including jewellery 'crafted from the flowers of the battlefield' and exclusive 'Culloden Battlefield Highland Malt.' It sounds like Fort William on steroids.

There are hills beyond Culloden as well, which we'd not quite gauged from the map. We plough on, between dark conifer plantations and remnants of ancient woodland, magnificent old Scots pine, each with huge limbs. Eventually we come down to Nairn, where we fail to find a café, and get a bit lost. A wiggly NCN 1 leads us towards Forres, which seems not to be getting closer, as we take yet another little detour to avoid the main road. Each time we see a hill in the distance, the route will inevitably go up there. But it's a sunny afternoon, bowling through wooded country and fields, with young bracken, bluebells and stitchwort by the roadside, and primroses still in flower in early June.

The ancient town of Forres brings us B&B in a superb old stone house with a friendly owner, and a good meal at the Mosset Tavern. I reckoned on 52 miles today, but it turns out to be 56, so Steve chalks up another four Bluck Miles. Maybe I'll add ten percent to each day's estimate, and try to claim a rebate later on.

DAY 31   FORRES TO BANFF   (61 MILES)

After a fine breakfast, we potter round to have a look at the Findhorn Community, an interesting collection of buildings mostly designed by their owners. It's bigger and less hippy than I imagined, and it would have been fun to stay here. Maybe they're on a higher spiritual plain where email enquiries don't reach them.

The road going east is again hillier than expected, and we're relieved to find a nice café in Elgin. We pedal onwards between woodland and farmland again to Garmouth. A short but excellent section on a disused railway leads us across the old Spey Viaduct, opened in 1886 as part of the Great North of Scotland Railway, with 'a central 350ft bowstring approached on either side by three 100ft plain truss girders'. Very impressive, even fifty years after the railway was closed, crossing the wide mouth of the River Spey, now overgrown with vegetation below us. There was once a boat-building industry in Garmouth and the nearby village of Kingston, with timber floated down the River Spey to be 'transformed into ships that sailed all over the world.'

Today is good for birds – a jay on the path, a woodpecker in a tree, and a couple of surprised goldfinches, almost close enough to pluck out of the air. We find ourselves on the shoreline at Portgordon, with eiders and mergansers in the water. As with many of these villages, the little harbour now has pleasure boats rather than trawlers, though an ice-house is a reminder of the days when salmon were stored here.

The whitewashed cottages at Findochty have stone

window and door surrounds, painted a different colour on each house, originally for weatherproofing, but now more of a local tradition. Soon we're in Buckie and pause for a massive sandwich, almost a meal in itself. Pressing on we come to Cullen, built confusingly on two levels, with a railway viaduct between the main street and the lower village of fishermen's cottages. Steve and I disagree about the route and head off in opposite directions, both knowing we're right. Half a mile further on we meet up again. We *were* both right! I took the NCN route and Steve followed his nose, underlining my excellent map-reading and his fine sense of direction. There's another rule somewhere here.

Portsoy and Whitehills are two more villages whose fishing industry has been replaced by leisure craft. Following NCN 1 all day confirms our suspicion that Sustrans have sent us up hills deliberately. We should be grateful, they've kept us off the A98 trunk road. Tired but safe, we pull into Banff, with Greek columns and Venetian windows on the Georgian buildings in the centre. Our reception at the B&B is slightly cool. I did ask in advance about parking the bikes indoors, but the landlady seemed rather disgruntled. We found an unusual bar in a posh hotel, but had a good meal in strangely faded surroundings, as if we had stepped back in time.

Hard work on the hills reminds me about losing weight. My Raven weighs about 28 pounds, and there's another stone or so of kit in the panniers, and nearly 13 stone of me. So I'm pushing 16 stone or more up the hills. If I lost a stone, our expeditions would be almost as easy as a training ride. I imagine the extra weight on top of the panniers as two-pound bags of sugar, but actually it's spread round my middle as a spare tyre. Surely I should be losing weight, cycling sixty miles a day?

DAY 32   BANFF TO DYCE   (67 MILES)

We have an interesting diversion from NCN 1 today, a bit of an experiment. The morning ride to Fraserburgh is hard work, with lots of hills we didn't expect without a detailed map. (Extra maps would weigh little and at least tell us where the hills are.) Several times we go down steeply towards the coast to cross river valleys, and it seems even steeper up the other side each time. One of these hills is signed as 20% (1 in 5 in old money), which neither of us can manage, and we both have to walk.

Fraserburgh sees us in a Subway café for an excellent custom-made sandwich. Then we set out on the best part of the whole trip, forty miles on a disused railway line, the Formartine and Buchan Way, almost all of it a solid surface on compacted gravel. An afternoon of traffic-free cycling, with hardly noticeable hills, as steam trains didn't go up much more than 1 in 60 (less than 2% in new money). Along this track we see a dark hare sitting in a field looking at us, and several yellowhammers. Steve asks again if they're not wongle-warblers, and I try to push him into a ditch.

Strichen has a good café, where I tackle the largest cheese scone I've ever seen. On we go through Maud and its railway museum (sadly closed today) and through Auchnagatt, Ellon, Uday and finally into Dyce. The surface is a little mixed at times, but mostly firm and gravelly. A delightful afternoon. There are calls locally for the railway to reopen, but don't hold your breath.

The B&B in Dyce is hard to locate. Steve has to phone and ask for directions, and we eventually find it tucked away close to the airport. The plumbing is odd, and the water is reluctant to drain away in the shower, threatening to overflow into the room. This is offset by an excellent meal in the nearby Dunavon Hotel on the main road. I planned 62 miles today but it was actually 67. I'm sure this is not all my fault. The maps must be wrong.

DAY 33   DYCE TO MONTROSE   (61 MILES)

After an early start, all goes well until we get lost in Aberdeen, underlining the need to avoid big places (though we also got lost in much smaller places). We're only a couple of streets adrift, but it's disconcerting in a big city. Local humourists have twisted one or two Sustrans signs round to face the wrong way.

We eventually find our way across the River Dee and eastward on NCN 1, passing the docks and a massive industrial complex. Fumbling our way through Aberdeen, we've taken two hours to cover fourteen miles, but it's so hot that we're ready for a cuppa in Portlethen. The café is full of mothers with very loud babies and toddlers – how glad we are not to be parents.

The wiggly inland route to Stonehaven on minor roads is a good deal longer than the A90 but has the special advantage of staying alive. Several bridges cross the new Aberdeen Western Peripheral Route (still under construction). We're tempted to cycle along the empty tarmac, but not sure where it comes out. NCN 1 becomes entangled with horrible road works north of Stonehaven, and we have to wheel the bikes over rubble to get back to something resembling a flat stretch of surfaced road.

Walking across a town square, we swerve round an eager Jehovah's Witness. A café on the corner has lovely cheese scones – but they're cheese and bacon! Why put bacon in a cheese scone? It's a cunning and successful plan to annoy vegetarians.

The Stonehaven to Inverbie route on minor roads is fine, except for a tiny bit on the A92, until we come to a large 'Road Closed' sign. Cyclists can usually squeeze past or persuade workmen to let us through, so we cycle on and risk it. A hefty stone wall has collapsed right across the road, and a large digger is plonked in the middle, mounds of earth on one side and piles of stone on the other. The digger driver kindly lets us struggle through, and we're able to help two women struggling through the other way, manhandling their bikes and kit over the rubble. Our good deed done for the day, and a dangerous detour avoided.

South of Inverbie we find a scenic but bumpy coastal route for four miles to Johnshaven, avoiding the A92. It's on a disused railway track, which could have been a good bit smoother. The main road is unavoidable for three busy miles, all of which are uphill. Finally we turn off onto minor roads, following NCN 1 over a viaduct, across a disused airfield and into Montrose. The accommodation is cheap and basic, and we could only find a pretty ordinary fish-shop-cum-café open for our evening meal. We're not impressed with Montrose.

But perhaps we should be. The Montrose Basin immediately behind the town is 'the largest inland saltwater basin in Britain', and underlines the sudden creation of the island we're cycling round. Archaeologist Neil Oliver explains that the thick layer of sand found here was left behind by 'a tsunami 50 feet high', caused by a massive earthquake off the coast of Norway 8,000 years ago. This massive wave cut us off from continental Europe in a single day. I view Montrose with more respect.

DAY 34   MONTROSE TO CRAIL   (64 MILES)

Another sunny day. Fifteen gentle miles on small roads into Arbroath, passing the impressive ruins of Red Castle in Lunan Bay, once owned by Robert the Bruce. A fawn in a small paddock is frightened and jumpy, bounding back and forth, then leaping over the wooden fence and away over the farmland. Another similar hare and more yellowhammers.

In Arbroath we glimpse the famous abbey, where Scottish nobles gathered in 1320 to proclaim the Declaration of Arbroath, praising Robert the Bruce and asserting Scotland's independence: 'As long as but a hundred of us remain alive, never will we on any conditions be brought under English rule.' Brave words. After a café stop, we follow a tarmac bike route out of Arbroath alongside the railway and into Carnoustie, where we're diverted off NCN 1 because of the golf. This happened at Troon two years ago. Shall we encounter more golf course diversions, or is this a space-time loop where the same golfers, yellowhammers and hares keep appearing?

A further trackside cycleway on NCN 1 brings us into Broughty Ferry, with another café stop and a chat with an elderly Dawes tandem owner (the elderly owner of a newish tandem). He's impressed with our Rohloff hub gears, but points out that our Ravens are filthy compared with his gleaming tandem. Cleaning bikes isn't much of a priority after a full day's ride.

We cycle on into Dundee, whose exports were said to be 'jute, jam and journalism', and which was once a major whaling port. Several whaling ships were also used as polar research vessels – Scott's *Discovery* and Shackleton's *Terra Nova* were both built in Dundee. We skirt round the city and ascend by lift up to the Tay Bridge, swiftly overtaking a group of schoolchildren so that we're not tangled up with them. The slightly weird central reservation cycleway is several feet above the roaring traffic, safely fenced off but not very relaxing, with two lanes hurtling by on either side.

Remaining posts from the original rail bridge are a poignant reminder of a winter storm in 1879, when the central span collapsed as a train was crossing. The engine and six coaches plunged into the Tay and all 75 people on board were killed. The Tay Bridge disaster was also commemorated by William McGonagall, famous as Britain's worst poet. If he was with us now he would write:

We had a grand ride across the silvery Tay,

Even if it was slightly uphill all the way.

The cycleway and pavement lead us into Tayport, and onto a rough track round the Tentsmuir Forest, a pleasant run through the trees, if a little bumpy. We meet a chap on a Moulton, whose tiny wheels must be uncomfortable on this terrain. He's younger and fitter than we are, and we attempt to overtake him without success.

After pausing in Leuchars for the third café stop in 45 miles, we find another roadside cycleway leading us into historic St Andrews, where the apostle's bones allegedly rest, home of golf and a famous royal student. One café proclaims 'William met Kate here' in large letters. (A café in Leeds could proclaim 'Robert met Caroline here' but doesn't.) The last ten miles into Crail were on the not-so-nice A917, but we've done 64 miles in all today and are not really tired.

Crail has some lovely sandstone buildings and a fine little harbour, with good views of the Bass Rock, north Berwick and even Dunbar, almost fifty miles away. It has good places to stay as well, but our hotel isn't one of them. When we arrive at five o'clock, the owner is asleep and has to be woken by a neighbour. He emerges unsteady on his feet, and his speech is slurred.

'There's been a wee problem with your room, just a bit of a leak in the plumbing, but it's all OK now.'

Steve is led to a sunny room with a sea view, and I'm taken to the room with the wee problem. Heading for the shower, my bare feet cross a wet carpet. The hot water takes ages to run, the cold tap bangs when turned on and off, and water leaks noisily into the toilet after flushing. Coming out of the bathroom, I notice the smell of damp.

We ask the owner for breakfast at eight o'clock.

'Oh, that's a wee bit early for me, shall we say eight-thirty?'

When we walk out in search of an evening meal, the

owner and his neighbour are sitting on the wall outside drinking large glasses of wine. We have a good meal at the nearby Golf Hotel and come back for an early night. The two men and their friends start singing in the street, just outside my room. Steve misses all this in his sea-view room. Eventually I fall asleep. Loud voices wake me in the dark, as the friends shout their goodbyes, slam their car doors and drive off. It is 2.45 a.m.

DAY 35 *CRAIL TO PORTOBELLO* *(64 MILES)*

I thought everything that could go wrong at a B&B had already happened. But at breakfast my grey scrambled eggs swim in a watery soup, and each forkful has to be drained. After eating two slices of thin white toast, I notice blue-grey spots on the next piece. The bread is mouldy. As we prepare to leave, the owner asks for £85 in cash, when I had booked for £75 and sent him a hefty £50 deposit. I am sorely tempted to give him nothing except my candid opinion of him and his hotel.

Instead I give him £25 and we collect our bikes from the corridor outside Room 12. We are the only guests, so how come I get the room with the wet carpet? The ten rooms we didn't see must be even worse. I won't name this hotel. Who knows, it may change hands and get much better? Perhaps the current owner will sober up and improve his plumbing, cooking, food hygiene and financial management. I hate complaining, but we should have done so. It was truly appalling.

We cycle away from Crail on the busy and rather unnerving A917. Anstruther – known locally as Anster

– has ancient buildings housing the Scottish Fisheries Museum, which 'embraces the entire history of the fisheries and fisherfolk.' No, we didn't have time. But it was a pleasure to cycle through Upper Largo, where retired admiral Sir Andrew Wood had a canal dug from his castle to the church, 'so that he might be rowed to the service by his old shipmates each Sabbath morning.' I wonder how much they enjoyed that, especially in the winter. Next stop Lower Largo, birthplace of Alexander Selkirk, the castaway and inspiration for Defoe's *Robinson Crusoe*. I was surprised to learn that Selkirk and the island were both real.

During a café stop at Leven, we have time to ponder urban decay and road safety. There are several run-down communities along the coast here. It's not a good sign when the first three shops you pass are boarded up. Perhaps they should set up as opticians. Despite us both wearing bright yellow tops, two cars pulled out of side streets straight in front of us as we cycled into the town.

On we go through Methil, recently voted one of the five worst places in Britain to visit, and Buckhaven and East Wemyss, all rather run-down after the mines closed and heavy industry moved elsewhere. Kirkcaldy is much larger and feels more prosperous, though its fame for producing linoleum has faded. The guidebook suggests that great men have been its most important export: Adam Smith, author of *The Wealth of Nations*, architect Robert Adam, and landscape gardener Lancelot 'Capability' Brown were all born in Kirkcaldy.

A couple of miles further on at Kinghorn, we cycle past a monument marking the spot where in 1286 a horse stumbled and threw its royal rider over the cliff to his death. Alexander III was said to be 'one of Scotland's wisest kings'. He wasn't bright enough to keep his horse away from the edge, was he?

Through Burntisland (burnt-*eye*-land, not *burn*-tisland), and so to the beautiful Dalgety Bay, on a helpful track. NCN 76 here is a good little road-and-cycle-path route along the coast. Suddenly there's a fabulous view – all three Forth bridges in the sunshine. We wriggle our way round Inverkeithing, and emerge onto the old road bridge, now restricted to buses and taxis and its fenced-off cycle lane, and much quieter than before.

North Queensferry appears far below and the other bridges draw the eye. On our left is the newly-restored rail bridge, the three familiar rust-red diamond shapes stretching out across the Forth. 53,000 tons of steel, 6.5 million rivets and goodness knows how much paintwork. They really did have to start again each time they finished, though now it's been coated with 'permanent paint'. Paint that lasts forever? I don't think so. As we gaze at this Victorian marvel, a train obligingly pulls across, like a tiny toy crossing a giant's Meccano set.

The train disappears and we look at the new road bridge on our right. The Queensferry Crossing takes the M90 across the Forth, and was opened by Queen Elizabeth in September 2017, fifty years after she opened the original bridge we're riding across. It's the world's longest triple-tower cable-stayed bridge, and the UK's tallest, its towers reaching up an astonishing 207 metres. It looks wonderful in the sunshine, like a three-masted sailing ship with its silver hawsers as the rigging.

The last ten miles into Edinburgh on NCN 1 are new to us. We got lost in the city centre and missed our way coming north on LEJOG five years ago. This time all goes well and we come in on quiet roads and a tarmac surface on the old railway line. Thank you Sustrans! Crowds are flocking towards Murrayfield for a Rolling Stones concert, and Steve checks for late tickets. Yes, a few left at only £400 each. But where would we leave the bikes?

I dislike cities, but I'll make an exception for Edinburgh. I have happy memories of staying with friends here many years ago. (Edinburgh is famous for its authors – James Boswell, Arthur Conan Doyle, Walter Scott, and Robert Louis Stevenson were all born here.) We cycle off through the Meadows and meet two Sustrans volunteers interviewing cyclists about their journeys. Our answers cause amusement – no other respondents have been cycling eight hours a day for ten days! (Anna Hughes needed a new rear wheel and chainrings in Edinburgh after 800 miles, but we seem to be trouble-free.)

Soon we're riding through the 320-metre-long tunnel beneath Arthur's Seat, built in 1831 for the Edinburgh and Dalkeith Railway, to bring coal supplies into the city. It's long been known as the Innocent Railway, as it was horse-drawn to begin with, when steam engines were still considered dangerous. Out in the daylight again, we follow the railway path on NCN 1 for another mile or so, but then turn off on the Brunstane Burn Path, a lovely route through the woods, emerging on the coast road. Seaview Terrace in Portobello is much longer than we thought, but eventually we find our B&B, infinitely better than the hotel in Crail.

Portobello was supposedly founded by sailor George Hamilton, who had fought at Puerto Bello in Panama in 1739. This sounds like an elaborate bluff to me. Wandering along the seafront, we come to the Beach House, which serves us a really excellent meal – super veggie food. This is our second evening with no internet access – Steve is suffering withdrawal symptoms, but I understand he is able to access data via his smart phone. Perhaps I might buy one, join the rest of the world, and save weight by not bringing my iPad.

DAY 36   PORTOBELLO TO BERWICK   (64 MILES)

The morning sea fret clears after a while. We ride through Musselburgh, an important seaport in Roman times, known as 'The Honest Town' since its citizens declined compensation in 1332 for looking after the dying Earl of Moray. James IV played golf here in 1504. Pedalling along the coast to Prestonpans, we vaguely remember hearing of this in O Level History. (Battle of Prestonpans, 1745. Bonnie Prince Charlie's forces win. Get your O Levels and escape into the sixth form.) A traffic-free path into Haddington, birthplace of John Knox, leader of the Scottish Reformation, where we stop for coffee. Haddington marks Two Thousand Miles done on our coastal circuit. And we're *still* not half way round!

It's much warmer when we emerge. Pausing on a stone bridge to apply sun cream, a kingfisher streaks along the river. We have a straightforward run along the River Tyne – remembering we're in East Lothian rather than Northumberland – and into Dunbar for lunch. Dunbar is the birthplace of John Muir, the famous explorer and early environmental campaigner. We're honoured to be riding on the John Muir Trail. There's also a lifeboat museum....

Soon we're cycling beside the A1 which is even worse than the A9. We're safely on a cycle path, but it's disconcerting to see and hear the traffic roaring past a few feet away. (Mike Carter cycled on the A1 itself, which I can't recommend.) Then we turn off and go down steeply into a little place called Cove, with a ford at the bottom and a much stiffer climb on the other side. While Steve struggles on, I see a man by the roadside with a new Dawes Galaxy. We sit on the grass and compare bikes, both pretending we're not really out of breath.

After four miles of gradual but relentless ascent on the A1107, we glide down into Eyemouth for another coffee stop. There's a cloudburst as we emerge from the café! We scramble to find our wet kit, racing off on soaked bikes to take shelter at the entrance to Eyemouth Maritime Centre. It's built in the form of a full-scale wooden ship, with a long bowsprit above us. Let's visit a museum! No, due to financial problems it's now permanently closed. We could have learned all about the hurricane of October 1881. The experienced fishermen saw there was a storm in prospect, but followed when the younger men took a risk and left port. The terrible result was that 19 boats were sunk and 129 Eyemouth men drowned, leaving 'nearly a hundred new widows, almost 300 children newly fatherless.'

Fifteen minutes later the sun comes out. The road's steaming as rainwater evaporates. Off we go with yet another slog uphill, and a wiggly road before the border sign – back to England at last, with Scotland's coastline all completed! We shake hands and take photos. I considered a man-hug, but the look on Steve's face says no. We are English after all.

Adding the distance from Carlisle to Thurso via Fort William, and another 627 miles from Thurso to the border, Scotland's wiggly coastline seems to be 2044 miles in all. That's twice as long as Land's End to John O'Groats!

A few more hills before we drop down into Berwick, where we find a lovely B&B with a very amenable owner. 'Bring your bikes in and leave them in this room, they'll be fine here overnight.' A good meal in the Queen's Head, and we're looking forward to the last couple of days, which should be easy with a shorter mileage.

If Edinburgh is my favourite city, Berwick could be my favourite town. It has often passed between English and Scottish control in the past, and is still surrounded by Elizabethan defensive stone walls. Local people may see themselves as Berwickers rather than Scottish or English.

Three bridges cross the Tweed here. The 1635 Jacobean Bridge has fifteen arches, increasing in size as they approach the town. Upriver is Robert Stephenson's magnificent Royal Border Bridge, completing the London to Edinburgh railway line in 1847. Trains pass 125 feet above the river on 28 arches. Between these two is the not-so-lovely concrete Royal Tweed Bridge, built in the 1920s to take the A1 into the town.

After ten days cycling, mostly in the sun, my face and neck are brown, and my arms below the T-shirt line. There's a sun-tan tide mark on each thigh, where the bike shorts stop. My hands have brown knuckles exposed beyond the track mitts. After a shower, I catch sight of a strange form in the mirror. Is this a pink man with brown limbs, or a brown man wearing a pink T-shirt and shorts?

According to Steve's navigation thingy we have climbed over 3000 feet today! This seems hard to credit – but we have certainly cycled 64 miles.

DAY 37   BERWICK TO AMBLE   (62 MILES)

Breakfast is served in our room – a decadent first! Overwhelmed with luxury, we leave the B&B, and I lead Steve down a cul-de-sac which ends in two flights of steps. They're so steep we have to unload the panniers and carry the bikes down. He teases me about my faulty navigation, and this time – just this once – he's absolutely right.

There's a heavy sea fret, quite damp for the first two hours. This turns out to be a slow section, with hard work on rough and muddy coastal tracks, where both we and the bikes get filthy. A pause at the Barn at Beal brings coffee and cake and a thorough wipe down for cycles and cyclists.

We were tempted to cycle over onto Holy Island, but it's only an island when the tide's in, so it doesn't count as part of the mainland. Anyway, Caroline and I have ridden across on holiday. Steve and I agree that honour is satisfied – though I'm not sure it counts if only one of us goes there.

Before the Norman Conquest this wouldn't have been a problem. Britain was bigger in Saxon times, with the coastline from Berwick to East Yorkshire several miles further out into the North Sea. The same is true of East Anglia, most of Kent, Sussex and Hampshire, parts of the west country and almost all of Wales. This would have made our coastal journey even longer, and with no bicycles. Aren't we lucky?

We managed a mere sixteen miles in the first two hours, but then get going more steadily. After a complicated road works diversion along country lanes, we come back to the A1, where the large signs read Newcastle north and Berwick south. *What?* We've gone horribly wrong somewhere! Retracing our route adds six wasted miles to reach Bamburgh. It's not my fault this time, we're both as confused as each other. From now on we take extra care with route-finding, and have no further problems. Crossing a slippery cattle grid, I fall off against a rickety wooden fence. Nothing much is bruised except my ego, and Steve manages not to laugh.

The café in Bamburgh is bulging with visitors, but it's good to have a stop. Bamburgh Castle towers over the village, covering an impressive eight acres in all. According to Malory's *Le Morte d'Arthur*, Bamburgh was Sir Lancelot's fortress, where he brought Queen Guinevere after their affair was discovered. Chivalry, castles and adultery! Except that Arthur lived in the seventh century, long before the castle was built – and may have been fictional. Good story though.

The medieval walls of the keep are ten feet thick, but all is not as it seems. The structure was 'over-lavishly rebuilt for the first Lord Armstrong' in the 1890s. Much of the castle is more recent than Bamburgh's local heroine, Grace Darling, the lighthouse keeper's daughter. In 1838 she and her father rowed a small boat out in a violent storm to rescue nine men from a shipwrecked steamer. Theirs wasn't a lifeboat, so the RNLI awarded them only a silver medal. The story is well-illustrated in Bamburgh's little Grace Darling Museum, which I have actually visited – though not on this trip, obviously.

On we go to Seahouses, Northumberland's smaller version of Skegness. Crazy golf, gift shops, an amusement arcade, soft play area for children – and lots more. NCN 1 winds inland for a few miles before returning to the coast near Dunstanburgh Castle, 'a brooding presence of stone on its tapering ledge of rock above the sea', and more ruinous than Bamburgh. We continue through Craster, home of kippers, and Alnmouth, one of my favourite little towns. We're both tired after eleven days in a row, and are happy to reach Warkworth, which also has an ancient castle, probably built in the 1150s by Henry II while repossessing Northumberland. The River Coquet makes a loop round the town, with its Norman church and medieval humpback bridge, which 'served the town from 1379 until 1965, when an unsightly new bridge was built beside it.'

The last few miles into Amble feel a bit of a slog, and we're relieved to get there. Our planned 55 miles today has somehow become 62, but every day seems to end at about 5.00 or 5.30 pm whatever the mileage. The Amble B&B is basic, and the Old Boathouse restaurant is fully booked, but they send us along the harbour front to the Fish Shack, which was good for both fish and a veggie option. Our last evening celebration included an extra beer for me, which may have been a mistake.

DAY 38   AMBLE TO HOME   (46 MILES)

Another lovely sunny day. We ride along the path round Druridge Bay, always a pleasure, looking out for unusual birds, thought they seem to have been told in advance to hide this morning. This was planned as an easy day, and so it turns out, pootling through Lynemouth and Blyth – both once coal mining communities, but now more an industrial wasteland – and then on through Seaton Sluice and Whitley Bay, still on NCN 1. Sustrans have done a superb job signposting, tarmacking, using local routes and linking them all up so that cyclists have little need to ride on the dreaded dual carriageways. Having said that, NCN 1 goes all the way to Dover, which still seems a long way off.

At Tynemouth we pause for a delicious sandwich at a café, and glide round to the Shields Ferry in glorious sunshine. I remind Steve of the last time we crossed the Tyne here, but he insists he's never been on this ferry before. One of us has had a memory lapse, and we both know it's the other one. I've been across on this ferry – who else could possibly have been with me? Oh, there was the time when my neighbour Mick and I did the Hadrian's Cycleway together. That might have been it. Steve beams with delight when I tell him.

We pedal gently through South Shields and Whitburn and soon arrive in Sunderland. Persistent problems with Northern Trains means a long wait for a train to Bardon Mill. Steve phones Julie and yes, she can meet an earlier train in Hexham with the car and the bike rack. We sit sweatily in the train and are both home before 5.00. I plunge into a bath and dump all my bike kit in the wash.

Accommodation for this trip was mixed as before, with no correlation between quality and price. One of the two excellent ones was predictably expensive, but the other was the cheapest of them all. Let's forget Crail. On our return I weighed myself and found I had lost seven pounds. Apparently Steve has remained exactly the same. Cheese scones versus carrot cake?

Trip Three was 735 miles, with an average of 61 miles each day. Our total mileage cycling round all of Scotland and Northumberland now stands at 2152. This still isn't quite half way. How much further round the rest of England and Wales? I hardly dare think about it. But next year we plan to do *two* trips, and see if we can't get right round to Cardiff. This will leave only one trip left for the final year, and so reduce the whole crazy journey from seven years to a mere five. If we get that far.

6

WEARSIDE TO HUMBERSIDE – SUNDERLAND TO HULL

DAY 39   SUNDERLAND TO WHITBY   (73 MILES)

After completing our second June trip and returning from Thurso, we felt we could do a little more. In September we cycled for three days along England's east coast. This was *before* the third trip described in the last chapter. Only a complete pedant would put this in chronological rather than geographical order. I'm more of a part-time pedant, so let's leave it here, bridging the gap between Sunderland and Hull.

The early train from Hexham is crowded – standing room only, squeezed in with our bikes between commuters. Most of them get off in Newcastle and we can sit down from here to Sunderland. The morning looks drizzly, but this may just be the Wearside fret.

Soon we've found our way out of the city without

getting lost, and onto NCN 1 again. The day brightens up with glorious sunshine and a strong westerly wind. We bowl along southwards, and turn off onto NCN 14 towards Hartlepool. There's a good surface on the disused railway track, but we've not reckoned on the overnight rain. At one point the path is completely flooded with black water too deep to risk on a bike. The only way forward is blocked by a steep bank crammed with bushes, brambles and nettles. The next fifty yards is a hard physical struggle, scrambling through with our bikes. Our feet are soon soaking wet, our legs badly scratched and stung everywhere. This is one of the few low points on the whole journey. Only a grim determination keeps us going.

Finally we escape into a housing estate and find our way into Hartlepool, cycling through the impressive marina, and turning inland through an extensive industrial wasteland. This is familiar territory for Steve but entirely new to me. Then one of the highlights of the trip, crossing the River Tees by the famous Transporter Bridge, now resplendent in bright blue. You drive, cycle or walk into a massive cage – another bit of road suspended from the bridge above – which glides across the river with you safely inside it. A bargain at 60 pence each.

The cycle route takes us through Middlesbrough – with just a little loss of direction and a narrow bumpy footpath, and on into the centre of Steve's home town of Redcar. The cycle path twists through some allotments, where a notice announces: 'NCN 1 – John O'Groats to Dover'. True – but why would you choose to announce it in Redcar?

Steve suggests it's because Redcar is a good place to

leave, and I soon see why. We pause for Steve to have a chat with his brother John the butcher – a free sausage roll for him, but nothing suitable for the vegetarian. Along the high street we pop into a café and wait a few minutes to be served. The waitress says they don't do food after three o'clock. It's one minute past three. We stand up and leave, before steam comes out of Steve's ears. A second café has the same story – no food after three. It's four o'clock before we can find a panini at a seaside café in Saltburn.

Pedalling up into more hilly country on NCN 1, we pass the highest cliff on England's east coast at Boulby, and drop down steeply into Staithes, where the explorer James Cook first worked as a young grocer's assistant. Once a busy little fishing port, whose isolation made it ideal for smugglers, Staithes is now mainly a spot for tourists, and many houses here have become second homes.

All is not well. Steve has pulled a muscle in his right leg and is going much more slowly on the hills. He encourages me to carry on alone, but no, we'll slow down and stay together. As we pass Whitby Golf Course, one of the greens is swarming with oystercatchers. And suddenly there is lots of sea! More familiar to coastal Steve than landlubber Robert, the waves coming in along a wide beach with *such quantities of sand* – as the Walrus said to the Carpenter. We formulate **Rule Eleven: We have to see the sea every day**. Otherwise it doesn't count and you have to do the whole day again. Let's hope this doesn't catch us out later on.

It's seven o'clock before we arrive at the B&B. Steve's in real pain, having bravely cycled twenty miles or so with only one good leg. He rests both legs in the B&B while

I slope off for a meal and a pint of Theakstons, both of which were very welcome. I did bring him some chips back.

I remember visiting Whitby, the ruined abbey on the cliff top and the statue of Captain Cook. His famous ships *Endeavour* and *Resolution* were built in Whitby, a whaling port in the eighteenth century. Several thousand whales were brought into the quayside here, and their blubber boiled down to make oil. The stench must have been appalling. Another local industry is Whitby jet, mined here since Roman times, and carved into all kinds of jewellery and ornaments. I assumed it was a soft stone, but it's fossilised wood 'subjected to chemical action in stagnant water and then flattened by enormous pressure.' Whitby is where a huge black wolf leapt from a ship whose crew he'd killed, raced up to the churchyard and once more became…. Count Dracula! Black jewellery and vampires – Whitby is a favourite with modern Goths.

Lying in bed and dozing, I'm worried about Steve. Will he be able to continue tomorrow, and if not, what shall we do? Does it count if I go on and he goes back? How would he get back? Should I go back with him? The answers to these questions are all the same – I don't know, let's wait and see what tomorrow brings.

DAY 40   WHITBY TO HORNSEA   (60 MILES)

Steve seems to have recovered a bit this morning, though we dawdle over breakfast, and pull out of Whitby very gently. No twinges and he seems to be OK. Luckily NCN 1 follows a disused railway line most of the way from

Whitby to Scarborough, though it's not all as flat as we expected. We bowl through Robin Hood's Bay, where the outlaw reputedly came from Nottingham to Yorkshire 'to help the abbot repel Danish invaders'. How likely is that?

After a long push up to a coffee stop, the café's full. The only free seats are sharing a table with a couple who we recognise – our ex-postman Colin and his girlfriend! Small world. We're about to set off when I notice my flat tyre. At least it's the front one, and a slow puncture too. I pump it up and we carry on. Does this count as a puncture if I'm still riding on it?

We cycle on into a sunny Scarborough, sometimes called the Nice of the North, but only by those who have never been to the south of France. It's really nothing like Yorkshire! Nobody calls Nice the Scarborough of the South. On our right is the once-magnificent Grand Hotel, opened in 1867 as the largest brick building in Europe, with '365 bedrooms, 52 chimneys, 12 floors and 4 turrets representing the days, weeks, months and seasons of the year'. It's less grand now, operating at the budget end of the market, with a series of health and safety problems. We cycle past the foot of the South Cliff funicular railway, which has been running up to the Esplanade above since 1884 and is powered by gravity – or more properly by potential energy, created by adding water to a tank in each car at the top and letting it out at the bottom. No, I didn't really understand it either.

The sun is shining, Steve's legs are OK – the tired one as well as the muscle-pulled one – and my front tyre only needs pumping up about once an hour. We pause for lunch in Hunmanby, where everything is served with coleslaw.

Perhaps it's farmed or mined near here. There are more hills between Scarborough and Bridlington, and it seems to be a long way, but we take it easy. We don't quite make it out to Bempton Cliffs, the spectacular bird colony with a 400-foot vertical drop, partly because the nesting season is over, but mainly because it is down a dead-end road (see Rule Three). On the prom in Bridlington, I *ping-ping* a couple to warn them of our presence. The man turns round with a broad Yorkshire reply: 'Two cornets, one with a flake please!'

We planned 64 miles today, though it came down to 60 with a bit of careful short-cutting. But with a late start, more hills than we realised, a couple of 'navigational episodes', and pumping the tyre up once an hour, I'm really tired by the time we get to Hornsea. Thankfully Steve is back in business with both legs functioning better after a night's rest, though still a bit slow on the hills.

The Hornsea B&B has an ageing-hippy feel about it, and we had a good meal in a posh restaurant where we are the only customers, apart from a few drinkers at the bar. The food's excellent – my goat's cheese, rocket and mushroom is served on a square pizza. Why should pizzas always be round? Perhaps you could choose the shape as well as the toppings. Mozzarella and sun-dried tomato on a triangle, please!

It's only later I realise this has been Day 40 of our projected 80 Days Around the Coast. We seem to be about half-way round, in only three fortnights. Or to put it another way, it's taken us three years to get half-way round. Only another 40 days cycling, and we should be back in Carlisle!

DAY 41   HORNSEA TO HULL   (57 MILES)

We order an early breakfast and we're away by 8.15. No time to visit the North Holderness Museum of Village Life, with 'reconstructed Victorian rooms, collections of farm gear and railway relics'. I bet you didn't know Hornsea Mere is Yorkshire's largest freshwater lake, albeit less than a mile from the sea. Isn't nature wonderful?

I've pumped the front tyre up again. Would it be quicker to change the inner tube? There's certainly less emotional effort. I hate repairs, and always think I'm going to get it wrong. If I pump the tyre up once an hour that should get me home, where I can change the tube indoors. What a wimp!

An hour and a half in the drizzle brings us into Withernsea, where heavy rain drives us into a café. It's a different world. Apart from the worst coffee I've ever tasted, we're twice the age of the other customers, but only half their weight. Even men and women in their twenties are overflowing the chairs, and can hardly prise themselves upright to waddle out. Since the railway closed in 1964 Withernsea has been slowly declining. You wonder how much further it has to go.

We wait until the downpour passes over, then make for the bikes. But the rain comes on again before we can leave Withernsea. We hide in a bus shelter, which reminds us of Scotland. A bus pulls up, and for a moment the driver thinks we're hoping to get on. Sitting in a bus shelter in the pouring rain in Withernsea, we're tempted to turn around and head direct for Hull.

After passing two villages in the damp, we come to

Easington, where some of the houses have been built from 'sea cobbles', large stones gathered from the nearby beach. It's cheaper than buying bricks. North of the village is the massive and hideous terminal where North Sea gas has been piped ashore since 1967. Finally we reach Kilnsea, a village so isolated that it actually has two shores – a sandy east shore on the North Sea, and a muddy west shore in the Humber estuary. The land's been eroded fast here – an earlier Kilnsea is mostly under the waves. Last year we could have cycled along a narrow peninsula to the lighthouse at Spurn Head, but a few months ago the access road was finally breached in a winter storm. Spurn Head is now a new tidal island. So that's saved us a few miles.

Turning round, we're relieved to be heading for Hull and home. Towards Patrington we hide in the trees for another shower to pass, reminding us of getting soaked to the skin on the road to Dumfries. Patrington has a fine little café, where two coffees and two cakes set us back a mere £4.90 – and they were all right too. Then we plod westwards along the A1033, which is fairly busy, but has a pavement where we ride illegally but more safely.

At Ryehill we turn north and find the start of NCN Route 66, which sets me off singing – *Get your kicks, on Route 66!* Steve tries again to push me into a ditch. The map warns this a rough surface, but it's not bad and a considerable improvement on a main road. The track is level, quiet and traffic-free – and less windy too. The breeze was behind us going south, but in our face strongly coming back from Kilnsea.

And so into Hull, where the NCN signposting is not

all it might be – or are we more tired and gormless than usual? We need to add this to the list of places we got lost. I've been to Hull several times to research my family history – my parents met here many years ago. I enjoyed wandering round the old town and the docks, and exploring William Wilberforce's house, with its graphic accounts of slavery and his fight for abolition. No time for that today, we're off to the station and home.

A slow train takes us to York, then an express to Newcastle. Steve manages to lose his ticket – I knew I shouldn't have given it to him. He's still got the bike ticket, and the nice ticket inspector lets him off, much to our relief. When you meet two old fools with bikes, it's more likely one of them would lose his ticket, rather than not buy one in the first place.

What have we learned from our September jaunt? Stick to June! The weather was not good for these three days. Having said that, it was foul for quite a bit of Trip Two up the west coast of Scotland, and that was in June. It will be a while before we forget the horizontal rain on the way up the Applecross Pass, or appearing in Durness like drowned rats.

This little coastal run round to Hull has clocked up another 190 miles, making 2342 for all of Scotland and the first little bit of England. It should also allow us to plan for only three further trips to get round the rest of England and Wales. If we are still daft enough – we're still not much more than half-way round.

* * *

After we came back from Sunderland at the end of Trip Three, we planned to keep cycling together once a week through the rest of the summer, and on into the Autumn and winter. But somehow it didn't happen. Steve and Julie focus on sailing during the good weather. We only got back into what might loosely be called training in the autumn, with an occasional weekly ride, usually 40 miles in our standard loop to the café in Brampton and back. With Steve's toasted tea cake and my cheese scone, I'm not sure we lost as many calories as we gained.

How many miles do you have to cycle to burn off a cheese scone? There's probably a scientific answer to this, but it's pretty complex, depending on several factors. How fast are you cycling? The harder you push, the quicker you burn off calories. Where are you riding? If two cyclists each ride forty miles at ten mph, one in Northumberland will burn off calories faster than one in Norfolk, because of the hills. Unless the one in Norfolk is riding into the wind – and only if they're identical twins who weigh the same to start with. How much do you weigh? How fit are you? If you are an overweight couch potato, the calories should come off more quickly than if you are already lean and fit. But the experienced cyclist can ride further and faster, even on the hills, so might burn off calories more quickly than the overweight newcomer. And then there is the scone itself to consider. How large is it? How cheesy? How much butter did you put on?

I weigh the same after our ride to Brampton as I did when we set out. So my answer to the cheese scone/calorie question is 40 miles. If I go further and faster and there are hills to climb, I'm going to need bigger cheese scones and more of them, or I'll fade away. Isn't science wonderful?

Our discussion about losing weight came to the same conclusion as usual. Steve said he couldn't be bothered, and I promised to lose a stone but then didn't. I intended to do lots of winter training on my static bike in the porch, but this didn't get much further than a New Year resolution.

In early January Steve and I set off for Brampton again, on our first ride for a good few weeks. Both of us admit to topping thirteen stone over Christmas, though he is seven pounds heavier than I am. I hope to keep this advantage throughout the year, so I can keep calling him Fatty. We find the hills incredibly hard work. Where's all that fitness we had cycling from Thurso to Sunderland? Lounging on a comfy sofa in the café in Brampton, we're appalled to see what our tummies look like – the spare tyres go almost all the way round. What a sight.

On the way home we're slowing down. Steve pulls ahead on a hill and it takes me a couple of miles to catch him up. How will I cope with the extra weight of the expedition again in June? In a sense I'm doing it already, except it's round my waist rather than in the panniers.

Just before we join the South Tyne Trail – a favourite off-road section which takes us back into Haltwhistle – I spot a dead tawny owl and stop to pick him up. He weighs nothing in my hand. Stiff as a board, but otherwise perfect, he's probably flown into a car and broken his neck. It's a privilege to hold this beautiful creature, with his feathered legs and large talons. I place him gently away from the road.

On a windy morning we take the train to Carlisle and cycle back home. Steve is going well but I'm working hard to keep up. He pulls away from me on a hill and I can't respond. He's taller, younger, and fitter than me, so he probably has a better power-weight ratio. What's the solution? Lose more weight than him and get fitter.

The next week we want to extend our mileage, so we take the train to Annan and cycle back via Gretna, Longtown and Brampton. Steve has got the bit between his teeth today and it's all I can do to keep up with him. He has to wait for me twice, much to my dismay. We're up to fifty miles now, and I'm shattered, while he seems fighting fit. At Hallbankgate we stop in the community café, and read about a local couple who are cycling Wall to Wall – Hadrian's Wall to the great Wall of China! We feel considerably less intrepid.

In early February we set out for Wylam on a bitterly cold morning. An hour later we're riding into Hexham alongside the River Tyne, and we're both frozen, so we stop for an early coffee. After sitting in the café for half an hour to warm up, we decide to turn back. It's a long pull up to the top of the Stanegate – the highest point on Hadrian's Cycleway – but just for once we're glad of the hill, which gives us a chance to keep warm. Don't go out if it's below freezing! You'd think we'd have worked this out before now.

By the end of March we finally get out for a really long run – an early train to Dumfries and a 70-mile ride back via Gretna, Longtown and Brampton. We're both tired but quite pleased with ourselves. We manage two more long rides in April. The first one means taking the train to Sunderland and cycling home against the wind, uphill and on tracks rather than road for much of the first half. It's a real slog and we're both completely exhausted when we finally got home.

This makes us think about the right kind of training, as this year we're hoping to complete two trips instead of just one. We don't need hill training for Lincolnshire and Norfolk in June, though it might come in useful for Devon and Cornwall in September. Have we bitten off more than we can chew here? A week later we are off again round the Big Loop, again with more hills than we need for Hull to Southampton. Why does the wind always seem to be in your face?

With only six weeks to go before Trip Four, I'm out of action with a foul summer cold, and feeling as weak as a kitten. Steve has it too, and it keeps going into May. I'm counting down the days to Monday 3rd June and hoping I'm off the sick list by then.

7

HUMBER, THAMES, DOVER, WIGHT – HULL TO SOUTHAMPTON

DAY 42   HOME TO CLEETHORPES   (42 MILES)

Free at last of our summer colds, we meet up at Bardon Mill station. Steve breaks a record – three TLPs before the train arrives! There's a noisy journey from Newcastle to Leeds, with young women downing cans of G&T at 10.00 am, but otherwise an uneventful three-leg journey into Hull.

We have some difficulty finding our way out of the city, but not enough to admit that we got lost *again*. Soon we arrive at the Humber Bridge, the world's longest single span when it was opened in 1981, with 44,000 miles of wire in cables suspended from two towers 533 feet high. It would be more impressive if the bike lane wasn't four feet below the main carriageway – exhaust fumes spew out into our faces all the way across. I'm guessing the architect wasn't a cyclist.

Wriggling through Barton-upon-Humber, we set off on NCN 1 again, finding ourselves still in Yorkshire. I assumed the Humber was the county boundary with Lincolnshire, but apparently not so. Thence through Burnham, Melton Ross and a couple of miles on an off-road track across fields and through a woodland edge. By now we really are in Lincolnshire, which is not yet as flat as I had hoped.

We pull into Great Limber, bemoaning the lack of a coffee stop. But look! The post office sells drinks and sandwiches. We sit on a bench munching, feeling English and tranquil and rural. Minor roads lead us off through Swallow and Beelsby, where we turn off NCN 1 and find a new NCN 110 signposted to Cleethorpes. Thank you, Sustrans!

Waltham is much more built-up and by 5.00 pm we're cycling through our very first traffic jam. Before long we're in Cleethorpes at a good B&B where our bikes are invited into the dining room! We don't feel bad about missing Grimsby and its commercial docks. After a pub meal – where I astonish Steve by only having a single pint – I take a walk along the sea-front – the usual amusement arcades, ice cream parlours and shops selling only 'donuts'. The lovely Victorian pier has recently been taken over by a business which claims to be The World's Largest Fish and Chip Shop. I think I'd emphasize quality rather than floor area.

We can see across the Humber to the Spurn Head lighthouse, and nearer the shore are two circular forts guarding the mouth of the Humber. Haile Sand Fort and Bull Sand Fort were built during the First World War with armour-plating over a concrete core. Now the military no longer need them, they're available as exclusive residences, very private and extraordinarily ugly.

Cleethorpes suffered badly in the 1953 floods. The sea broke through all flood defences from the Humber right round East Anglia and on to Deal in Kent – over 500 miles away by our coastal route. At least 24,000 houses were flooded and over 300 people were drowned. It will take us eight days to cycle to Deal. Let's hope it stays fine and we're not washed away.

DAY 43   CLEETHORPES TO SKEGNESS   (56 MILES)

After a good breakfast, sharing the dining room with our bikes, we're away by 9.00 in fine weather. Steve pauses to buy orange juice and I stand astride the bike outside the shop. A chap walks up with a friendly wave.

'Aye aye, where are you off to?'

'Skegness today.'

'Skegness? Not on a *bike*?'

No, I've got a helicopter folded up in my panniers for when we get tired.

We tried the main road out of Cleethorpes, but it was too busy – like the road into Cleethorpes – so we find a smaller one, helpfully marked yellow on the Sustrans map to recommend it to cyclists. This takes us on to Tetney Lock and North Cotes, where a wrong turning brings us unexpectedly into Fulstow. We find our way back onto the yellow road – only yellow on the map of course, though a stripe along the road would be very helpful at the moment.

Riding along flat roads at last, we pass through wonderfully-named villages – Covenham St Bartholomew, Saltfleetby St Peter, Theddlethorpe All Saints. This was when *everyone* went to church. Thence into Mablethorpe, once chosen by Tennyson for solitude on the day his first poems were published, reciting verses to his brother on the deserted beach. Today overweight holidaymakers are ferried from the Golden Sands Holiday Park to the amusement arcades on the Jackson's Land Train, 'with realistic train noises and songs played during your journey'. A cartoon railway engine pulls coaches full of people who can't walk half a mile. Steve and I glide past, waving at the occupants, who all ignore us. We've overtaken a train – it really is quicker by bike! This is nothing compared to Anna Hughes, who arrived here after riding 121 miles in a day from Wells-next-the-Sea. She's a true athlete – though she was only 28.

The first of our promenade rides is along a wide concrete path and through Sutton on Sea. After the 1953 floods – which reached two miles inland here – extensive new sea-walls were built. The concrete is a little bumpy in places, but good to cycle on, except where the sand has blown across, making it almost impossible to steer. You can ride a bike with care through mud or gravel, or even stony ground, but cycling across loose sand doesn't work at all.

In the afternoon we turn inland looking for minor roads to avoid the busy A52. At Chapel St Leonards we ride round in a square and back onto the main road close to where we left it. From Ingoldmells – site of the first Butlins Holiday Camp – we're directed by a helpful café owner back onto another concrete sea-front leading directly into Skegness, only after several hundred yards of amusement arcades. Sounds drift across the road – bored bingo callers shouting numbers into their microphones.

Apart from the famous poster declaring that Skegness is 'so bracing', I knew nothing about it. (Mike Carter's back wheel buckled here, but that happened in other places as well.) In *The Road to Little Dribbling* Bill Bryson contrasts the town's continued popularity as 'the ninth most visited place in Britain' with its isolation: 'Lincolnshire is a long way from anywhere, and Skegness is about as far into Lincolnshire as you can get'. I think Skegness is in just the right place, tucked away in Lincolnshire, so you can't come across it by accident.

We're only a few streets away from our B&B when the rain comes on in torrents, and we dive into a café. It's about to close, and we're forced to hide under a Victorian shop awning before a short and wet ride to the hotel. These have been two relatively easy days to start with. We have an excellent meal at a nearby Italian restaurant, still keeping to one beer each, though one of us ate rather too much. We should have removed our yellow rain tops *before* entering. The owner hid us in a corner away from the other diners, taking us for workers from a building site. Our sophisticated conversation might convince him otherwise, but it was too late by then.

DAY 44   SKEGNESS TO KING'S LYNN   (73 MILES)

We're happy to leave Skegness. A few winding and windy miles brings us into the little town of Wainfleet All Saints.

It's delightful today – but a week after we returned home, Wainfleet was completely flooded when the River Steeping burst its banks, and almost everyone had to be evacuated. At least nobody was drowned.

After a series of infuriating detours, where we keep coming back again to the A52 in another space-time loop, we've wasted several miles. Where are the road signs? Perhaps they removed them in the war to confuse potential German invaders, and never put them back. Finally we reach Boston, passing a fabulous windmill on the way in, and stop for a sandwich and coffee. The famous church tower known as the Boston Stump is visible for miles, and from the top you can see Lincoln Cathedral, almost thirty miles away.

Six hundred years ago Boston was an important seaport, despite being several miles inland. Ships still come to the docks along the River Witham, but Boston is now known (rightly or wrongly) as Britain's murder capital. At the next table is a First Responder gearing up for a busy night shift, who has a way with words. 'What goes in the top must come out the bottom,' she says, as I head off for the loo.

After a slight wobble finding our way out of Boston, Steve coins the term Lincolnshire Miles – poor signposting and thus definitely not our fault. We've done five such extra miles today and three yesterday. Eventually we're back onto NCN 1 and through Frampton and Fosdyke Bridge. Then we get lost finding our way into Holbeach, which isn't where it should be. Why do they keep moving these villages?

After a good café stop – asking a local pays off again

– we feel a bit better and pedal on again, as NCN 1 winds its way through vast flat fields, with scores of vegetable pickers lifting cabbages and loading them onto wagons. Ten of them are riding on a contraption drawn by a tractor, bending over and planting the next crop, like human seed drills. Most of them are from Eastern Europe. Who will work this land in a post-Brexit Britain?

We leave NCN 1 at Gedney, as it would lead us to Wisbech and away from the sea. Minor roads north of the A52 lead us towards King's Lynn. Although we're most of the way around The Wash, we haven't yet seen the sea at all today. This causes some alarm, due to Rule Eleven – the ocean *must* be viewed every day. We decide that two views of Obvious Tidal Influence (OTI) count as one view of the sea. The tide's out and we count four OTIs in all, mud banks on rivers flowing into The Wash. We cross the River Nene on a swing bridge with its own bike track at Sutton Bridge. Robert Stephenson's earlier bridge here didn't last, and the 1881 docks collapsed a month after they opened. We cross quickly before anything else happens. Sutton Bridge marks 2500 miles on our coastal circuit. Past half way at last!

This is a long day and we're tired when we reach King's Lynn, whose centre is full of wonderful historic buildings. The fifteenth-century St George's Guildhall is the largest in England to have survived in one piece, and contains the only remaining theatre where Shakespeare is said to have *performed*. Even more astonishing is the town's maritime and commercial history. As early as the fourteenth century King's Lynn was 'the third most important port in England', according to Neil Oliver, not only for fishing, but also to receive 'iron, pitch, timber and wax' from elsewhere, and to send out 'cloth, grain, lead wool and skins' to wherever they were needed. On the map it appears a good way inland now, but as we walk along South Quay to a restaurant, we can see all the way up the River Great Ouse to the open sea. We didn't need those four OTIs after all.

DAY 45   KING'S LYNN TO CROMER   (65 MILES)

It's an easy start out of King's Lynn on NCN 1, where we catch up with an Australian couple cycling a similar route. We ride along and chat with them, passing through a forest which turns out to be the Queen's back garden at Sandringham, with a great avenue of mature trees. The house – a mock-Jacobean mansion built in 1870 by the then Prince of Wales – is well hidden and there is no sign of Her Majesty.

The Aussies are behind us when we stop for a drink, but they catch us up and hold forth on the evils of Australian bike helmet legislation. They apologise for going on about this, but when they get onto the evils of dog mess, Steve and I decide it's time to move on.

A lovely gentle ride through Norfolk now, with more and more period flint houses – and posh new ones too, also in flint, copying the vernacular style. After a café stop in Burnham Market, we ride through Burnham Thorpe, birthplace of Lord Nelson. His local pub the Plough, renamed in his honour in 1798 after the Battle of the Nile, has been closed for some years, but plans are afoot for refurbishment.

We turn up at the main gates of Holkham Hall. NCN 1 is signposted through here but electronic gates are closed to all but authorised visitors. A tiny side gate forces us to remove our panniers to squeeze through, expecting to be thrown out at any moment. *Get off my land!* We glide down the main drive in splendid isolation, waving to imaginary peasants on either side. The Hall itself, begun in the 1730s and only completed three decades later, is fairly described as 'a vast Palladian mansion', with posh fountains in front. The interior is probably just as grand, with paintings by Raphael and Rubens and others of that calibre. Tourists approach en masse via a rear car park and miss out on our magnificent view.

A track leads away from the Hall towards Wells-next-the-sea (known locally as 'Wealth-next-the-sea'), which is less idyllic than I had imagined, with amusement arcades and lots of tourists. It must have looked different in 1953, when the floods threw a 300-ton coaster onto the quayside. Everything looks quaint but not spectacularly prosperous. Maybe the posh houses are round the back.

Equipment malfunction! Steve's left pannier has lost a screw and threatens to detach itself from the rack. He binds it up with temporary strapping – but posh nautical Wells has a *chandlery*, where he buys a little bolt (actually a pack of four, three of which he doesn't need). Ten minutes later the problem is sorted.

Soon we leave NCN 1 again as it turns inland, and head off on NCN 30, the Norfolk Coast Cycleway, well-signposted by Sustrans. We somehow miss a turn on the last few miles into Cromer, ending up on the horrible

A148. After missing *another* turn down a wooded lane, the road ahead is closed and blocked by metal fences. Riding back up the lane, we see the NCN sign we missed, and turn into the grounds of Felbrigg Hall, a fine Jacobean building described as 'one of the most elegant country houses in East Anglia'. We ride through the park feeling very grand. Even the jays in the oak trees and the green woodpecker seem part of an ancient landscape.

At the far end of the park there's a Road Closed sign immediately in front of us, but we ride on regardless. A second and a third sign insist the road is closed, but a few cars are passing in both directions. Emerging from this confusion, we accidentally enter Cromer at exactly the right place, and the B&B is easily found. A gentle day's cycling in the sunshine.

Cromer was originally inland, but the coastal village of Shipden was washed away in medieval times. The lifeboat here saved hundreds of lives in the Second World War, and its coxswain Henry Blogg is famous among lifeboatmen. We had holidays here when I was a child, but it's changed a bit since then.

DAY 46   *CROMER TO LOWESTOFT*   *(58 MILES)*

NCN 30 leads us out of Cromer on a dry and breezy morning, though the forecast is howling gales and driving rain. After only ten miles we stop for coffee in Mundesley. Steve is fretting about the weight in his panniers. He asks in the Post Office about a box to send stuff home, as in Tobermory, but then in the café he decides to plod on with all the kit he has.

What to take on a cycling tour? Cyclist A believes he'll never get a puncture or break a spoke, or need a multi-tool with allen keys on. His chain will never break. Cyclist A travels light. Cyclist B knows these catastrophes can and will happen, so a full tool kit must be carried, making the bike heavier.

I'm Cyclist A and Steve's Cyclist B. He carries spare spokes and pliers and a chain-repair thingy. I teased him about this until an earlier Hadrian's Cycleway trip, when we both still had bikes with derailleur gears. After a two-hour train ride, we set off from Ravenglass station – and my chain broke. Using the aforementioned thingy and a spare chain link, Steve mended my chain in fifteen minutes, washed his hands, and didn't even say *I told you so*. I was speechless with admiration for his forethought and expertise, and I don't tease him now. Except about the spare spokes hidden in his kit, which neither of us will ever need. Hopefully.

So what do you really need? Rear panniers, a bar bag for things used during the day, water bottles and a bike lock. And all the maintenance stuff – multi-tool, puncture repair kit, spare inner tube, chain links, lubricant, cloth rag and rubber gloves. Spare shoe cleats? We take an eccentric spanner – not one with an odd personality, but one which fits the eccentric bottom bracket, to tighten a slack chain when needed. Shall I take another spare tyre, as well as the one round my waist?

That's just for the bike. How many pairs of bike shorts and socks do you need? How many T-shirts? You have to wash your kit each evening – or every other evening at least – and try to get it dry overnight. What about when it rains? I weighed out my clothes on the kitchen scales, while Caroline gave me that *I married a harmless lunatic* look. Bike shoes, socks, shorts, cycling longs, T-shirts, long-sleeved tops – you need them all. Then there's safety and comfort and wet kit – high-viz tabard, helmet and cover, track mitts and full gloves, sweatbands, waterproof jacket and overshoes. Shall I take a cover for the bike itself?

While we're thinking about safety, here's a heartfelt plea to cyclists young and old who want to look cool on the bike. *Don't Wear Black!* You can't be seen by motorists, lorry drivers and white van men, all of whom can easily flatten you and your bike. Wear bright clothes and stay alive!

Turning up at the pub in sweaty clothes, however bright, can make you feel unwelcome as well as uncomfortable. You need what we laughingly call evening clothes. I take lightweight trainers, socks, pants and trousers, non-cycling T-shirts, and a sweatshirt or a fleece top. Back to the kitchen scales. I wear boxers at night, but Steve takes his pyjamas. Extra weight.

What about everything else? Toilet kit – a tiny tube of toothpaste plus the ordinary necessities. Don't forget the deodorant! Steve takes a full first-aid kit, but at least you need sun cream, lip balm and nether-region cream of some kind. You don't want sunburn or chapped lips, and you need to avoid chafing in the saddle-contact area.

The other stuff goes into the front bar bag where you can get at it. Cash, cards and tickets in the wallet. Pens and notebook, itinerary and B&B bookings. Mobile phone and charger. Spare glasses, emergency crunchy bars – and maps. In Scotland I took OS maps as I already had most of them, but for England and Wales I relied on the excellent Sustrans maps – less detailed but much lighter. It all weighs something and has to be lugged round. I dread to think what Steve's kit weighs, but he can't decide what to send home.

Despite the route being well signed, we miss our way and add on a couple of Norfolk Miles in the country lanes. We pass some thatched barns as big as churches, one of them dated 1581 on a plaque set into the flint wall. Ancient storage on a grand scale! Another plaque at Sea Palling marks the completion in 1959 of an eight-mile stretch of sea defences from Happisburgh (pronounced *hays-borough*) to Winterton. There's nothing new about our losing battle with the sea. Daniel Defoe visited Winterton in 1725 and found half the village was made of wood salvaged from shipwrecks. At Happisburgh 400 sailors were drowned in 1801 when the unwisely-named HMS *Invincible* broke up on a sandbank in a storm. But Happisburgh history is the oldest of all, because of a discovery on the muddy shoreline in 2013 – human footprints almost a million years old! They were made by 'pioneer man' – *homo antecessor* – who looked quite a lot like us. We humans are a lot older than we think.

It's a *long and winding road* – I start singing again, and Steve tries to push me into the verge – which leads not to your door (as in the song), but into Yarmouth for a sandwich. Steve takes a long pull on his ice-cold mango drink, and suddenly goes red in the face. 'Freezeburn!' he says, putting his head in his hands. His glasses fall on the floor and I think he's going to pass out. All I can do is mumble, 'Keep breathing, you'll be all right.' He can't hear me. After a few long seconds his eyes open again. He's a bit shaken, and sips the drink carefully, looking at it with suspicion. My diagnosis is that he's had a funny turn.

Yarmouth is recorded in the Domesday Book, and it later developed into a medieval shipbuilding centre. Daniel Defoe waxed lyrical about the harbour, where he found 'the finest quay in England, if not in Europe', running through the centre of the town. By the early nineteenth century a thousand herring boats were based in Yarmouth harbour, until overfishing led to a decline. We're only slightly lost before finding the promenade, a good flat concrete path on the sea-front, just as the rain comes on properly, belting into our faces with a powerful wind across the grey-brown North Sea. It's a *very* wet hour down to Lowestoft, and bitterly cold.

Lowestoft has an ancient rivalry with Yarmouth, with frequent 'sea fights' in the 1590s recorded in Camden's *Britannia*. Finally the Yarmouth men damned the mouth of the River Waveney so Lowestoft trading vessels couldn't reach the sea. A bit extreme? I wondered if this rivalry still persists but thought it best not to ask.

The B&B is basic, but after a wander round we find an Indian Restaurant called the Spice Den, where we have a really splendid meal, washed down with four pints of Kingfisher (two each, let's be sensible).

DAY 47   LOWESTOFT TO FELIXSTOWE
(OR SO WE THOUGHT)   (70 MILES)

Riding out of Lowestoft, it's wet and windy as forecast. After a few miles we pass through a village with a wonderful flint and thatch church with a round tower. It looks exactly like the one we saw yesterday. Is this the Norfolk space-time warp? Shall we end up back in Cromer? No, there are over 150 round-tower churches in East Anglia, half of them in East Norfolk, so it's not surprising that we've seen a couple of them. Flint rubble was often the only building stone available locally, and wasn't thought safe for corners – hence the round towers. But some of the naves have perfectly good flint corners, and the round towers were probably copied from the style of German churches. Don't ask me why.

For once our route-finding is accurate, even on unmarked minor roads, but the rain and wind increase alarmingly. After a café stop in Southwold – a prosperous fishing port a thousand years ago – Steve buys new waterproof trousers, having torn the originals. We ride slowly along Southwold's lovely harbour, thinking how much nicer this would be if the wind were not blowing rain into our faces. Eventually we find the footbridge across the River Blyth and a track into Walberswick.

The Suffolk Coast Cycle Route (NCN 42) would take us from here to Dunwich, which I wanted to visit to see what is left, since coastal erosion swept Saxon, Norman and medieval settlements into the sea. Even the church fell into the sea in 1920. But time is pressing and we cut the corner off, by-passing the RSPB reserve at Minsmere. Instead of marsh harriers, bitterns and avocets, there's a glimpse of Sizewell's nuclear power station. We pull into Leiston for a larger-than-expected lunch. I hadn't realised the cheese toastie comes with salad and chips. Filling though.

As we leave the café, I walk across a drain cover and

think how awful it would be if I dropped my bar-bag key down there. Five seconds later Steve realises he's lost his bar-bag key! But it's not down the drain, he left it in the café and soon retrieves it.

The country lanes lead us into Snape and the Maltings, home of the Aldeburgh Music Festival. It's not just a famous concert venue – you can eat and shop here, view art exhibitions or go birdwatching. We do none of these, but cycle past in the rain and wind, grumbling. We also have to miss Orford Ness, as the Butley River ferry only operates on weekends and Bank Holidays. There's less traffic as we ride through Alderton and Bawdsey, and we can soon see why. The road is a dead end with only a foot ferry across to Felixstowe.

Wheeling the bikes down a tiny jetty, we find a stick with a white disk on the end marked 'Wave Bat for Ferry'. Assuming this is an invitation to summon the ferry – rather than a bat to propel the ferry through the waves – I pick up the bat and wave it, feeling rather foolish (and slightly pedantic).

It works! The ferry emerges from the other side, and we're taken across the River Deben with our bikes by a silent ferryman, whose only word is 'Thanks' as Steve hands him the money. Perhaps he has things on his mind. Or maybe he's a magician – as we step off his ferry the rain's gone, the clouds are a brilliant white against a clear blue sky suddenly full of swifts, wheeling round screaming and hoovering up insects on the wing. We glide along with twenty of them swooping and diving overhead, speedy and graceful at the same time. All wind and wet is forgotten.

At Felixstowe the guest house has no record of my

booking! The owner's apologetic, but they're full up. Either he hasn't registered my booking or I've made a gormless mistake. Steve is very forgiving as we cycle round Felixstowe trying to find somewhere else. Everywhere is booked up. It looks like the station or a beach-side shelter, neither of which are appealing.

Steve's brilliant solution is to ask the fully-booked Felixstowe Premier Inn if there's another one nearby – and there is! Ipswich is ten miles away, and an hour later – thanks to Sustrans NCN 51 taking us off the appalling A14 – we're booked in by a nice woman from Ukraine. She agrees to secret Steve's bike behind reception, which somehow prompts yet another TLP. My Thorn is carried upstairs and sleeps overnight in the room with us. We've done 70 miles rather than 60 today, but we have a roof over our heads, and Steve kindly doesn't mention Bluck Miles.

DAY 48   IPSWICH TO SOUTHEND   (76 MILES)

Our enforced inland detour is a blessing in disguise. The Felixstowe to Harwich ferry is suspended today due to bad weather, and the planned route to Brightlingsea and Mersea Island is out of range. We cycle through Ipswich's impressive marina, a long way from the coast at the head of the River Orwell. Defoe suggested the town should become a whaling port for Greenland, where blubber could be boiled down for oil. Mercifully the citizens of Ipswich ignored him.

We head out on NCN 1 towards Colchester. There are yellowhammers in the hedgerows and a kestrel glides past us at head height, only fifteen feet away. A much closer view of a green woodpecker, but sadly he is dead by the side of the road. Lovely plumage!

The Centre of Colchester looks interesting, but with a long day ahead there's no time to explore. We take a short cut from the winding NCN 1 to get into Maldon, a place I've always wanted to see. At university I had to decipher *The Battle of Maldon*, an Anglo-Saxon poem celebrating the 991 conflict between Byrhtnoth's Englishmen and Olaf Tryggvason's invading Vikings (Summary: English fought bravely, Vikings won easily.) As the oldest recorded battlefield site in England, I imagined Maldon as a peaceful backwater with a helpful interpretative sign. Today it's heaving with cars and crammed with people enjoying their Sunday afternoon. We've done 50 miles and would like to see the restored nineteenth-century sailing barges in the harbour. Again there's no time, so we head off south, and the rain comes on again for an hour.

Cycling from Lincolnshire and Norfolk into Suffolk and now Essex, we've noticed increasingly obvious signs of wealth. Houses seem to get larger, electric gates more imposing, Range Rovers and large BMWs more frequent. A red Ferrari roars past. *Who wants to be a millionaire?* Aggressive driving becomes more common.

We reach Burnham-on-Crouch jetty in the nick of time. A woman waiting there tells us the last ferry is in ten minutes. Actually it's two minutes – the three of us jump aboard, the ferryman sees nobody else, so we're off. Unlike yesterday's ferryman, he's friendly, chatting and laughing with the woman, who's been across simply to retrieve her sunglasses. With yachts everywhere, we're not surprised to learn Burnham's been called the Cowes of the East coast. It's still raining.

With the River Crouch safely negotiated and 64 miles behind us, we plod on to Rochford and finally Southend. There was much to look at during this long day, but we spent our energy getting back onto the route. Aside from being a seaside resort, Southend's has the world's longest pier, dating from 1899, well over a mile long, with its own train and a lifeboat station at the far end. At the B&B the beds are not yet made up and the shower drains very slowly. Not one of the best.

DAY 49   SOUTHEND TO SITTINGBOURNE   (58 MILES)

The forecast is for continuous rain today. Our landlady suggests a shortcut to keep us away from the thundering traffic on the A127 to Basildon. So we keep to the seafront and then beside the railway, riding defiantly on a track regularly marked 'No Cycling'. At Leigh-on-Sea there's a path through towards Benfleet, north of Canvey Island, but overnight rain has turned this field-edge track into a mile-long corridor of mud. We slither along until I fall off, much to Steve's amusement.

Soon we're walking rather than cycling, with so much mud inside the mudguards that we can barely push the bikes forward. After a mile or so we turn onto a gravel surface and use sticks to poke some of the mud out. We look at each other and the bikes, caked with claggy mud, and are reduced to helpless laughter.

Turning north at Benfleet, we try to avoid the thundering traffic on the A13, a hellish dual carriageway.

The little road running alongside leads us into a cemetery, round the graves and out again. Death or the A13? A lorry driver appears at this exact moment – another guardian angel? – and directs us over the bridge to the old London Road on the other side of the dual carriageway. Not perfect, but a lot safer.

The rain has washed some of the mud off our shoes, but our bikes are still completely filthy. We can't turn up at a B&B like this. Steve finds a garage with a jet wash, and for a pound each we give the bikes and panniers and me a thorough hose down. If it were not still pouring rain, the man on the till might come out and ask what on earth we're doing. But at last we're completely mud-free.

Eventually we come into Stanford-le-Hope, and wriggle our way down to Tilbury. It was here that Queen Elizabeth (the First) – wearing a white velvet dress and a soldier's breastplate – made her famous speech: 'I know have the body of a weak and feeble woman; but I have the heart and stomach of a king, and a king of England too.' (That's all very well, your majesty, but it's us going off to fight the Spanish Armada, not you.) Sadly the exact spot is unknown, probably hidden inside Tilbury's massive container port.

The ferry terminal is deserted, but full of cars. What's going on? It's a foot ferry, you idiot, the cars are for people commuting across the Thames. Julie emails to say the main ferry has engine failure, and we ponder riding west to get a bike bus through the Dartford tunnel. But the reserve ferry turns up on time, and we go across to Gravesend.

Gravesend is the headquarters of the Port of London

Authority's Thames Navigation Service, with pilot boats guiding ships between the London docks and the wider estuary. This has long been one of England's most-used crossings – a vital link between East Anglia and Dover. In the fourteenth century, Gravesend's ferrymen were running both the 'Long Ferry' upriver into London and the 'Short Ferry' across to Tilbury, which has run continuously up to the present day – even when there's engine failure.

We stop for lunch, where it's now my turn to pay. On previous trips we've paid on alternate days, but Steve suggests we pay for one week each, and square up at the end. So far I haven't spent a single penny, but now I have to pay for everything for the rest of the trip. We've cycled through six counties in this first week – Yorkshire and Lincolnshire, Norfolk and Suffolk, Essex and now Kent. The weather may be gauged by the state of the Sustrans maps – Essex and Kent are almost falling apart, having been much consulted in the wet.

Now we're back on NCN 1 so we should be fine, on a solid off-road track to Higham and then a minor road into Rochester, with its fantastic castle. (The massive square tower of the 12th-century keep is said to be the best-preserved in England.) We cross the Medway and head round the south shore – on a path beside the road – and on into Gillingham and Rainham (most appropriate today). Steve buys newspapers to stuff inside our wet shoes this evening. It takes an age to get to Sittingbourne, and a cloudburst with real thunder and lightning doesn't help, as we try to get our bearings and find the B&B. We pull uphill on London Road, with water pouring down the gutter towards us.

We're both soaked to the skin. As yesterday, there were lots of good things to see today, orchards and oast houses and all. But for most of the time it was head down, try not to slip over, try to avoid the appalling traffic and the selfish driving of Kent's BMW owners (other vehicles were also driven selfishly at times).

Although we look like drowned rats, we're welcomed at the B&B with towels and kindness, a winning combination. Soon the towels are all wet, but we're warm and dry and our kit is hanging up and only damp.

This has been the wettest day in six years of cycling together, but the evening makes up for it. Steve's sailing friend Tony, who lives not far away, picks us up in his Volvo and whisks us off for a good pub meal and a couple of hours of friendly chat. Tony was in a terrible car accident last year and has had multiple operations, but seems to be on the mend, and hopes to come up to Northumberland at some stage. It will be a pleasure to see him again. A real tonic after a truly terrible day's cycling.

DAY 50   SITTINGBOURNE TO DEAL   (65 MILES)

There's no time to visit Sittingbourne's Dolphin Yard Sailing Barge Museum this morning. The sun's shining and we need to be away. Not all our stuff is fully dry, so I change into the other cycling kit. Some cyclists manage with only one shirt and one pair of shorts and socks, but pulling on wet kit is not pleasant. I left a new rain jacket and overshoes at home, thinking the old ones would do for June. What an idiot! They would have kept me a lot drier and warmer.

Safely out of Sittingbourne on the ever-reliable NCN 1, we pass through a little marina near Conyer, on an inland part of the Swale estuary, south of the Isle of Sheppey. We should have gone out to Sheerness but we didn't. An egret flaps across the water beside us, waits for us to pass, and then flaps back again. These delightful pure white herons are spreading northwards – we've seen them in Northumberland.

In Faversham we stop at the excellent art café, opposite a road leading to the parish church, with its huge tower and spectacular stone spire. It's a lovely town altogether, with Tudor and Georgian houses in evidence. Out in the countryside again, the orchards are full of apple trees, as befits the garden of England, and hops trained on tall wire trellises – the beer-garden of England?

Then on into Whitstable, whose harbour has the largest oyster hatchery in Europe. A row of two-storey fishermen's huts has been renovated as holiday lets. This is the start of a long ride round the coast on NCN 15, often on a concrete promenade. Through Herne Bay – another fishing village the Victorians turned into a resort – and into Reculver, where the huge towers of the ruined St Mary's Church, nicknamed the Two Sisters, were used as a landmark for shipping. Soon we find ourselves in Margate. Several places have 'No Cycling' painted on the concrete, though it's also clearly signed as a National Cycle Route. At one point a woman in black – an anti-cycling warden? – tells us firmly to dismount, but we ignore her and ride on. Will she phone ahead to the cycling police?

Margate saw the first covered bathing machines, allowing Victorian ladies to change and enter the water without fear of embarrassment. Today the sea-front is covered with amusement arcades and a funfair. People wander and ride up and down on the promenade. Idiots cycle with a dog on a lead, or while on their mobile phone. Both are daft and dangerous. But here comes a young man riding along the prom while *playing a guitar*! How cool is that? Not at all, you're a silly show-off, a danger to pedestrians, bringing shame on the cycling community. That's told him.

I'm keen to see the famous Nayland Rock Shelter, where T.S.Eliot sat and wrote part of *The Waste Land* in 1921. Many years ago I wrote a thesis on Eliot and have always been interested in his life as well as his poetry. The scruffy shelter is still there a century later. A fine blue plaque commemorates this important literary event, but it's mounted on the breeze-block wall of the adjacent public toilets, hinting at the obvious anagram of T.S.Eliot. Well done, Margate.

Now the NCN route goes through North Foreland Estate, so private that electronic barriers across the road stop anyone from sneaking in without this year's Range Rover. The lighthouse here was lived in until 1998, when local residents removed the keeper for driving a Ford (or perhaps because the light was being automated). We pedal through slowly, hoping to annoy the residents by energetic waving and being scruffy, but they're hidden behind tall hedges and electronic gates.

Around the corner of coastal Kent, we stop in Broadstairs for a coffee at The Old Curiosity Shop (1508), the very place which inspired the Dickens novel, now turned into a café. Dickens spent his summers in

Broadstairs, as the town is keen to remind everyone, with Christmas Carol Donuts, the Barnaby Fudge sweet shop and Great Expectations Casino. (Not really, I made them up.)

We emerge from the Old Curiosity Café with Steve slightly ahead while I'm fumbling with my track mitts and helmet. As I turn up the path to catch him, a young woman wheels her granny across the steep pavement. One wheel goes down the kerb first, tipping granny forward. She shouts 'Whoa!' and rolls her eyes at me. We both have the same thought and say it out loud together: 'You can't get the staff'. Granny and I start giggling, but her granddaughter misses the joke.

Before long we're in Ramsgate, and ride past a fine sculpture commissioned by Sustrans and funded by Pfizer. A pair of hands, eight feet high, emerges from the ground and cradles a molecule, celebrating innovative medicines developed in East Kent. Impressive if slightly weird. And we can see France! At least until Brexit, when we'll probably be towed out of sight.

Round the corner in Pegwell Bay, we ride past a newly-restored Viking longboat. This is the *Hugin*, a replica sailed across by a Danish crew in 1949 to celebrate the 1500th anniversary of the arrival of Jutland warriors Hengist and Horsa in Kent. The boat is looking splendid with sixteen oars on each side and a bright yellow dragon head on the prow.

We follow NCN 15 into Sandwich, a lovely medieval town, where we join up with NCN 1 again. Unwilling to leave the gaming table for a meal, the Earl of Sandwich famously asked for a slice of beef between two pieces of bread. This is how words pass into the language. Steve and I could have been ordering a tuna mayonnaise Ramsgate or a cheese and tomato Folkstone.

It's a sunny afternoon, there are few hills, we're going well and almost there. Coming into Deal, we end up on the dual carriageway. That can't be right. Heading back towards the town, another cyclist tells us the bridge is closed. It's a swing bridge which is jammed *open*, with no other way across. A man in the adjacent boatyard sends us back onto the dual carriageway, telling us we'll be safe as the traffic is *crawling*. And so it turns out. Half an hour later we're on the other side of the swing bridge, only a stone's throw from his boatyard.

A woman and a passing cyclist give us directions, both pointing towards another private road. This one has a *sentry box*, where two young women wave us through into the golf club and exclusive estate. A nice quiet road into Deal – but what a struggle.

Staying at a pub – with a small room and no breakfast, grouse grumble – it's disconcerting to find earplugs on the bedside table. But it's Tuesday and there's no karaoke or late-night noise from the bar. Or if there was, we were both unconscious.

DAY 51   DEAL TO HASTINGS   (65 MILES)

After a huge breakfast in a sea-front café – full English for Steve and full veggie English for me – we head off in an overcast but dry morning. Gliding along the promenade, we pass Deal Castle, an astonishing structure shaped like a Tudor rose, and built in 1540 by Henry VIII (not personally). Soon we're in Dover and the very end of NCN 1 – have we done all of it? All 1194 miles? Dover to Shetland – yes! Steve and I have done John O'Groats to Dover, and I've cycled all of Route 1 on both Orkney and Shetland.

The Channel Tunnel has had a serious impact on Dover. You don't need a ferry to reach France, and the town looks in decline. It could have happened a lot earlier. There were nineteenth-century plans for a tunnel, and in 1880 the English and French both started digging through the chalk, using 'a fantastical burrowing machine'. They had each advanced more than a mile when the English took fright and halted the project on security grounds. (I'm not making this up.)

It's not as flat as I thought today, but there's a magnificent view of Dover Castle as we plunge down into the town, close to the massive harbour, with a cross-Channel ferry coming in – they do still exist. A lengthy drag up out of Dover on the west side, at the start of NCN 2 – shall we do all of this one as well? I think so! We are soon on top of Shakespeare Cliff, the famous 300-foot chalk headland, and the tallest of Dover's white cliffs. Of course you can't see them from the top.

A mile or so further on at Abbot's Cliff, Steve gives a shout of recognition as we swoop downhill. A peculiar structure on the left turns out to be a First World War 'sound mirror.' These concrete structures were built around the coast as early warning devices, focusing the sound waves from enemy aircraft engines to a central point, to be picked up by an operator using a stethoscope.

In the 1930s radar made them obsolete, but several remain.

Coming down into Folkstone for a coffee, we're undecided about which way to go. That's nothing new, but this time we have *three* options – the coastal promenade, inland on NCN 2 or the Royal Military Canal, which leads to Rye and has the advantage of being straight. We potter along the sea-front to Hythe, where a local cyclist says you can't ride through beside the canal.

The Romney, Hythe and Dymchurch Railway brings memories of a childhood holiday, sitting in miniature carriages pulled by steam-powered locomotives. We decide to stick to the sea-front, and all looks well, bowling along the promenade towards Dymchurch. Then the rain comes on and we have to stop to put on our wet kit. It's easier to get waterproof overshoes on when you're sitting in the dry, not standing in the wet. We carry on in nasty solid rain and wind, properly set foul.

We're *cy*-cling in the rain, Just *cy*-cling in the rain,

It's a very wet *fee*-ling, we're *soaked through* again....
Steve tries to push me into the sea wall, but I pull ahead and keep singing.

Riding through Dymchurch, we cross the little railway again. We should have re-joined the road to head inland, but the sea-wall hides our view and we plod on along the promenade. Soon we're at New Romney, then Littlestone and Greatstone, an hour's struggle in the rain with no café. Eventually we see the towers of Dungeness Nuclear Power Station in the distance. We've come much too far. If it weren't raining we'd get a grand view of France, with the Channel at its narrowest here. Dungeness has almost 4000 acres of shingle beach, some of it 50 feet thick, though much depleted by recent extraction.

At Lydd-on-Sea the road turns back on itself and we head north-west across Romney Marsh, whose promoters describe it as 'a hundred square miles of paradise for walkers and birdwatchers'. Today it looks bleak for walking, and the birds are all hiding under whatever vegetation they can find. The only advantage is that the wind is now behind us and we can get through the rain faster.

We stop at a café with undrinkable coffee – even with three sugars to take the taste away, neither of us could finish it. The rain stops at last and we carry on, with a good cycle path beside the road back towards the coast. It's a bit overgrown, and we ride through some dense foliage with tiny yellow flowers, which soon are plastered all over us and all over the bikes and panniers.

A young stoat pops out from the yellow-flowering greenery onto the path, closely followed by two siblings. The three of them twist and tumble around each other in fun as we glide towards them, almost holding our breath. We're only a few yards away when they see us and vanish.

We ride on through Camber (remarkably flat) and into Rye, a gorgeous little medieval town with narrow cobbled streets, looking for a better café. Steve asks a woman if there's a Costa, and she replies in a cut-glass accent, 'Tosh, tosh, there are lots of *independent* coffee shops.' The one we find is lovely, with a helpful map of Rye on each table, so we can work out how to find the NCN 2 route out of the town.

Fifty miles done and it's only 4.00 pm. We're feeling

fine, until we come to Fairlight, with a spectacularly long and steep hill. We both think we can make it up here – and we're both wrong. I give up and Steve pedals slowly past, but soon comes to a halt. Gasping for breath, we push the loaded bikes up this endless hill, under a leafy tunnel of trees.

Finally we zoom steeply down into Hastings, site of the famous battle with the Norman French and William the Conqueror. Actually it was six miles inland at Battle, a village named after the…. Battle of Hastings. So why isn't Hastings called Battle? Because the battle was at Battle. Do try to keep up.

Pedalling along the promenade, we pass pubs, fish shops and amusement arcades. The spectacular cliffs are neatly set off by the Humbug and Gift Shop nestling beneath. We glide along the sea-front into St Leonards for our B&B.

'Our computers are down, you'll be in Room Six.'

'We've already paid, by the way.'

'Oh that's different, you'll be in Room Three.'

I'm past caring. Both rooms are on the second floor, which is a struggle after 65 miles. There must be an easier way to carry two panniers, a front bag and two water bottles, perhaps attaching the bottles to each other, or to the panniers, or both. I'm working on it. We wander into the town for a welcome pizza and another early night. By the time the Ten O'clock News comes on, we can only just keep awake.

The political background to this trip is that Theresa May has thrown in the towel after failing to sort out Brexit. We watch the news open-mouthed as the race to be the next Tory leader and our Prime Minister gets under way, without asking anyone except Conservative MPs and party members. In what parallel universe do they think Boris Johnson would make a good Prime Minister?

DAY 52   HASTINGS TO LITTLEHAMPTON   (66 MILES)

Yesterday's forecast was so bad that we considered calling today a washout and taking the train. But that would be cheating. This morning the prospect is for showers rather than lengthy downpours, so we set off along the sea-front in a howling gale. We start feeling sorry for ourselves, until we see a homeless man curled up in a sleeping bag under a promenade shelter, where he's spent a cold night barely protected from the wind and rain. We've had a comfy warm night in a B&B after a hot meal. So let's get things in perspective and stop whinging.

Hastings to Bexhill is a wet and windy ride along the promenade, but then NCN 2 turns inland to avoid both Eastbourne (which you might wish to avoid anyway) and steep hills on the South Downs leading up to Beachy Head. It may be a safer route for suicidal cyclists, if they don't have a heart attack on the hills instead of throwing themselves off a 500-foot cliff.

After some meandering we come into Polegate and notice we have done sixteen miles without a café. Again a local woman gives us helpful directions, this time to an excellent coffee shop. Another guardian angel? We exchange rainy experiences with two women cyclists. One of them has a Rohloff hub with a belt drive instead of a chain, which looks dodgy to me. Steve says I'm prejudiced and there are similar belts in the car. I bet they're not driving the wheels.

There's more gentle hilly wiggling before we get back to the coast at Seaford, passing Martello Tower 74, the most westerly of a chain of more than a hundred similar towers reaching from Aldeburgh in Suffolk round to here. Seaford marks another milestone – Three Thousand Miles now completed. In a village further on two brave men are re-tiling a church steeple, each dangling from a single rope. Let's hope *they* have a guardian angel.

The route goes inland for a mile before entering Newhaven, bringing us to a lunch stop after another sixteen miles. Soon we're back on the sea-front beyond Peacehaven with only thirty miles to go, feeling pleased with ourselves. Then we hit the promenade, with a powerful wind and rain coming off the sea. Head down and just keep on going – *we're cy-cling in the rain* – through Saltdean and Rottingdean. A vast Victorian building on our right is Roedean, the poshest girls' school in Britain. Don't get me started about private education, I'm in a bad mood already, with a howling gale driving the rain into my face.

On another day Brighton would be very pleasant. It has been called 'the queen of British seaside resorts', and its huge marina was once 'Europe's largest man-made yacht harbour' where over 2000 boats may be moored. It even has the world's oldest electric railway, opened in 1883 by Magnus Volk, a local engineer. But today the rain is lashing down and we're just trying to keep going.

The rest of the day seems endless, as we bash on through the industrial wastelands of Shoreham (nicer parts of Shoreham are also available). We pause here in a delightful café, setting off refreshed at 4.30 pm with fifteen miles left. Going through South Lancing and Worthing the wind is really fierce. I'm struggling to keep going at six miles an hour, even on the flat, and Steve is flagging. It's no better through Goring, head down and pedalling against the wind and rain. Finally at Ferring, after yet another 'No Cycling' section of promenade, we turn inland for a mile or so with the wind at last behind us.

The South Coast Cycle Route signs are not always clear. After some awkward manoeuvring and a tiny stretch of horrible dual carriageway, we're back into the howling gale on the sea-front again. It's only a mile or so before we turn inland along the river Arun and into Littlehampton, past the harbour and marina and boatyards. We've taken over two hours to do the last fifteen miles and ten hours from Hastings. I'm well relieved to see the Littlehampton YHA.

Here we're greeted by Les, a charming South African who checks us in, leads us to the bike shed, suggests good places to eat, and generally makes us feel welcome. An excellent meal at a local restaurant is washed down with a couple of pints of Sussex Gold. We're feeling good now, but this was one of the hardest days we've spent cycling together. We've often covered this mileage before, but not with the continuous howling gale and stinging rain in our faces. Steve is particularly weary, though we don't discover exactly why until we get home.

DAY 53   LITTLEHAMPTON TO SOUTHAMPTON (62 MILES)

An easy start from Littlehampton on the NCN 2 into Bognor Regis. Windy but dry, despite the forecast of more heavy showers. I put my wet kit on in case, and get hotter and hotter as the morning wears on.

We miss a turn somewhere – Bugger Bognor! After wrestling with a gate, crossing a field and finding ourselves on the horrible A259, we turn off down a path which doesn't look right. But a local woman walking her dogs gives us directions on a minor road and safely into Chichester. Sadly the magnificent cathedral is wrapped up for repairs.

Plodding on towards Emsworth on the NCN 2, we decide to avoid Hayling Island, reducing today's ferry journeys from three to two. We'll miss 'an abundance of seaside entertainments' as well as 'unspoilt beaches covered with grassy dunes.' We'll just have to cope. Instead we take NCN 222 south into Fratton, where Steve locates the first house he and Julie bought in 1981 for the princely sum of £17,500. He takes pictures, estimates it's worth over ten times that today, and skilfully navigates us back to the coast at Southsea, where we could have seen Henry VIII's 1545 castle, sea forts, and the wreck of the *Mary Rose* – but we didn't.

A white Vauxhall taxi squeezes me into the kerb and misses me by only a few inches. Bastard! Two streets further on, he stops down a side road. Years ago I'd rush down there to express my outrage. Not now. This is the benefit of regular meditation, and the realisation that taxi drivers are often younger and bigger and more aggressive than me. (Elderly small placid taxi drivers are also probably available.)

We progress round the sea-front to Portsmouth, gliding towards the Spinnaker Tower and the Historic

Dockyard, where we can see HMS Warrior, 'Britain's first iron-hulled, armoured battleship', launched in 1860. Round the corner is HMS Victory, made from 6,000 trees and held together with two tons of copper and iron bolts, with four acres of sail and 27 miles of rigging. Portsmouth is the birthplace of engineer Isambard Kingdom Brunel, who designed and built the *Great Western*, the first steamship to cross the Atlantic. We have lunch in a Caffé Nero with a large shelf of books twelve feet off the ground. Highbrow reading?

Down the ramp to the foot ferry we go, and across Portsmouth Harbour into Gosport in strong sunshine. We can see the Isle of Wight! Anna Hughes went across there to get her coastal mileage up to 4,000. I think we'll be closer to 5,000 by the time we get back to Carlisle. If we ever do get back there.

With twelve miles to go along Southampton Water, the time's tight for the last ferry across the River Hamble at Warsash. There's a long inland detour if we miss it, and no sign of a jetty at the end of the road. A local man sends us down a tiny path with no signpost, warning us that the ferryman often knocks off early.

We wiggle along a rough track to a bright pink shelter, where a man digging for bait confirms that we're in the right place. But where's the ferry? Eventually a small bright pink object emerges from further upriver and chugs across towards us. It doesn't look like a ferry. It pulls up end-on to a slab of old wood beside the rocks, and we wheel the bikes onto the front end. The ferryman reverses away across the Hamble. The estuary's five yacht marinas make it one of the most concentrated boating centres in England. There might be half a billion pounds-worth of craft within only a few hundred yards.

Having negotiated our two-ferry day, we're soon into Southampton, where the *Queen Mary 2* is a vast floating hotel towering over the harbour. I once came to Southampton on a day trip from primary school to see the original Queen Elizabeth (the ocean liner, not the woman addressing the troops at Tilbury). The city is teeming with traffic, but Steve's sense of direction locates the B&B while I'm still trying to follow the map. Perhaps it comes from sailing. The guest house is a bit basic, and we're due back here again in September. But it's only a short walk to a good Italian restaurant, where they produce a delicious vegetarian calzone – a massive Italian Cornish pasty with pizza dough. Yummy!

I make the mileage for this trip a respectable 756, averaging 63 per day, and bringing our total to 3098. That's not counting winter training. Perhaps there should be some sort of credit we could build up, with inland miles included at a lower rate. After all, if we hadn't done any inland miles, we'd never have got round the coast. This is part of my cunning plan to claim we've done at least 5,000 miles, if not more.

SOUTHAMPTON TO BARDON MILL BY TRAIN

We've plenty of time to catch the train this morning, and an uneventful six hours between Southampton and Newcastle, where we board a local train to Bardon Mill. Two thirds of the way round, with only two more trips to go! Steve's been complaining about the weight of his panniers, so we each put everything onto the scales before unloading them. My panniers and bar bag weigh about 19 pounds, about what I expected. If I weigh 12 stone 7 pounds and the bike weighs about 28 pounds, I've been pushing about sixteen stone around.

Steve emails me later to say that his kit weighs almost *seventy pounds*! This explains why he was falling behind in the foul weather – he's dragging *twenty* stone around! I know he has more bike tools, a laptop, an electric toothbrush and his shaving kit – and he's taller than me, so his clothes are a bit bigger. But his kit is *fifty pounds* heavier than mine. This doesn't bode well for September. Devon and Cornwall are much more hilly than East Anglia and Kent. That electric toothbrush will have to go.

8

SUMMERVAL: HILL TRAINING

It's odd to think of summer training rather than winter training, but our next trip is only twelve weeks away, and there are lots of hills ahead of us in the west country. Six days after returning, we take our regular 40-mile run out to Brampton. With no panniers it should be easy, but our legs are like lead as we struggle into the breeze. The last fortnight was relatively flat, unlike Northumberland. Summer training is thus definitely needed – and a thorough pruning of Steve's kit list. He'll not get round Devon and Cornwall with all that luggage!

By July we set off to ride round the Big Loop, but it was too windy for us, so we turned around after our café stop in Alston. 40 miles instead of 70 and we're still tired. It's not until we're nearly home that I notice Steve has his bike shorts on inside out again It's a good job his padded inserts are black. Mine are red, which would make my backside look like a weird baboon. But then I don't put mine on inside out.

Because of the foul weather, it's mid-August before we get round the Big Loop. As I'm heading down to Steve's house, he rides up to meet me, and we find a steeper route including Suicide Hill, the local name for the 1 in 4 road to Whitfield. (A little walking is required here.) Then we ride up to 1500 feet at the county boundary with Cumbria, with a fierce wind in our faces, before descending into Alston for coffee. The ride up to Hartside Top takes a full hour, with the wind against us all the way, and again we have to pedal *downhill* for a while on the descent into Melmerby. It's not natural. By the time we get around to Brampton we're both tired, and the last twenty miles to get home is a real slog.

I'm a bit apprehensive about Trip Five, with the steep hills of the west country in prospect, but I do have a secret weapon. I've lost a stone! Having weighed in at 13 stone over Christmas, I've recently tipped the scales at an astonishing 11 stone 12 pounds, so I'm feeling very pleased with myself.

With three weeks to go, we set off round the Big Loop again, anti-clockwise this time. It's drizzling as we ride to Brampton, and on the road leading to Melmerby it starts to rain properly. The cloud is very low on the Pennines ahead of us. I pull ahead of Steve and arrive at the café first, so I sit down for my coffee and cheese scone. Just as I'm starting to worry, imagining Steve lying in a ditch, he wanders in.

'I'm suffering from Premature Turn-off', he says with a grin.

A frank and unexpected admission of reduced libido? No, he took a wrong turning and didn't realise for about a mile. Bike in gear, brain in neutral. He admits these are Gibbon Miles, but that's fine, I didn't have to cycle them.

It's a long steady ride up Hartside from the wrong side – Melmerby is lower than Alston, so there's more height to gain this way. On the way up a shower passes over us, but I'm pushing hard, and the five miles to the top takes only 42 minutes. This is only seven miles an hour and doesn't look impressive – but it's *all* uphill, and it took almost an hour the first time. A young chap on a road bike overtakes me and pauses at the top. He and his pal are cycling from Hawes to Middleton-in-Teesdale today and camping. They have hardly any kit – just a tent and sleeping bag strapped to their handlebars and seat posts. Neither of them seems to have any clothes apart from their cycling kit. How do they get dry overnight? Maybe they don't.

Steve soon catches up and we plunge down to Alston – five miles in twelve minutes! Coming out of the café, we decide not to attack the big hill leading up and over to Whitfield. We'll go home the sensible way. The sun is out now and we bowl along in a warm afternoon, with the drizzle and rain forgotten.

Everything is now set for our September trip – or so I thought. After the farce in Felixstowe, I'm extra careful to get confirmation of our B&B bookings. Almost all are fine, but a guest house in Clevedon hasn't responded to emails or phone calls. This reminds me of the hotel in Crail, so I lose patience and cancel. The second I book an alternative B&B, the owner of the first place rings to confirm. Aaargh!

With two weeks to go, Julie and Caroline join us

on their electric bikes for a gentle 40-mile ride out to Brampton and back. It's August Bank Holiday, and the cafés in Brampton are closed. So we keep going to Hallbankgate, where the excellent community-run shop and café provides us with coffee and tea cakes.

Six days before setting off for Trip Five, Steve and I catch an early train to Dumfries for a long flat run back home. By 9.00 we're having our first coffee, ready to set off on an overcast but dry morning. An hour later we pass Caerlaverock Castle, and remember coming here on the first day of Trip One, more than three years ago now. What a nice café they had! It doesn't open for another half-hour, but the same kind woman lets us in, and the scones are as good as ever. We don't tell her how far we've cycled since we last met.

Pressing on towards Annan, the drizzle gets thicker, so another stop seems appropriate. I'm not sure all this caffeine is good for me, but they do have nice carrot cake. When we emerge it's nearly midday, we've had three stops already, and the drizzle has turned into proper rain.

Riding through Gretna without getting lost, we take the NCN 7 route to Longtown and then the B6071 for a straight run along to Brampton. I don't like this road, which has some heavy traffic, so I ride a bit harder. By Brampton we've done 52 miles in four hours cycling, at an amazing 13 mph! This doesn't count the stops of course, we couldn't ride for four hours without refreshment.

In Brampton instead there is *more* carrot cake! Steve calls me Fatty, but I just point at his bulging tummy. Pulling away on the last lap, I feel decidedly tired, due to my efforts between Longtown and Brampton. The rain eases off at last as we get closer to home, and we agree not to stop for a *fifth* coffee in Bardon Mill, but to head for our respective homes, and meet up on Sunday for Trip Five.

For the next couple of days I spend time fretting about my kit and the bike. Which cycling tops shall I take? Do I need a torch for September evenings? Are those crunchy bars and my spare glasses really essential? How will the Raven behave with two full trips between services? How difficult can it be to change the brake blocks? Eventually all is ready – or so I hope.

9

SOLENT TO SEVERN – CYCLING PAST PLUTO

At Bardon Mill station on a sunny morning, I'm delighted to see Steve has squeezed his kit into the smaller panniers. He must have jettisoned the bricks he carried round in June. Our train is a few minutes late, and loses time on the way into Newcastle, reducing our connection time to three minutes! We jump out onto the platform, race up the ramp and down the other side for the Birmingham train, load the bikes in a cavernous luggage room and dash for our seats. The train pulls out seconds after we sit down. That's the closest we've come to missing a train. With no Plan B, we might not have got to Southampton today.

There's a more relaxed connection in Birmingham, but the Southampton train has little space for bikes. It's a struggle to hang them vertically in a tiny alcove. The train itself is crowded, perhaps my fault for picking a Sunday start. I'm sure there was a good reason.

We find our way back to the same Southampton B&B,

with another good meal at the Italian restaurant. Steve produces my account of Trip One, which he reads through and scribbles on, with occasional nods of approval. I tease him about this extra weight, and he passes the manuscript across to me with a grin. *You're writing the book, mate, not me.*

The soundtrack to this trip is turmoil over Brexit. New prime minister Boris Johnson lost his first three votes in Parliament, we can't leave without a deal, and he's unable to call an election. His brilliant plan is to *shut Parliament down* because it won't do what he wants. Do we live in a democracy or a dictatorship?

DAY 54   SOUTHAMPTON TO WOOL   (60 MILES)

We sleep in, have a poor breakfast, and miss the turn as we set off. Our trip begins with a ferry across Southampton Water – if we can find the jetty. It's coming back to me now. Some ferries don't run every day, so the Sunday start was to avoid these problems. We fumble our way down to the terminal, where a little catamaran takes us across to Hythe, past moored vessels from different centuries. The ancient Calshot Spit lightship is being restored in a nearby dock, close to a vast cruise ship – a floating hotel with tiny people wandering round the top deck, ten storeys above us.

At Hythe we pull up at the end of a 700-yard-long pier, with an electric railway to take you into the town. We wheel the bikes instead, walking over sleepers inscribed with sponsors' names. The train rumbles slowly past us, looking slightly ramshackle.

In no time we're in the New Forest, heather in bloom and ponies everywhere. It was only new after the Norman Conquest, and is no longer a forest – more heathland and patches of woodland. Very nice though. We bowl along admiring the view and feeling pleased with ourselves – until we come into Lyndhurst instead of Brockenhurst. We've missed an obvious turn somewhere. We're not lost – we know where we are, it's just not where we planned.

A café stop provides time for route-planning, and we head south on the busy A337 into Brockenhurst. Steve turns off on the right earlier than expected and I have to follow him. Yelling doesn't work – he can't hear well at the moment. We're out in lovely moorland again, but this isn't the right road. After three miles or so we find a turn which brings us back onto NCN 2 towards Christchurch – and the rain.

There's no time to explore Britain's longest parish church, with the country's oldest bells, cast in 1370. It's been spitting a little this morning, but on the promenade at Bournemouth there's a steady rain blowing off the sea. *We're cy-cling in the rain, We're doo-ing it again....* Everything seems very familiar – grey sea, wind and rain in your face, beach huts and amusements arcades – the only thing missing is the No Cycling notices. Bournemouth boasts 'seven miles of golden beaches', but there's nothing golden in view today, as we struggle on to the end of the prom. Steve knows a good café where we linger for most of an hour.

We're in no hurry to get back out into the rain, and we can't raise the energy to explore the British Typewriter Museum. Britain has about 2,500 museums, and we've missed seeing quite a few. But even if we cycled past three museums a day on each trip – and some days we pass none at all – that would still be less than ten per cent. It's obscurely comforting to know we've only ignored a small proportion of them. Even our ignorance has its limits.

I was looking forward to a ride through Sandbanks, with some of the most expensive property in the country – posh houses range from £6 million to £16 million. Sadly we're denied the chance to gawp at all this wealth, as the Sandbanks Ferry has broken down. Instead we wind our way north of Poole Harbour – the world's second largest natural harbour, after Sydney in Australia – with its marinas and sailing clubs, and a distant view of Brownsea Island, a nature reserve and birthplace of the scouting movement. Then we ride on to Upton and tackle the A351 down to Wareham, which is very busy but has a safe footpath all the way.

South of Wareham, we're soon back onto the NCN 2 for the last few miles into Wool. A wasp gets inside my helmet and stings the top of my bald head. Ouch! I've not been stung for many years, and had forgotten how much it hurts. Meanwhile, half a dozen vintage cars come towards us, their owners wrapped up against the elements, even in June. The last one is a magnificent Stanley Steamer, the famous 'flying teapot', a hundred years old and worth a fortune.

In Wool our B&B has a *Sold* sign on the gate, but mercifully the existing owners are still in residence for the next few months. We meet up again with Steve's sailing friend Tony, down here for a folk festival. Another pleasant and convivial evening, with a good meal in The

Ship. The mileage today is 60 rather than the planned 55 but these are as much Gibbon miles as Bluck miles so they don't count against me.

DAY 55   WOOL TO BRIDPORT   (56 MILES)

We set off from Wool for a gentle ride on NCN 2 along the Frome Valley, through Morton, Woodsford and West Stafford. There's a sign to Hardy's cottage – only a mile or so uphill – and I can't resist. The National Trust Visitor Centre has coffee and delicious fruit cake, but the cottage itself doesn't open for another hour. Too long to wait, so we're invited to cycle up the access track to have a look from outside. A lovely picturesque cottage, very Thomas Hardy. Another one we almost visited but didn't. There's an odd example of life imitating art here. In my novel *Mr Woodreeve's Reflection*, Matthew Innes visits Dorchester to do research on Thomas Hardy. Now I'm sort of doing the same thing – am I turning into my own fictional character?

Steve's under the weather with a cold, so we pause in Dorchester to stock up on medication. Then we head south on NCN 26 with a good tarmac path beside the busy A354, bringing us into Weymouth, where we find the vegan and veggie Café Piccolo, much to my delight. Weymouth has the earliest sea-side promenade, constructed in the 1770s after an hotel was built facing the sea. Promenades often began as sea defences, but then attracted visitors who wished to walk along and enjoy the sea air.

There's a wiggly route, not always easy to follow, to the Isle of Portland. We didn't get lost, the road was in the wrong place. I'd hope to go down to Portland Bill, but the isthmus at Wyke Regis seems far enough. We look along the eastern end of Chesil Beach, an astonishing 18-mile strip of shingle, keeping the sea away from the Fleet Lagoon, home to a wide variety of wading birds.

There's some not very pleasant urban climbing to get out onto the busy and rather scary B3157, which leads into Portisham and safety. We climb steeply uphill towards the Hardy Monument (Nelson's admiral, Thomas Masterman Hardy, not the novelist), a massive 72-foot high tower on the top of Black Down. A spectacular view can be had from the top – except that it's closed.

After missing out on a second Thomas Hardy experience, we have a lovely afternoon riding through Dorset villages with their honey-coloured stone and thatch. Very picturesque, very Thomas Hardy (novelist). Finally we reach Bridport and find our way down to West Bay for the B&B, close to the mouth of the River Brit. There was a flourishing rope-making industry here, using hemp, but this disappeared when sailing ships were overtaken by steam-powered vessels. We watch open-mouthed at the chaos as Boris Johnson *prorogues* (shuts down!) Parliament for *five weeks*. What on earth will he do next?

DAY 56   BRIDPORT TO EXETER   (57 MILES)

The morning is overcast and breezy, and the cloud is down on the hill-tops, making them look like little mountains – which is what some of them turn out to be. We're riding on minor roads through quaintly-named villages – Whitchurch Canonicorum and Wooton Fitzpaine – and then the first of the long and fiercely steep hills, slowing us down quite a bit. It's two and a half hours for 20 miles before we struggle into Axminster. By accident we find the River Cottage Café, crammed with Hugh Fearnley Whittingstall books, but serving neither scones nor tea cakes.

We were a couple of miles from Lyme Regis, but chose not to go there, to avoid the A35. (Anna Hughes cycled along this busy dual carriageway, but we're not as brave as she is.) Lyme Regis is famous for a scene in *The French Lieutenant's Woman*, but its real heroine is Mary Anning, who found the first fossil ichthyosaurus on the beach here. She could fairly be called the mother of palaeontology, but sadly she's best remembered for a tongue-twister. *She sells sea shells on the sea shore* was written about her, a poor local woman trying to support her family, and she was never properly credited for her discoveries.

I made the mistake of putting my wet kit on this morning, thinking it was going to rain, so now I'm sweltering and drenched in sweat. But we have a good run down into Seaton, at the mouth of the River Axe, crossed by an 1877 concrete bridge, one of the earliest in Britain. The hills seem longer and steeper today. There are two endless pulls up out of Seaton and then Branscombe. How can the road *still* be going uphill? Maybe it's a space-warp, like an Escher drawing where you go round and round and always uphill. And hills take forever! Bowling along at fifteen miles an hour, each mile only takes four minutes. But heaving the bike up a steep hill at four miles an hour, each mile takes fifteen minutes. So a two-mile hill can easily take half an hour, or even longer if you're reduced to three miles an hour. It's a long time to be pedalling uphill without a break.

We zoom down into Sidmouth for a late lunch. The cliffs frame a Georgian resort with royal connections. In 1819 the Duke and Duchess of Kent moved here with their new-born daughter Victoria (yes, that Victoria) *to escape their creditors*. How very different from the home life of our own dear queen!

We imagine the hills are now behind us for today, but there's another *long and winding road* steeply out of Sidmouth and away from the coast. I hear a raven croaking, and start thinking about vultures. There's something odd about cycling between delightful picture-postcard houses in local stone and thatch, while gasping for breath and being unable to speak.

At last we're down to Exmouth – an important port in the sixteenth century, used by Sir Walter Raleigh. I remember ancient adverts for *Raleigh, the all-steel bicycle*, which as a child I associated with Sir Walter. Like Hadrian on his Cycleway, Raleigh would have created a stir riding around on something that wasn't yet invented. The beautifully flat Exe Estuary Trail leads us into Topsham, with buildings dating from the seventeenth century, when the village was a port. We're in a farm B&B, where the bikes are stored in a locked shed inside a locked barn. We almost wouldn't mind if someone stole them in the night, as we're so tired from the hills.

Shock horror! The High Court finds the prorogation of Parliament is *illegal*. What happens next? In the pub we ponder the route for tomorrow, which looks very main-roady. Inland routes are untested for either hills or mileage, but the main roads so far have been horrible. Steve suggests a train by-pass to Totnes. This obviously breaks some rules, but upholds the rule of staying safe.

DAY 57   EXETER TO SALCOMBE   (50 MILES)

It's overcast but dry again. We begin with an easy flat run round the Exe estuary to Starcross – site of one of the pump houses on the 'atmospheric' section of Brunel's railway in the 1840s. This created a vacuum to pull the train along via a piston. No, it didn't catch on somehow.

We ride down into Dawlish and its nature reserve, where 180 bird species have been recorded. This is how cycling should be, with an off-road tarmac surface with no hills. But NCN 2 runs out at Dawlish, and we duck into a café to ponder. A woman follows us in, noticing our Ravens outside, as she's about to acquire one of her own and wants to know if she's made the right decision. Steve tells her Ravens are a *nightmare*, but she's not fooled, and the three of us have discuss the wonders of Rohloff hub gears, Thorn Cycles in general, and our respective cycling adventures. She says the main roads on our route are *horrible*, so we decide on the radical train option. How many rules does this break?

Steve has to wait an age to get our tickets, queuing behind a woman trying to book her trip to Hexham! But we can only get as far as Newton Abbot, on a local train where you can take your bike but not book it in advance. From there to Totnes it's Inter-City, where you *can* book bikes in advance – but not on the day! This means cyclists can be turned away from local trains with bikes on board, and also from regional trains with *no* bikes on board. They could just make more room for bikes.

Dawlish station only has a bridge to cross the track, and we have to lug the loaded bikes up a long flight of steps to reach our platform. Sitting on the train, I lean across to examine a spot of what looks like rust on my chainstay. Ouch! Pain shoots up through my spine as I sit down again – the seat has flipped up and I land heavily on a metal bar. Loud profanities fill the carriage, and just for once *Steve* is embarrassed to be seen with *me*. I have bashed my coccyx and it really hurts.

The A381 south from Newton Abbot is horrible, but not as long as I'd imagined, and by 12.45 we're in a café in Totnes. We've broken some rules by coming inland by train, bypassing Teignmouth, Torquay, Paignton and Brixham. We've missed an impressive harbour and quayside, palm trees and tropical plants, the Dart Valley Railway, and a full-size replica of Francis Drake's *Golden Hind*. But we've avoided a long ride on main roads, and we're still alive (if badly bruised), so we've come out ahead. I feel bad about missing Dartmouth and its long naval history, featuring not only Walter Raleigh (and his bicycle) but also the pilgrim Fathers, who came here in 1620 for repairs to the *Mayflower* and *Speedwell*.

Instead we've reached the start of the NCN 28, which looks like a good route. The pull up out of Totness is extremely steep, and again seemingly endless. It's an off-road section at least, but the track soon forces us down into first gear. We both grind to a halt and push. When it steepens even further, we start wondering if we can even *push* a loaded bike up here.

My image of a Devon afternoon is gliding along a country lane, pausing every so often to pick luscious ripe blackberries from the hedgerow. This did happen a couple of times, but a lot of it was slogging up steep and narrow lanes, with deep banks either side and no view over the high hedges – and cars trying to get past. Most drivers are considerate, but not all. The larger and taller the car, the less patient the driver tends to be. I'm safe up here in my Range Rover (other high and mighty vehicles are available) so I don't need to pay attention those smaller and lower down.

At last we descend (steeply) to East Portlemouth and the ferry across to Salcombe, home to a wealthy yachting community in the summer, when visitors increase the local population tenfold. They are drawn to the fine natural harbour, surrounded by almost 2,000 acres of tidal creeks. Plenty of creeks up which to go! We wrestle our bikes down steep stone steps onto the boat, and struggle up a longer flight of steps on the far side. There's a long pull out of Salcombe to our pub B&B, where the landlord complains repeatedly about me not answering the phone (he copied the number down wrong). We've reduced the projected mileage today, due to the train journey and a more direct route on NCN 28, but these have been some of the hardest 50 miles I've ever cycled. The painful coccyx is still there in the evening.

DAY 58   *SALCOMBE TO ST AUSTELL*   *(72 MILES)*

Friday 13th begins with the grumpy landlord, who brings us a basic breakfast and treats us to a lengthy account of his problems, ignoring our attempts to divert him. *I don't know why I'm still doing this, I'm not making any money, I pay a fortune in rent, and nobody comes in here any more.* I wonder why that is? If he tried listening to the customers instead of moaning at them, his bar might soon be full again.

There's a sunny day in prospect, but it hasn't broken through yet. The A381 is busy for the first ten miles into Modbury, where we have an early cuppa before heading off north to try to find our way back to the NCN 2. We're still surprised by the steepness of the hills. Sustrans have put up tantalising signs which seem to mean *this way to the NCN 2*. And they do! We arrive safely in Ivybridge, after our hilly detour, and bowl along into Plymouth.

Everyone seems to have sailed out of or into Plymouth at some stage – Drake and the Armada, Cook the explorer, Darwin the naturalist, and the return of the pardoned Tolpuddle Martyrs from Australia. We ride round looking for the Torpoint Ferry, and a woman tells us it's just around the corner. And so it is, with a fine jetty and the boat just coming in. We jump on with more heavy lifting of loaded bikes. Half way across I check with another cyclist – this is the *Torpoint* Ferry, isn't it? He gives me a funny look. Ah, no, he says, this is the *Edgecombe* Ferry. How could we have got on the wrong ferry? At least it's not going to France.

It's only another three miles or so to get back on track- and we're in Cornwall at last! How many counties are left? The hill leading out of Crafthole again appears to be endless, and then we *plunge* into Downderry and Seaton. There's a sign here saying 'Looe 7' but it's going inland, so we wriggle round on the shorter coastal route. The road immediately heads up into the sky again. By the time we get into Looe we could easily have ridden the inland route. We're going to be late, with several extra miles and these *incredible* hills.

The road from Looe to the Bodinnick Ferry is flatter and I'm flying along in the sunshine. I keep thinking of my father, and how much he would love doing exactly what I'm doing now, riding through Cornwall and watching the world go by. I remember cycling along beside him as a boy. For a minute or two I almost imagine I have *become* my father, bowling along in the lanes, but at the same time being myself, remembering how much I owe him, and all his kindness towards me.

Waiting for the ferry, Steve is exhausted, and decides to stay and eat in Fowey. Its reputation for smugglers and pirates has faded so he should be safe. At least the ferry is a nice little RORO, so no heavy lifting of loaded bikes is needed. On the other side, Steve revives a little and follows me up the hill. Then it evens out a bit for the ride into St Austell, though we have to cycle right through to reach the B&B. Our 56-mile day has somehow become 72 miles and we are both done in. Where have all those extra miles come from? I think they are detours rather than Bluck miles, but Steve isn't so sure.

The restaurant looks understaffed, and the next table is scattered with sprinkly stars – a birthday, or perhaps an engagement celebration? The couple are very cuddly and loving, though the girlfriend leaves half her starter, and then toys with a massive bowl of pasta while large glasses of red wine are swiftly emptied. The manager is a pal of the boyfriend, and sits down for a lengthy chat, rather diluting the romantic atmosphere.

DAY 59   ST AUSTELL TO HAYLE   (58 MILES)

It's sunny this morning, and I apply sun cream – in September! Two miles out of St Austell we turn left, cycle up a steep and rutted track, leading only to a farm. We descend back to the road, wondering if Sustrans have got this wrong. No, there's the sign we missed, pointing to a lovely tarmac path, just the other side of the fence. This is neither a Bluck nor a Gibbon mile, but a Gormless Git mile, and not the first.

We plunge down into Mevagissy, ride round twice in a complete circle, find the road, and start walking up into the sky. So on into Portmellon, and up into the sky *again*. My legs are made of jelly – perhaps due to my flying epiphany yesterday afternoon – and Steve cycles up three hills where I have to walk. But riding in first gear isn't much faster than walking, and I'm able to catch him at the top.

Following NCN 3 down towards Caerhays Castle, I sweep round a right-hand bend too fast and am sliding onto a grass verge which suddenly appears to be vertical. After a brief Cornish-wall-of-death moment, I'm safely back on the tarmac, heart pounding but still upright. Brake *before* the bend, you idiot!

Steve and I have several discussions about today's route, as I'm really tired. Plan A is the Lizard today and Land's End tomorrow, but that seems too far. Plan B is the Lizard tomorrow and ignore Land's End – which we've been to anyway – but wouldn't that be cheating? If we take the St Mawes Ferry to Falmouth, instead of the King Harry Ferry to Trelissick, there's a more direct route to the Lizard, avoiding the Helford Ferry and reducing the mileage. We zoom down into posh St Mawes just as the ferry arrives. We offload our panniers to get the bikes down twenty steep stone steps, and when we turn round, the couple behind us have carried the bags down unbidden.

After the ferry ride across Carrick Roads, we pull into Falmouth and the captain announces: 'Please remain seated while my highly intelligent crew member secures the vessel.' The man rolls his eyes and ties us to the jetty. We carry the bikes up more steep stone steps. Half way up I scrape a cleated shoe on the stone, and imagine plunging into the sea with the bike on top of me. At the top the same couple bring the panniers back to us again. The kindness of strangers! I wonder if they'd like to ride our bikes to the Lizard while we drive down in their car?

Falmouth is crowded with tourists, and has a fine Maritime Museum which traces the history of the sailing ships which made it an important Atlantic port. No, we didn't go in. Riding out of Falmouth – up into the sky again – it's harder to find the way, as we're off the signposted NCN routes. Eventually we're en route to Constantine and Gweek, but I'm confused by the route. It's all Gweek to me….

A sign says 13 to the Lizard – too far we reckon. Turning off to Helston, we pass within eight miles of the Lizard, but the A3083 is extremely busy and uninviting. Have we cheated by not going to Britain's most southerly point? Don't care, we're still alive! If you keep two rules by avoiding main roads and not getting killed, you can be let off the last few miles to the Lizard. I bet it was horrible. It's 'a tongue of wave-washed rocks marking the southern tip of mainland Britain'. Who needs that? The locals opposed building a lighthouse, as they wished to continue plundering wrecks – though this was in 1619. Let's not go there. The Lizard also has 'an international reputation for its distinctive flora', but this isn't a botanising holiday.

We're again very tired as we ride over to Hayle, but are rewarded with an excellent meal at The Terrace, at the expense of cycling two miles there and back. A projected 65 has become a mere 58 miles today, which is just as well.

DAY 60 *HAYLE & LAND'S END* *(58 MILES)*

Another welcome day with no luggage, as we can leave the panniers behind for a trip to Land's End. The couple running the B&B – let's call them Sue and Dave – are quite chatty over breakfast, but I have to bite my lip.

Sue: We often have agency nurses in here during the week, lovely blokes, mostly from Africa. John's from Nigeria, isn't he?

Dave: Yes, Oxford he comes from.

Robert: That's an unusual part of Africa.

Dave: No, he *lives* in Oxford. Ask for a specialist, he said, don't be put off by the GP. And I got to see the specialist, so there you are.

Sue: So, not *all* Africans are like that, are they?

Robert: Mmm.

Chuntering quietly over this casual racism, we gather

our day stuff and cycle into Hayle. This was once a centre of copper and tin mining and a busy port, but now is much frequented by tourists. Along the NCN 3 we gain height at Gwallon, with a fantastic view of St Michael's Mount in the sun as we descend to sea level, as if our road leads straight across the causeway and up to the fairy-tale castle.

We ride along Longrock Beach on the South-West Coast Path and into Penzance. At the far end of the lengthy promenade, two portly men are walking towards us, deep in conversation. As we ride past, one says to the other: 'Well you see, that's funny, I tried it on the banjo and it didn't work at all.' (Which tune wouldn't work on the banjo? Discuss.) Riding through the town, there are fine views of the harbour and St Michael's Mount, and as we go around the coast road to Newlyn and then Mousehole, the sea looks gorgeous in the sunshine. Mousehole (*Mouzel*, not Mouse-Hole) is a delightful little place, with narrow twisting streets. It was once Cornwall's main fishing port, though it's now always tinged with sadness. In December 1981 the local Penlee lifeboat, the *Solomon Browne*, set out with eight crew to save eight others on the *Union Star*, a coaster whose engine had failed. Vast waves threw the lifeboat onto the deck of the coaster. All those on both vessels perished, and half the bodies were never found.

Of course from Mousehole the road goes up into the sky again. This was supposed to be an easy day, with no kit to lug around. We wind our way across to St Buryan and down to the Land's End Experience, a theme park at the end of Britain, turning this beautiful and remote spot into a complete nightmare. Weaving our way between Harry Potter and the shopping outlets, we find a massive café selling Cornish pasties and horrible coffee from a self-service machine. Several obese people are stuffing themselves with calories here, making us feel quite slim. It was the same at John O'Groats – do such places attract overweight people?

We have memories of beginning LEJOG here six years ago, and vow never to come back. After a couple of miles on the dreaded A30, we have a fine ride along a minor road through St Just and Zennor to St Ives. We pass the former Geevor Tin Mine at Pendeen, which offers visitors an underground tour into the claustrophobic shafts and tunnels, perilously close to the sea. No thanks. It also has a Hard Rock Museum – probably geological rather than musical history.

Thinking of missing museums, Zennor could well have had a D.H.Lawrence Museum. The novelist and poet lived here for two years during the First World War, before being ordered to leave. His wife Frieda was German. People imagined she might be sending coded messages – perhaps using her line of washing – to her cousin Manfred von Richthoven, the flying ace known as the 'Red Baron'.

Visibility is a bit limited in the deep lanes with high hedges, and it's clouded over, slightly chilly with the mist coming in from the sea. *Mull of Kintyre...* We pass a few more abandoned tin mines on our left, the engine houses and chimneys a reminder of a once-thriving industry. The last mine closed only twenty years ago and there are rumours of revival. Tin is needed again for technical thingies.

Steve's going well this afternoon. When I pause at a

field gate to put on another layer of clothing, it takes me five miles to catch him up. He's always three or four bends in the road further on, and never seems to get any closer. We come down into St Ives for a cuppa, lost in the maze of narrow streets near the harbour – which used to be Cornwall's main pilchard port. Then we have to climb up into the sky yet again, and I have to walk as Steve pedals up in first gear. Did I mention he's nine years younger than me?

We've come a good bit further than planned today – 58 miles instead of 46 – partly through cycling down to Hayle for another good evening meal at the Terrace. Are these Bluck miles? Have I measured things wrong? At the end of Day 60 we should be three-quarters of the way round Britain's coastline! It's been a lovely sunny day, but we really are exhausted.

Back at the B&B, I ask to square up with Sue for the two nights and there's no card machine. *Cash please, if that's all right, I don't want to make you short.* He's not in the kitchen with us, but I can hear Steve saying: *Too late, he's already short.* Sue's phrasing also gives me a worrying thought. Is she a Cornish witch? *Pay up, I don't want to have to make you even shorter.* What do you mean, paranoid?

DAY 61   HAYLE TO TINTAGEL   (63 MILES)

We're apprehensive about today, with the need for an early start and some careful navigation. It's heavy drizzle and all our wet kit on for the run down into Hayle and along the road to Gwithian. We can just about see the Godrevy

Island lighthouse, made famous by Virginia Woolf. But by 8.30 the cloud has lifted a good bit. It's dry as we bowl along the clifftop road and steeply down into Portreath.

Steve and I remember this well as Day One of LEJOG. We head off as before on the Cornish Mineral Trail, but this time we turn north. Our plan was to wriggle round on minor coastal roads, but we've learned our lesson, with the lung-bursting hills and winding lanes adding extra miles. Plan B is to take the A3075 to Newquay. It's busy, but straight and not too hilly – and it's not the A30.

We detour round Newquay to save time, missing out on Cornwall's biggest resort, Britain's surfing centre, and the 'new quay' itself – which dates from 1439. The plan is to join NCN 32 for an inland route to Padstow. Of course we miss the turn for this minor road (I won't say who was in front), and it's another four miles on the A 3059 before we get into St Columb Major, where we hide from a sudden shower in a convenient bus shelter. Just like Scotland!

Parking the bikes in a narrow street, we wander into a new vegan café. I ask the waitress idly who St Columb was and she googles it for us. Columba the Virgin was a fifth-century woman who ran away rather than marry a prince. He caught up with her in nearby Ruthvoes, and chopped off her head! I hope he was sent on an anger management course, and then turned into a frog.

We climb out of St Columb – steeply of course – and then rather more gently along the NCN 32 and down into the fishing port of Padstow, which is *heaving* with tourists. The Black Tor Ferry isn't due for a while, so we have time for a cuppa.

Coming out of the café, there's now a *huge* queue for the ferry, but when the boat arrives through a narrow channel between the sandbanks, we're beckoned down to go on first. This is to get the bikes out of the way before squeezing the passengers on behind us. It's a fair-sized vessel, but about twenty people are still left waiting on the jetty for the next trip.

After crossing the River Camel, we're surprised to land at Rock on the beach rather than a jetty. We push the bikes across the sand, and then off we go through St Minver (a Welsh nun who fended off the devil by throwing her comb at him) and St Endellion (a virgin of whom nothing is known). We're making good time, but the weather is closing in, with heavy drizzle each time we reach higher ground.

Before Delabole we turn off the main road (which is increasingly misty), to get away from the traffic. The lane gets steeper and steeper, but looks to be a dead end rather than the way into Tintagel. So we turn around, up into the sky again on another lane, and meet a car at the next junction. Their Satnav says Tintagel is down this left turn, so we follow them down there, and find our way to the B&B at last. Several miles and another pint of sweat wasted.

Tintagel Castle – birthplace of King Arthur! The legend of Uther Pendragon's romance with the Duchess of Cornwall goes back a long way, but its popularity owes more to Tennyson's *Idylls of the King* than any historical evidence. Even if it's true, it was centuries before the castle was built. Very romantic though.

In the pub later Steve has a signal again, and discovers

the steep lane would have brought us into Tintagel by an easier route, if only we'd had the courage to follow it. Ye of little faith! So 56 miles has become 63 miles, though we are agreed that these are another new category of TAD miles (Tired and Deluded). No sign of the wonderful new Tintagel Bridge as yet.

DAY 62   TINTAGEL TO BRAUNTON   (65 MILES)

We should be OK today if we can get to Bude in reasonable time. It's a lovely sunny morning, so we ride into Tintagel in search of the new bridge linking the village and the famous castle. Sadly it's only accessible via a walk which will take some time. Another wonderful experience missed.

The B3263 to Boscastle is severely hilly, particularly at the end, working its way down to the 'deep, narrow, fiord-like harbour', where there's a Museum of Witchcraft. A ride on a broom is what we need. The pull up out of Boscastle on the far side lasts for *four miles* and takes most of the next hour. Each corner must surely be the top, but the road goes up again and again. To avoid the A39 we turn off left through Higher Crackington, and then go steeply down into Crackington Haven at sea level. There are wonderful Cornish cliff views here, though we're focusing on the road and squeezing the brakes. On the other side there's a long drag uphill to re-join NCN 3. We're back onto Sustrans recommended routes for the rest of the day, so there should be no more route-finding problems.

After a couple of miles the road plunges down alarmingly and announces a 30% gradient. That's 1 in 3 and the steepest we have ever seen! We *heave* on the brakes and descend at a stately 7 mph, not trusting the next bend, but still gawping at the fantastic cliff scenery. This is Millook Haven, where the other side is also 1 in 3, so we walk slowly, only just able to push our bikes up here. We pause at the top to regain our breath, and ride on past Widemouth Sand, where the 'hotline' between Downing Street and the White House runs under the beach, so that Boris Johnson can chat with Donald Trump. Then down into the surfer's paradise of Bude, where we're happy to stop for lunch, even though we've only done about 20 miles.

What follows is a surprisingly strenuous afternoon. I thought the Sustrans-recommended yellow route would be across a plateau, but the hills are again steep and endless. By the time we get to Bradworthy I'm wondering when we'll ever reach Bideford, where there's still another 16 miles to go. How late will it be when we get to Braunton?

Soon after Bradworthy we reach the highest point at last. At West Putford there's a sign for the Gnome Reserve, with over a thousand gnomes and pixies, with more mysteriously appearing all the time. Mike Carter visited them, but I'm prepared to miss the gnome fairground and the gnome space centre. We're on the flat at last, and then a *long* run downhill – gentle and very satisfying. The moorland and farmland give way to delightful ancient woodland, mainly mature oak and ash and beech, with dappled sunshine filtering through. Better even than visiting the gnomes.

Despite all the hills, we've done 20 miles in two hours when we come down to Bideford at 4.30 for a coffee. Bideford's famous Long Bridge with 24 arches has spanned the River Torridge since medieval times.

Apparently a philanthropic merchant saw a local woman drown while trying to cross the river, and so he financed a causeway and a bridge. We ride across, suitably impressed and thankful. There's a wonderful flat run along the Tarka Trail on a disused railway to Barnstaple, an ancient borough which was an important port until the railways arrived. We should thank Dr Beeching for making this railway disappear, giving us sixteen miles of flat traffic-free cycling at the end of a hard day. This speeds us up a little, and it's only 6.30 when we arrive in Braunton.

Our projected 57 miles today has become 65 miles, and an awful recognition is dawning. The difference in scale between my map-measurer and the Sustrans maps means I should have added ten per cent to get the correct mileage. For some days I have failed to do this, so the mileage has been longer than projected. These are Bluck-Map miles, as Steve reminds me on more than one occasion. Sorry, Steve!

The B&B is not at all as expected. It's do-it-yourself with no contact with the owners except by phone – who may be in a different part of the same building. The accommodation is fine, but you have to make your own breakfast with the stuff provided. It was advertised as a conventional B&B where they make the breakfast for you. But by now I'm too tired to care.

DAY 63   BRAUNTON TO BISHOPS LYDEARD
(55 MILES)

We wrestle with an uncooperative toaster and coffee machine, and head off with less breakfast than expected.

But it's another sunny morning and we're away by 8.00 – just as well as it turns out. Our coastal route towards Ilfracombe is flatter than NCN 27 and gives us lovely sea views, but adds a few miles and then turns out to be hilly after all. Ilfracombe has North Devon's major holiday resort ever since the railway brought Victorian tourists here. Now they have to drive – the station closed in 1970.

Beyond Ilfracombe we stay on the main road to get round to Coombe Martin. There were silver mines here in the Middle Ages, only closing in the nineteenth century. We look for a left turn on the NCN 51 but the road is closed. We'd normally blag our way in here, as we've almost always been able to wriggle through somehow. But this closed road leads up into the sky, so we decide to stay on the A399 and follow the detour signs. Several miles later we turn off left and find ourselves on an extremely narrow lane leading steeply on a poor surface down into Parracombe – the valley where you need a parachute?

Then we walk and bike-crawl up the other side of the valley. Even the A39 begins to look inviting by now, so we stay on it until it brings us down a steep wooded gorge, plunging down into Lynmouth behind a massive lorry which squeezes past the cars coming uphill. At one point the lorry and the cars come to a standstill on a sharp bend to negotiate a safe way through, and an imbecile in a little white car behind us scoots past everyone and roars off down the hill.

Lynmouth has earlier literary refugees than Zennor. In 1812 the newly-wed poet Shelley and his sixteen-year-old bride Mary Wollstonecraft hid here for two months from her furious parents. But the village is best known for the terrible flood of August 1952, when nine inches of rain fell on Exmoor and rushed down the river valleys towards the village. Whole buildings were swept into the sea, 34 people were drowned and 400 made homeless.

We wander into a café and get chatting to a couple who ask about our intrepid cycling. The café owner is a cheery no-nonsense woman: 'I've no sympathy for you, why don't you come down here in a car like normal people?' It's a fair question, and we have plenty of time to ponder it, while pushing the bikes up Countisbury Hill on the other side of the valley. It starts at 25% (1 in 4) and really is a *long and winding road*, which seems to go up forever.

We begin to wonder if we'll make Minehead in time for the train to take us along to Bishops Lydeard, to stay overnight with my friends Chris and Hilary. We remain on the busy A39 all the way into Porlock, including the final exhilarating plunge down the infamous Porlock Hill at over 40 mph. (There was once a water tank at the top, so motorists could fill up their radiators after struggling up this steep hill.)

We're a wee bit tight for time, so we keep on the main road for the last few miles into Minehead, where the sea's half a mile away, as it's low tide. We arrive in time at the station – just as well, since there was no Plan B. Then there's a lovely ride on a *steam train* on the West Somerset Railway, passing through Dunster, with its wonderful medieval buildings, and Watchet, where Coleridge is said to have met an old sailor whose stories were later immortalised in *The Rime of the Ancient Mariner*. Very literary, the West country. So down to Bishops Lydeard and an evening in good company. Hilary is my oldest friend – we were at primary school together in the late medieval period.

DAY 64   BISHOPS LYDEARD TO CLEVEDON
(68 MILES)

Our plan to take the train back to the coast this morning would take two hours out of the day, so instead – after a lovely breakfast, thanks to Hilary – we head off on the back roads into Taunton. An excellent run in the sunshine, avoiding all the traffic. The moment we pause in the town, a man walks across the road to show us the way down onto the canal towpath. This is NCN 3 which will take us all the way to Bridgewater.

Now all the massive hills are done, Steve pauses to tighten his brakes. He's been planning to do this for several days. Better late than never. We ride along the canal towpath, remembering how we first came here on LEJOG. We were surprised to pass a concrete plinth with a model of Jupiter on top. After more such planet-plinths, including the Earth, we came to Jupiter again! Was the canal built in a circle? Were we in a time-warp? No, there really are two Jupiters! We didn't recognise this as the Somerset Space Walk, a scale model of the solar system, with a set of planets either side of a bright yellow Sun – eight feet wide, fourteen tons of concrete – which we had somehow not seen.

At each end of the canal of course is Pluto. There's a Pluto in Taunton and another in Bridgwater. We cycled past both of them, hence the title of the book. There's also an *Inspector Morse* episode where Sergeant Lewis has to sort through hundreds of parking tickets for a vital clue. Morse asks impatiently why he's not finished yet, and Lewis replies: 'I'm doing me best sir, but it's a bit like cycling to Pluto'. This phrase entered our private vocabulary – an endless task which must be accomplished, and which is of inestimable value. Cycling *past* Pluto seems even more impossible – and yet here we are.

Steve and I are passing the planets on the Somerset Space Walk as before, noticing this time that the sun is hiding behind a large bush. As we ride past Saturn, there's the railway just beyond. A train passing behind Saturn – what a picture that would make! Two hundred yards further on, a train whooshes past, closely followed by another in the opposite direction. We've just missed a train behind Saturn, which sets us off giggling as we wobble along the towpath.

We cycle past Pluto into Bridgwater for refreshments. We're going well and not at all tired after 20 gentle miles. Still on NCN 3, we're riding towards Glastonbury in lovely country lanes, when we pass Sedgemoor Battlefield, site of the last real battle in England in 1685. The Duke of Monmouth declared himself king in Taunton, which surprised and annoyed his uncle James II. The rebels were defeated, rounded up and tried by Judge Jeffries. (400 hanged, another 800 transported as slaves.) One of the rebels was a young Daniel Defoe, who fled into a churchyard and saw the name *Robinson Crusoe* on a gravestone.

Soon we're in Cossington, and turn off north on NCN 33 for a gentle run into Burnham-on-Sea. Cutting through a tree-lined path by a roundabout, a man who's obviously drunk blocks my path. As I swerve round him, he slaps me hard across the back and shouts, 'I've lost my umbrella!' I think that's the least of his problems.

A sign in Burnham points the NCN 33 onto the concrete promenade – and straight into the sand! Perhaps it's been driven onto the prom by tide and wind. We decide to stick on the road and wiggle our way round, before picking up NCN 33 again. There's a new bridge across the River Axe, not marked on our map, and we find our way to Bleadon. It's an unpleasant surprise to find here's another *Bleadon Hill* here, but it doesn't compare with the hills in Devon and Cornwall. There are a few hills and lanes to get through before we reach Winscombe, where we head off, as on LEJOG, along the wonderful Strawberry Line, mile after mile of off-road flat disused railway with a good gravelled surface. Thanks again, Dr Beeching!

It's late afternoon and we're up to 60 miles already. A great day's cycling, slightly offset by a long final drag round the B3133 to get onto the sea-front at Clevedon and our pub B&B. Like so many places, Clevedon was a fishing village which became a Victorian tourist resort. Its magnificent pier was once a terminal for steamer companies, with twenty ships a week mooring here in the 1930s. John Betjeman declared it the most beautiful in England. Sadly (and ironically) it collapsed in 1970 while being load-tested for insurance. But it was swiftly restored and re-opened, as impressive as ever. We're soon eating upstairs in the restaurant, looking out over the pier. The whole sky is bright orange as the sun sets over the sea.

Devon and Cornwall have been by far the hardest

sections so far. Surely Wales can't be harder that this? 62 miles has become 68 miles but it was all flattish, so I'm not being teased too much.

DAY 65   CLEVEDON TO CARDIFF   (66 MILES)

We make a prompt start, as we have a rendezvous in Pill with Megan and Sophie from Sustrans, who are cycling out from Bristol to meet us. Walking across the road, a man notices my unusual bike. He's a Sustrans volunteer on the Strawberry line, and is doing LEJOG in stages to fit in with work commitments. I extol the virtues of Thorn bikes and Rohloff gears. Should I be on commission?

There's a good run on NCN 410, part of the Avon Cycleway, along to Pill – where the café is sadly closed on Fridays. We meet up with Megan and Sophie, and slope off to the local pub instead for coffee and a chat. They present us both with Sustrans T-shirts, either for supporting the movement or just being old and intrepid.

We notice their bike-locks are much more serious than ours – Bristol has its fair share of bike thieves. They lead us up to the Avonmouth Bridge and then head off back to work in the city centre. We glide across above Avonmouth, which replaced Bristol as a major port after its massive Victorian docks were completed. The NCN 41 route alternates between pleasant wooded byways and the edge of massive industrial areas, highlighting the best and the worst of the local landscape.

It seems quite hard work to find the Severn Bridge approach. A missing NCN 4 sign leads us astray, over a dual carriageway, down an overgrown track into the land of the British Transport Police, where *Thieves and Trespassers will be Prosecuted* – but only if they're caught!

Riding through Severn Beach, we pass over the eastern end of the Severn Tunnel, carrying the railway from Bristol to Newport. Completed in 1886 after fifteen years, it's lined with 76 million bricks, and at four miles was the longest underwater tunnel in the world for more than a century. No, it's underwater, we didn't see it.

Samuel Plimsoll – he of the Plimsoll line, showing how low a ship lies in the water – was born in Bristol. It's hardly surprising that people known for maritime exploits were often born near the coast – Nelson and Brunel, Grace Darling and Mr Plimsoll.

Finally we're riding back towards the original Severn Bridge – the new one has no bike track. (Before the bridge was opened in 1966, three ferries at Aust took 800 cars a day across the estuary.) We have a spectacular crossing of the Severn Estuary on the two-mile long bridge, way above the water level, to cope with the massive tidal range – 40 feet and more in spring, three times higher than the UK average. We began in June by crossing the Humber, and now we finish 700 miles further on by crossing the Severn into Wales. The cycleway is again set below the main carriageway, at just the right height to get exhaust fumes in our faces. Again I express my displeasure towards non-cycling architects. It's not rocket science.

We skirt round Chepstow, and NCN 4 takes us through country lanes. With no cafés we can see, we're hot and tired after three hours without a break. Finally in Caerwent we find a pub where we have orange juice and baguettes in the garden – and both of us apply sun cream. Steve's looking a bit red.

The Celtic Trail on NCN 4 takes us on a good flat route into Newport, and the only other transporter bridge in the world. It's not as impressive as Middleborough's design or decoration, but still fascinating – and we only just make it. Arriving at 4:17 for the 4:20 crossing, we learn that it's the last one for today. As well as nearly missing a ferry or two, we nearly missed a bridge!

There's a steady ride for the last dozen miles into Cardiff, where we're a bit disorientated, but eventually find our hostel. It's more basic than the one in Fort William, where Steve walked into the wardrobe. I'll not book us in here when we return to Cardiff for Trip Six next year. We were planning a celebratory feast but we're too tired to look for Cardiff's best Indian restaurant. A pizza place will have to do.

This has definitely been the hardest trip. We've been tired all afternoon on several days, either because of the mileage or the hills – or the advancing years? I don't remember LEJOG being like this. We've sometimes gone to bed at 9:00 or so and slept through till 7:00 in the morning. It's probably a cumulative effect of cycling for twelve days in a row. For Trip Six maybe we'll take an easy day in the middle. Cardiff to Lancaster will probably be enough – we can do the last 180 miles in a final little trip.

56 has somehow become 66 miles today. How did that happen? I fear it's the Bluck-Map miles problem again. Steve rolls his eyes and heaves a theatrical sigh. The things he has to put up with. This fifth trip has been 728 miles in all (average 61 miles per day), bringing our grand total

up to 3826. Only another 800 or so miles left, and we'll be back in Carlisle. But that's enough for this year.

TRAIN HOME FROM CARDIFF

We walk the bikes a mile or so down to the station, safe from the city traffic, in our 'evening wear' rather than our bike kit. There's no need to ride the bikes anywhere today. We mop up the time at the station with coffee and baguettes and reading the papers – Steve with *The Times* and me with *The Guardian*, both dismissive of the other's choice. I regard *The Times* as a Murdoch parody of what it once was, and Steve condemns *The Guardian* as a pinko liberal paper for the chattering classes. What do you mean, prejudiced?

The platform is crowded with beery football fans, chanting and shouting at 10.30 in the morning, gently shepherded onto a train by rather gloomy policemen. Two young women have reserved seats in the same carriage, but wisely decide to find another part of the train. One policeman looks much more cheerful, and is gently teasing his colleagues. When the train pulls out, they have to stay put with the football fans, while he's left on the platform for duties in Cardiff. He walks away whistling.

Mercifully our train is a good deal quieter, though still full. I cunningly arranged to set out on a Sunday because of ferries not operating on particular day – not realising that returning on a Saturday might make it a bit noisy. Avoid weekend journeys in future!

Leaving Birmingham, the man with the refreshments trolley spends so long describing his wares over the intercom – with feeble attempts at humour – that passengers may die of thirst before he reaches them. A passenger starts to remonstrate with one of the train crew, who asked him to move out of a reserved seat. Voices are raised and there's soon a full-blown argument. The senior train guard has to intervene. At Darlington a young policeman boards the train and escorts the irate passenger off down the platform, still protesting loudly. He may be under the influence of alcohol or other mind-altering substances. How difficult would it be to move your seat?

A twelve-hour day with Steve is completed with no TLPs! This must be some sort of record.

10

WINTERVAL THREE: THE LONG DELAY

We're both still feeling tired a week later. It's October before we slope off for a 40-mile ride, and it's bitterly cold. Steve's going fine but I'm sluggish and working hard to keep up with him on the hills. No more waiting for him at the top!

The following week we take an easy run up the South Tyne Trail to Lambley Viaduct, a magnificent Victorian stone bridge, carrying the Alston railway 33 metres above the river on nine elegant stone arches. The line closed in 1976 but the viaduct has been restored and preserved. The view of the river and wooded hills from the viaduct is spectacular – and it's only eleven miles each way.

Then the weather closes in, and we leave it for a couple of months. After Christmas I've mysteriously gained the stone I lost earlier in the year. My new year resolution is to cycle every day, outside or on the exercise bike in the porch. But visitors arrive bringing wine and chocolates. Then I get a foul winter cold which lasts six weeks and makes exercise impossible. Even twenty minutes on the spinning bike leaves me exhausted. Gradually this gets easier, and soon the digital display tells me I've covered 20 kilometres (12 miles) in half an hour. That's twice as fast as in the real world. How come? There are no hills in the porch, and no wind resistance. If I found a flat piece of land with a constant tailwind, I probably could manage 24 mph – at least in theory.

By March I've not been out on the Raven for *five months*, the longest gap for years. Next week we really must get going again. One ride a week, a month at forty miles, a month at fifty and a month at sixty. That should do it. Steve's busy with websites and Heritage Centre work and sailing. I can sneak in more rides and lose all that weight before we set off again.

The Raven is looking a bit tired. I order slightly heavier Schwalbe Marathon tyres to insure against punctures. The front rim is badly worn, and Palace Cycles in Carlisle have to build me a new wheel, as well as the service. Cycling isn't as cheap as you think. The bike feels lovely as I ride home with new tyres and tubes, tight chain and brakes all perfect. The wheel cost just over £100, but the old one lasted 10,000 miles or more, so that's only a penny a mile.

At last we arrange a ride together. The westerly wind feels a bit brisk, so we catch the train to Carlisle and cycle back with the breeze behind us. There's a new flood defence scheme in Carlisle – not long ago this side of the city was waist deep in water. We notice the hills more than usual, and we're both apprehensive. We should be off to Cardiff in 12 weeks for the last lap around Wales and Lancashire. Steve has been going to a keep-fit class, but my rides on the spinning bike have toughened up my legs, and I have to wait for him a couple of times. I reckon when we get to Cardiff it'll be me struggling to catch up with him.

* * *

This turns out to be our last ride for months. Coronavirus hits the UK, and we have to stay at home for 12 weeks! We'll probably not be cycling from Cardiff to Carlisle in June. I'm allowed to exercise on my own – but what am I training for? Eventually Steve and I are allowed out for a socially-distanced ride together, but all the cafés are closed, so we have to sit at either end of a long bench to eat our own snacks. Back home I receive this generous email from my cycling pal:

Whatever happens this year if for some reason we do not compete the ride round the coast can I just say a big thank you to you Robert for allowing me to intrude on LEJOG and then everything we have done since and most of all for putting up with me. The memories are fantastic and it has been an excellent experience – despite rain, wind mud, a few dodgy B&Bs and some Bluck miles, oh and my TLPs. I have enjoyed every mile (he lied, nearly every mile). Thanks for the memories Steve

We can both think of miles we didn't enjoy, hills we'd rather not have pushed the bikes up, and the rain and wind in our faces. But overall they've been super journeys so far, and I do hope we're able to complete the circuit. It'll probably be next year now, June or even September

2021, if our legs still work by then. I'd hate to think our Thorn Raven partnership is over – but it will be on hold for several months at least.

I email the B&B owners between Cardiff and Carlisle, cancelling everything on Trip Six and wishing them well. I hope their businesses are still there next year. Several of them took the trouble to respond and return our deposits with lovely messages. Thank you, Gill from Machynlleth, and also Andrew from Llanelli: *just stay safe yeah and look after your family dude... look forward to you staying with us when this virus crap is all behind us.*

By mid-April, with the first 10,000 deaths from the virus recorded, not being allowed out on the bike is the least of our worries. Actually I could go out, but not with Steve and only for an hour's exercise (the most allowed under lockdown). A ten-mile cycle ride is a quarter of our shortest loop, and hardly worth doing. My newly-serviced bike, with its new tyres and chain, its oil-change and new brake pads, sits in the porch, looking back at me: *ready when you are pal.*

Steve's next email shows he's thinking on similar lines: *Today I serviced both of our bikes. My bike now has a new chain, a pair of new mudguards, an oil change, a clean, and adjusted brakes. Unfortunately it has nowhere to go.* How long before we're able to get going again? Nobody knows. At least we're both ready, though he seems to be putting on weight as fast as I'm losing it. Maybe I'll get up hills ahead of him again. But he's been sneaking out in the evenings on his bike to do a short hilly loop locally. I'd better get going. The last thing I want is to find he is fitter than me.

Caroline and I cycle over the steep hills to Whitfield to have a socially-distanced lunch with our friends Jenny and Bob. On the way back we ride along the ridge for a couple of miles, and are rewarded with a wheatear and a red grouse – and a skylark sitting on the wall opposite and singing for us. The other three all have electric bikes and can cycle uphill much faster than me, almost without trying.

It's May before Steve and I are allowed out again. A couple of loops out to Brampton and back is all we can manage at first. He persuades me to cycle up to Alston, and I know what's in store. He's keen to ride on a path beside the narrow-gauge railway line. It's a rough surface, but at least it's flat. We've misjudged the weather – windy and squally, and it suddenly starts to hail! Hiding under a little stone bridge, with wind howling through, we're safe from Covid but we might die of pneumonia.

Next week we do the same ride in reverse, starting out with lots of uphill, including the famous 1 in 4 towards Whitfield. Both of us still think we can cycle up here – and we're both wrong, we still have to walk. It takes ages to reach the top above Alston, average speed only 7 mph. But then it's mostly downhill and we're back home for lunch after 40 miles. Of course we only paused in Alston for five minutes to eat a snack, rather than the normal half-hour in a café.

Looking for a different route, we head off north to Wark Forest. We've not been here for ages and I remember why – it's rough going for six miles on forestry tracks, and then a hilly ride into Bellingham. The Tea Room is closed, so we sit outside the Heritage Centre for our refreshments.

Water and bananas are not the same as coffee and cake. I'm expecting an easy ride back, but Steve wants to try the Redesmouth road. Is it by any chance further and hillier, I ask? Of course it is. About 48 miles in all and I'm really tired by the time I get home.

The summer seems to be full of rain. After another no-cycling month I email Steve to suggest a ride, and he replies: *What is a bike ride? Who are you and why are you contacting me?* He's beginning to wonder if we can do the final trip even next year. With no obvious end to the Coronavirus pandemic in sight, we might be booking everything and then cancelling again. If we leave it two years I'll be 74 when we complete the circuit! Will the legs still work by then?

I ride out to Brampton on my own a couple of times in August, where the café has reopened for socially-distanced coffee and cheese scones. Food and drink on separate tables? I'm almost down to 12 stone again, after being 13 stone at Christmas. I've lost another stone! No, it's not *another* stone, it's the same one I've put on and lost all over again. If I lost *another* stone I'd be floating away into the clouds.

No more cycling until the end of September, when we pedal off to Brampton and back. Steve's a bit rusty and tires easily. We ponder again about whether to attempt the last lap next year or wait for 2022. Neither of us are getting any younger.

But the next week we head off to Wylam together, and we're there in a shade over two hours. With a strong westerly wind, we're much slower on the way back. By the time we reach the Abbey Café in Hexham, Steve's flagging. We plod on towards Haydon Bridge, but his legs have gone and he waves me off ahead. When I get home and have a bath, there's an email to say he got back before me! He phoned Julie and got her to come and pick him up. This is definitely cheating.

That turned out to be our last ride of 2020. The weather turned unpleasant, we got lazy and couldn't be bothered, we were in and out of lockdown and tiered restrictions, the cafés were closed again. In December I managed to twist my right knee painfully, with three weeks of hobbling around before it was rideable, by which time it was Christmas, with incredibly short days.

* * *

Early in the new year there was another lockdown due to the pandemic, and we soon had to accept that we're not going to do the final trip this year either. At least I've not booked everything only to have to cancel it again.

It's March before Steve and I get going again, with three little rides of only 20 miles, the first together for *five months*, due to lockdown, winter and idleness. Caroline and I have another ride out with Jenny and Bob, with me still working hard to keep up with their electric bikes. Next week I ride out to Wylam along the valley, a bit over fifty miles, with the happy coincidence of meeting my friend George outside a pop-up café, where he buys me a coffee and the first cheese scone for months.

During April and May Steve and I manage to get out each week to Brampton, and I'm going a bit further on my own. Three rides up to Alston and over Hartside Top (1900 ft), down the other side to Melmerby, where there's a café sort of open – and back the same way. 60 very hilly miles. The ascent of Hartside from Alston starts at 53 min, then 45 min, then 40 min. But I'm pooped by the time I get back on the bike in Melmerby, and grind up the other side really slowly. In early June I ride up Hartside in an astonishing 33 minutes, but only with a strong wind behind me. Plunging down towards Melmerby, cyclists labouring up the other way are going very slowly, and half of them are walking. To avoid this I keep going round the Big Loop to Brampton, and end up at home having done 66 miles. I'm knackered.

Steve and I cycle out three times with his neighbour Dave – once to Wylam, once to Brampton, and then a real adventure. Steve drives us to Greystoke, beyond Penrith, and we cycle right round the northern lake mountains, with café stops in Threlkeld and Caldbeck. It's a good bit more hilly than we thought.

Starting up yet another a hill, Steve gives a sigh as I pass him.

'Have you got a toast rack?'

Has he lost his mind?

'Sorry, say that again?'

'Have you got a tow strap?'

It's not his mind that's going – it's my hearing.

Another trip around the Big Loop on my own, and I'm completely exhausted. But my weight is down below 12 stone at last. I start planning Trip Six again for *next year*, with detours and changes to avoid all the trunk roads and dual carriageways I had foolishly ignored. This all adds miles of course, but means we may be able to get an easy day in the middle of the trip.

Coming back from a gentle ride round to Brampton, the gear-shifter suddenly goes slack. With only a single low gear, I glide down into Haltwhistle and phone Caroline to pick me up in the van. The gear cables have worn out after about 15,000 miles – the day before the annual service is due! I take the Raven over to Arragon Cycles in Penrith, who diagnose the problem and sort everything out. A new rear sprocket is also needed, swiftly ordered from the ever-efficient St John Street Cycles in Bridgewater. It's a minor inconvenience being without the bike for a few days, but I could have been stranded almost anywhere, including half way round the last trip with Steve. What seemed like a catastrophe was actually a stroke of good luck, thanks to the excellent Arragon for servicing and St John Street Cycles for online ordering.

We drive over to Penrith again for a ride around the Eden Valley. This is the third ride we've done from Jack Thurston's *Lost Lanes North*, and they've all been good. However, when he says the route 'climbs steadily from Crosby Ravensworth', he didn't add that it goes on *forever* uphill. We were just saying how lucky we were that those endless hills in Devon and Cornwall are all behind us – and now here's another one! But a good day out anyway. We continue with *Lost Lanes North* once a week where possible, even driving over to Ravenglass for a delightful gentle ride along Wastwater and back.

In September I drive up to the north of Scotland, staying at Tongue for a couple of days to cycle two big loops in magnificently wild country. Then south and west to Lochcarron for a final attempt at the Applecross Pass. I'm keen to break 60 minutes for the ascent, but there's a good bit of traffic on the north roads now, mainly due to the North Coast 500, where people hire motor homes (or worse still Porsches) at Inverness, and drive round all the single-track roads for an adventure. I'm repeatedly forced to a standstill by vehicles negotiating their way past each other. Then the mist comes down and I can't see where I'm going. And I'm getting older! I planned each mile at a certain speed to reach the summit in just under an hour. But as the road gets steeper I fall behind schedule, and by mile three – still not half-way up – I'm panting and struggling. At last I reach the summit and fly downhill to Applecross and round the rest of the hilly loop. Never again.

I must have gone over a big pothole somewhere, as the rear wheel is catching the brake alarmingly. Back home at Arragon Cycles, the diagnosis is a new rear wheel build – again! So the Raven is out of action for a week or more. This doesn't matter at all, as I'm desperately tired after returning.

Caroline and I take the bikes to Fife for a week's holiday and have a couple of gentle rides, one of them with my cousins Matt and Lara and their daughter Lizzie, who at twelve thinks she can ride faster than me. Not yet!

Steve and I settle into an autumn and winter pattern of going out once a week for forty miles, usually to Brampton. On a fine October morning we decide to head east to Corbridge, into the wind for once, but in glorious sunshine. On the way back the wind has moved round and is right in our faces, bringing dark clouds and heavy rain stinging our faces so hard that we have to seek shelter. We arrive back home frozen.

I'm getting quite a bit of pain in my left knee, both on bike rides and walking around. Sue the physio has a go at it with ultrasound and says it's ligament damage, which will only clear up slowly, due to the advancing years. Heigh ho.

* * *

In February we finally make the decision to go *this year*, so I book all the accommodation with my fingers crossed. I take out cancellation insurance for the first time. There's a temptation to think about Covid, whether the trains will be running normally, and how my knee will stand up to a long trip. Not to mention apprehension about our fitness and weight after a two-year gap with no long trip.

I book the train tickets and bike reservations, with the same difficulty as usual. Passengers have a single ticket from Carlisle to Cardiff, but you have to contact different train companies to book your bikes. Crewe to Cardiff reservations can only be made two weeks in advance, and only by phone. Thank you, Transport for Wales! Another reason for a national rail system. Now, when I was a lad…

On a very windy morning, Steve and I take an early train to Dumfries and ride back with the wind behind us. We're flying along, with an average speed of *fourteen* miles an hour! This is unheard of, but it's wind-assisted so the record won't count. In the café in Brampton we get chatting to a chap who's just cycled from Thirsk and is heading for Edinburgh. Two hundred miles in a day! And this is over some fierce hills, with a powerful westerly wind. We feel decidedly less intrepid. But we're both more or less ready for the last lap.

Having booked everything, there's the sudden threat of a rail strike. What's Plan B for getting 300 miles to Cardiff? On our final ride round the Big Loop, the week before we set off, Steve leads me up Hartside for the first time ever, and however hard I push, I cannot catch him up. Well, he is nine years younger than me.

11

WALES AND LANCASHIRE – CARDIFF TO LANCASTER

An early start for the 0714 train to Carlisle, and we're soon on the London train bound for Crewe. An announcement claims First Class passengers 'are currently enjoying complimentary food and drink as they conga up the aisle.' We resist this tempting advert for an upgrade. The connection at Crewe is only nine minutes, but there's a lift to change platforms, so we don't need to heave loaded bikes up flights of stairs.

In Hereford station we're slowly passed by *Britannia* – not the woman with the trident, but a wonderful old steam engine (number 70000), which I first saw as a young train-spotter. Now in splendid British racing green, she glides past pulling maroon and cream coaches.

Out on our bikes, we wiggle round and stop for a bite to eat. Steve heads off anti-clockwise round Cardiff Bay, though I'd planned a more direct clockwise route. Our projected 12 miles becomes 16 and Steve generously admits these may be counted as Gibbon Miles.

After a couple of hours on cycle routes beside busy main roads, where our average speed is barely 8 mph, we arrive in Barry, where we're invited to take our bikes into the room! Most convenient. I almost decline a second beer with our meal, but Steve orders another Peroni and I hate to see him drink alone.

Barry has been described as 'a town with two faces' with a large dock area formerly used to export coal, and also 'the gaudy arcades of a popular resort'. There's also apparently a large scrapyard half-full of old steam engines, which may count as another museum we missed.

DAY 66   BARRY TO SWANSEA   (53 MILES)

It's overcast this morning finding our way out of Barry. This includes pushing the bikes up a road so steep that lines have been cut into the stone pavement to give pedestrians more of a grip! We take a wrong turning, push the bikes up a narrow overgrown track, and emerge more or less where we were. Steve offers this as a Gibbon Mile, but I decline – it was only half a mile, and may well need to be offset against future Bluck miles.

Porthkerry Country Park gives us a delightful traffic-free ride through the trees, the first of several today. There's a big tanker floating past, and Steve says the land beyond is Cornwall, but it's probably Somerset. We pause in Rhoose for a route-finding discussion. Along the coast or inland? A wiggly or a straight route? Main road or country lanes? The B4265 seems busy, so we turn off (missing the Aston Martin factory), and ride through charming villages – St Athan and St Mary Church. A Sustrans route leads us through the narrow winding streets of Llantwit Major, a delightful town with a long history, and then on into Wick (not the one in Caithness, unless the space-time loops are getting bigger).

After a café stop in Bridgend we head out north on NCN 885 with drizzle coming on gradually. We link up with the NCN 4 Celtic Trail, for a slightly damp traffic-free ride through woodland, guide by an excellent Sustrans map. The rain is more persistent as we approach Port Talbot, riding past a house with a large disused hovercraft in the garden. I imagine a couple with different opinions. 'Will you get rid of that bloody machine?' 'No dear, I'll fix it up for when the sea level rises.'

We emerge from a track into a tired-looking estate, with six police vans and a dozen officers. 'It's all kicking off round here,' one explains. But local residents are standing around harmlessly and the disturbance seems to be over. None of the police can give us directions when Steve asks. 'No, we're from somewhere else, you see.'

Port Talbot is another place with two faces. The massive steelworks have been under threat for years, limping on with massive losses, while the nearby sand-dunes have been reclaimed and turned into the holiday resort of Aberavon, with the Afan Lido, 'the largest leisure and entertainments centre in Wales.' No, we didn't go there.

It's still wet and I'm tired already, so we head into town for a café stop. As we're munching our paninis – the chill cabinet explodes! Safety glass all over the floor and a shocked group of staff. Steve offers advice on replacement, with his expertise as a trustee at a local Heritage Centre and its café. A good man to have around when things explode.

With all our wet kit on, we emerge into the rain to search for the NCN 4 again. There are 'navigational problems' in a busy Port Talbot, but Steve's GPS and his sense of direction lead us out onto a well-signed route next to the busy A483 and then into Swansea.

Like many coastal communities, Swansea was a fishing village before the Industrial Revolution. By the mid-nineteenth century over 10,000 ships used its expanded harbour each year! The massive industrial boom declined after World War Two, turning the valley into 'an industrial moonscape of scarred tips and derelict factories.' But there has been massive urban regeneration, and Dylan Thomas – who was born here – wouldn't recognise the place. In the restaurant I astonish Steve by restricting myself to a single pint of Doom Bar.

DAY 67   SWANSEA TO LLANELLI VIA GOWER
(52 MILES)

An early but cloudy start for a lovely day on the Gower peninsula, beginning with a gentle ride round Swansea Bay down to Mumbles, all flat and traffic-free. In a little tree-lined section an unwary magpie flies straight towards me at head height, swerving up at the last moment. Yet another reason for wearing a bike helmet. The world's first rail passenger service, the Swansea and Mumbles Railway, began in 1807, and was drawn by horses for many years until steam engines came along. Mumbles has recently been chosen as the best place to live in Wales – but the houses are pretty expensive.

There's some hilly work to get around to Bishopston,

but the cloud is lifting and it's sunny by coffee time in Parkmill. A robin flies in and wanders round the café floor, before the owner chases him out. 'That bloody robin! He flies in here four times a day.' (If you swept the floor occasionally, there wouldn't be so many crumbs for him.) The loo has a high cistern with a chain, and a fully detachable seat, which is disconcerting.

The Gower Peninsula is Britain's first Area of Outstanding Natural Beauty. In the south near Pilton Green is Paviland (or Goat's Hole) Cave. A small human skeleton found here in 1823 became known as the Red Lady of Paviland because of the discoloured bones. But it's actually a young man from 34,000 years ago and 'the oldest anatomically modern skeleton found in Britain'.

We decide to skip the wiggly roads down to Oxwich and back, and so proceed on the A4118 to Scurlage, where we turn off to Rhossili at the far end of the Gower for another café stop. Lots of gorgeous countryside to drift through, with grand views down to the spectacular Worm's Head. There's a stiff breeze in our faces, but when we turn round it pushes us on quite quickly to Sturlage, tough young men on road bikes are whizzing past us. One of them stands by the roadside staring at the ground. I pull up to ask if he needs help. 'No problem mate, I've dropped an earpiece somewhere. It's a First World problem!' There's a moral here somewhere.

Along the pleasant but rather busy B4295, we ride into Gowerton for yet another café stop. I remember my father saying how much he had enjoyed cycling on the Gower, many years ago when it was much less developed. Today it's quite different from the rural idyll pictured in his photo album. There are still a few unspoilt villages, but lots of wealthy homes overlooking the sea, with Range Rovers much in evidence.

The final ten miles from Gowerton to Llanelli are excellent on NCN 4, much of it on a separate metalled track through woodland, with a tunnel of trees above us. A super ride in the sunshine. The only drawback is the last stretch into Llanelli, a bit rough in places, and today exposed to a strong headwind. We're really early, so we go in for a *fourth* café stop, drinking Fentiman's Mandarin and Orange (Robert) and Ginger Beer (Steve), which is made in far-flung Hexham.

At the restaurant in the evening Steve orders bottled water as well as beer. His fizzy Welsh liquid is more expensive than petrol! We can now add water-bollocks to the wine-bollocks (and occasional beer-bollocks) we've found. After being 'filtered through the mineral-rich landscape of the Pembrokeshire hills', this water is 'lovingly drawn from and bottled on organically farmed land.' Taste the difference!

DAY 68   *LLANELLI TO TENBY (ST FLORENCE)*
(55 MILES)

There are swans on a lake behind the restaurant at breakfast, and swifts wheeling round. We're off for another early start, with a strong wind in our faces for at least part of the way. But it's a lovely sunny ride out of Llanelli, with birds and flowers in abundance, white ducks on a pond, a redstart on the track, and dozens of early purple orchids lining the route on NCN 4.

After this good traffic-free run, we're onto minor roads into Kidwelly, riding along a track with a drop on one side, and glimpses of weed-covered water. This is what remains of the oldest canal in Wales, dating from 1766, used for many years to bring anthracite coal down to the coast for export, but almost invisible as a canal now. Kidwelly is a medieval town still dominated by its massive castle, familiar from the opening scene of *Monty Python and the Holy Grail*, and is twinned with Teentrainer. Round the coastline, we come to Ferryside, with a ferry since medieval times, but no longer. It's a good deal hillier than we had anticipated, but fairly soon we're drifting down into Carmarthen for coffee with the first 20 miles done.

Carmarthen Castle is a whopper, originally built in the early twelfth century, captured by Owen Glendower in 1405, recaptured by parliamentary forces during the Civil war, and dismantled on Cromwell's orders (though still used as a gaol until the 1920s). Most of these huge castles were built by the English to subdue the Welsh, but it didn't always work.

There's some hard cycling to get along to St Clears, with an endless hill reminding us of Devon and Cornwall. This inland town once has a quay which could accommodate ships up to 500 tons. After another monster climb into the countryside, through green lanes with high hedges full of foxgloves and pink campion – but on the narrow side for cars to pass – we decide not to divert to Laugharne (pronounced *Larn*) to visit Dylan Thomas country. We could have visited the Boathouse, a museum full of Thomas memorabilia. But we didn't.

Going downhill on a pavement cycleway, we glide swiftly *through* (rather than round) a bus shelter. A couple of sharp showers where we hide under trees, and then on upwards. Each bend must surely be the last, but somehow the road winds up yet again. We pass close to the six flat miles of Pendine Sands, where land speed records were attempted in the 1920s. Parry Thomas was killed here in 1927 when his drive chains broke. Now, did I oil the chain before we set off?

Steeply down to Amroth for a coffee on the coast, at one end of the 168-mile-long Pembrokeshire Coast Path. Very low tides here can reveal a drowned prehistoric forest, with tree stumps and fossilised acorns. Then, surprise, more steep hills. I have to give up and push two or three times, while Steve ploughs on bravely in first gear. I can almost walk as quickly as he's riding, and it gives my quads a bit of a rest. At the top I usually feel a bit better and can mount up again and zoom away for at least the next fifty yards.

Steve's navigation is infinitely superior to mine. Left to my own devices, I'd get lost with monotonous regularity, but his GPS and sense of direction almost always get it right. I was good at map-reading on Scottish mountains, but this was looking at contours on an OS map rather than road signs. It's different in a town! Steve has the ability to turn written information into a mental map, but I'm easily confused.

Back down to sea level again, we ride through some peculiar tunnels to reach Saundersfoot, where a dozen boats, each with six rowers, are struggling across the bay in a fiercely-contested race. One boat is well ahead, but as we round a corner, the winners are already ashore, punching the air with delight.

Guess what? Up into the sky again. We're both really tired after only 50 miles today. It's a combination of four factors – Wind, Hills, Age and Panniers – and we're completely WHAPed today. As we approach a busy A478, we both have the same thought – let's cut across country to St Florence. And so we do, cutting off the corner and riding through reasonably level lanes, rather than down to sea level and steeply up again. I'm sorry to miss out on Tenby. The harbour has been called the most beautiful in Britain, and there are medieval walls, pastel-coloured houses, fine beaches and lovely views. Bill Bryson described Tenby as 'everything you could want in a coastal retreat,' so maybe I'd better come back here and check it out.

In the pub our room has three Buddhas! Two slightly twee paintings – a smiling face, a hand raised in blessing – and a photograph of a genuine Thai figure in meditation pose, very beautiful and serene. Pictures of the Buddha have come to be used as room decoration, suggestive of peace and relaxation. The atmosphere would be very different with three pictures of a crucified Jesus. We have a peaceful night after a good meal and a couple of beers, thanks to the chef, the brewer and the meditating Buddha.

DAY 69   TENBY (ST FLORENCE) TO HAVERFORDWEST (51 MILES)

Sunny and breezy this morning, and we're looking forward to turning the corner, when the westerly winds won't be in our faces so much. We could have done this the other way round, but we were only going to do Scotland at first, so we set off clockwise from home near Carlisle. We've had the wind in our faces from Dover to Land's End, and now again for a few days in South Wales. But if we'd ridden anti-clockwise like Anna Hughes and Mike Carter, we could have had headwinds from Bristol to Land's End – and also across all off the far north coast of Scotland.

We compliment the pub's landlady for providing a really good breakfast.

Landlady: Oh thank you, I'll tell the chef.

Robert: Please tell him we had an excellent meal last night as well.

Landlady: Oh thank you, I'm glad you enjoyed it.

Steve: Yes, we went down the road to the other pub.

He said this after she'd gone, and it wasn't true, but it did set us off giggling.

There are one or two further endless hills again as we set off along the Celtic Trail, though not as steep as yesterday. At Lamphey we head off south to Freshwater East and Stackpole, where there's a wonderful stretch of ancient mature woodland. The huge oak, ash and pine trees either side of the road make me think of ancient Britain, when the whole country was supposedly covered with woodland. It's said you could once climb a tree in Dover and not touch the ground until London. Except you'd be starving, and London wouldn't be there yet.

We turn off south again to Bosherton and Buckspool. This is Ministry of Defence land now, with tanks and lorries everywhere, Keep Out Notices and chain-link fencing. Down we go to St Gowans, along a rough track for a couple of wobbly miles. I'm behind Steve, so he doesn't see me slide into the gravel, turn the bike over and perform an elegant sideways roll, landing on the soft grass. I look around, but there are no witnesses. I'll tell him later.

There's some spectacular cliff scenery along this track, and as we reach the end, a group of birders are gathered to look at a cliff nesting site known as Elegug Stacks, two tall detached pillars of limestone. Elegug is Welsh for guillemot, and here they are in their thousands, with razorbills, fulmars and kittiwakes further along. This area has been an MOD firing range since the 1940s, with humans largely absent for decades. This has produced new habitats for wildlife, who've got used to noisy guns. So we can thank Hitler for a successful bird reserve!

Back onto tarmac and through Castlemartin. I'd hoped here to visit a little bay known as *Blucks Pool*, which my father photographed on a cycling trip, but it's a mile off the road, so a bit beyond our endeavours. It does exist, though, and maybe I'll go there another day. As we reach the end of the peninsula at Angle, there's a sweeping descent down to sea level, a glide through the village – and a café on the beach, open on a Sunday!

Thence back along the north side of this peninsula and into Pembroke, whose castle is truly spectacular. The circular keep is 80 feet high and the walls 20 feet thick. Henry VII was born here in 1547. There is also a museum of Gypsy Caravans and Romany Crafts and Lore. Don't ask. We find a tiny café and get chatting with the owner, who unlocks the shop next door to show us his plans for conversion. He's got a lot of work to do!

We ride out of Pembroke on the magnificent Cleddau Bridge, half a mile long and now toll-free, with 10,000 crossings each day, saving a 28-mile diversion or a ferry crossing. During construction in 1970 a section of the box-girder bridge collapsed, killing four workers. Poor design and poor site organisation combined – but it did lead to new standards and hopefully prevented further disasters.

There's a tarmac NCN 4 route through woodland and into Haverfordwest, where we take a while to find the guest house. The owner has just emailed me with an invoice for £80 (which I paid in January) and when we arrive he asks, 'Do I need to get the veggie sausages out, or are you both normal?' I'm tempted to tell him exactly where to put his veggie sausages. There should be laws to protect us against this kind of casual food racism. What do you mean, grumpy old vegetarian?

As well as the cliff-nesting guillemots, today has been good for birds. In a patch of woodland, a pair of bullfinches are only arm's length away before they scoot off. I put up a skylark on the clifftop track, bursting into his own perfect version of *The Lark Ascending*. Later there's a single swift, flying low in front of us as if to show us the way – and a jay, a heron gliding across, and a motionless buzzard in the top of a dead tree.

DAY 70   HAVERFORDWEST TO CARDIGAN (59 MILES)

I simply follow Steve out of Haverfordwest, as he seems to know what he's doing. We cut off a corner to avoid a couple of hills, and then go steeply down into Nolton

Haven. This was once a port loading anthracite from a colliery up the valley, but only during warmer weather – the winters were so wild that boats could not be insured. The first of today's big hills leads out northwards. I walk for a bit, but Steve ploughs on in first as usual. He's younger than me.

At the bottom of the next big hill at Newgate there's a stream which divides English-speaking South Wales from the Welsh speakers of the North. That's the theory, and we do hear more Welsh spoken from now on. The Celtic Trail map suggests an inland detour to avoid this hill, but we'll go the short way – with another little walk for the older of the two cyclists. Then we turn off the main road and through farmland and country lanes into St Davids, all on NCN 4. We seem to have gained two or three miles with the initial shortcut.

St Davids is of course the birthplace of the patron saint of Wales (in the sixth century), and also Britain's smallest city – only really a large village on top of a hill.

Why is the magnificent cathedral at the bottom of the hill? Why does the floor have a noticeable slope on it? Two more unanswered questions.

There's a good run on NCN 4 from here to Fishguard, with only two or three steep or long hills. We're riding through farmland with foxgloves, pink campion and bracken in the high hedgerows. Also nettles to sting the unwary cyclist, as I lean into the hedge to let another car to squeeze past.

Fishguard saw the last invasion of Britain. French troops landed in 1797, most of them conscripts searching for food and alcohol. They were overcome by local reservists, including Jemima Nicholas, who rounded a dozen of them up with a pitchfork.

A lovely ride out of Fishguard, gently up a wide wooded valley, instead of plunging down to sea level only to climb up again. There's a dead fox on the road, a young one struck by a car. At Cilgwyn we bypass Newport to take another couple of miles off. It still seems a long afternoon, but then another wooded valley, steeper and almost gorge-like, leads us into St Dogmaels and thence into Cardigan.

Our bikes are taken down a ramp into the pub cellar with the beer barrels – another new location for the Ravens overnight. I ring my friend Keith to apologise for not visiting him tomorrow as planned. It's too much of a long day. Sadly the kitchen is closed on a Monday, as is much else in Cardigan, and we are reduced to a fish and chip restaurant on the high street. We're both a bit tired after five days cycling, and slightly apprehensive about a long day tomorrow. But we do have a cunning plan.

DAY 71   CARDIGAN TO ABERYSTWYTH   (70 MILES)

We've been forewarned about the A487. Mike Carter described it as 'the worst road of the trip yet', with blind bends, hilly and narrow, tall hedgerows and 'heavy, speeding traffic...the most dangerous combination for a cyclist.' Point taken, we'll go inland on NCN 82, hoping to see the sea at Aberystwyth and so not have to repeat the day. Our bikes are retrieved from the cellar for an early start, a pleasant run along another wooded valley at the start of the Tefi Trail. A coracle is hanging up on the front of a pub in Cilgerran – more preparation for rising sea levels? A buzzard flies along the road right in front of me and out through the trees.

There's a difference of opinion about the route at Cenarth, but Steve is right as per usual. More hills than I had counted on going up the valley, as the road twists from one side to the other instead of following the river in the valley bottom. A good coffee stop in Newcastle Emlyn, and then a great deal wigglier, up and down in glorious wooded scenery. Not too much chance to admire it all, as we seem to spend half the time heaving the bikes up yet another long hill. Then we're suddenly whizzing down the other side, focussing only on getting round the next bend without hitting a car coming the other way. Some gentle squeezing through, as quite a few drivers don't know how wide their cars are.

Two buzzards swoop across the road close to Steve, one maybe defending his territory. Then there are *three* buzzards seeming to fight in the sky, perhaps a pair seeing off an intruder. Round the corner comes a grey open-top 1930s Bentley! The occupants wave as they glide by. A couple stand with mugs of tea, staring at a red kite in the sky above them. Three more Bentleys drift past, two sporty grey Continentals and a demure black saloon. Nobody waves. Then two more Continentals and a maroon saloon. More Bentleys than buzzards! A classic car tour – Posh People Drive Round Wales. What do you mean, prejudiced?

Eventually we emerge from this buzzard-Bentley parallel universe full of steep hills, and find ourselves eating a welcome panini in Lampeter, Britain's smallest university town, and once a centre of the Welsh woollen industry. With 37 miles done and another 30 left, we're properly tired. Surely the upper Tefi valley can't be even steeper? At least the sun is out.

The afternoon is a really pleasant surprise. As we cycle higher into the valley, the road gets flatter! There's a good run up the B4343 to Tregowan for another coffee stop, and the final 20 miles is quite delightful. We turn off for several miles on a disused railway line, then up another gently sloping narrow track, in the middle of fine woodland again.

And so into Aberystwyth, where the guest house is empty with no reply on the phone. Eventually Steve contacts the owner and we're directed to a house in the next street, where our two single rooms are ready. Call me old-fashioned, but when you can't be bothered to meet the guests, it's not a guest house, it's an air B&B – or in this case an air B and no B since it's room only. Some gnashing of teeth, but at least we have a room each.

DAY 72   ABERYSTWYTH TO MACHYNLLETH
(27 MILES)

This is planned as a bit of a rest day. Aberystwyth is the main tourist resort in west Wales, with a long promenade which has been damaged by recent storms but is being repaired. There's a bit of a fuss finding somewhere suitable for breakfast. Then off we go up the obvious long hill out of the town – more than a mile in all – and on to the inevitably hilly route to Borth, where, after seeing four red kites hovering above us, we stop for coffee after a mere six miles. This must be a record.

Borth has the legend of a Welsh Atlantis, a land lost

to the sea. It's not entirely fictional, as extreme low tides reveal huge stumps of a forest of ancient trees, perhaps 5,000 years old, when the coastline was 20 miles further west. Inland is Cors Fochno (Borth Bog), 'a desolate wilderness of semi-liquid peat', which may be 20 feet deep. Let's not go there to find out.

Then a nice flat run leading to a few miles on the dreaded A487. It's not horribly busy, but quite uncomfortable. Finally there's a cycle path into Machynlleth, where we're allowed to dump the panniers at the hotel. We pedal off unburdened to the Centre for Alternative Technology. A bit of a struggle to get there, as a huge new bridge is being built, and the cycle path is diverted round road works – pairs of huge concrete pillars with nothing on top of them as yet. Machynlleth has long been the lowest crossing point on the Dyfi before the river widens into an estuary.

A quiet but hilly back road brings us into the CAT, which has expanded a lot since I last visited, with an interesting mixture of old and tired buildings with new and quite exciting developments. Their ground-breaking ideas about solar and wind and water power have become mainstream by now, so that they're often preaching to the converted. In the café Steve asks if there is a meat pasty, and the woman tells him – with the merest hint of a smile – that it's all vegetarian. My chick pea and cauliflower pasty is delicious, with a lovely fresh salad, the best lunch I've had this trip. Steve is reluctant to admit that veggie food is any good, but he somehow manages to put it all away.

Back in the hotel, the landlady carries a full pint along the bar for a regular, when her colleague turns round and the two women collide. The landlady bends her elbow and delivers the beer without spilling a drop. What skill! I dine on delicious Glamorgan sausages with superb chips and a mushroom sauce. Veggie food is getting better. After a lovely sunny day, we're rested up a bit, with four solid cycling days coming up.

DAY 73   MACHYNLLETH TO PWLLHELI   (61 MILES)

I've had a bad night with hot and cold sweats for much of the time. Perhaps I've caught a chill wandering round the CAT in a thin T-shirt. This morning I'm a bit more settled, but still with a headache and a bit of a chesty cough. We were joking last night about catching the train home, but it doesn't sound so funny right now.

We ride gently out of Machynlleth and west along NCN 82 beside the A493, which is not too busy, and a little loop at Pennal gives us a break from the main road. At Cwrt we continue on the NCN 82 up a minor road, uphill for a mile and more, a really hard pull, with a little walking at the top for both of us. Then there's a lovely ride down the valley into Tywyn – high hedges either side and honeysuckle growing through the hazel, catching the scent as we glide past. A male wheatear springs off a rock and flaps away.

Tywyn is the terminus of the famous narrow-gauge Talyllyn railway, dating from 1865, which runs seven miles up the valley to quarries – but never reached Talyllyn. There's a railway museum, but we content ourselves with a café stop.

It takes us a while to find the right way out of

Tywyn, signposted as a dead end, but finishing with a bridge leading to the other side of Broad Water. Then a flattish ride back onto the A493 and an easy run towards Barmouth. There's a fun ride across the bridge next to the railway line, on wobbly wooden planks, as a train rumbles past us. In the water underneath, huge jellyfish float past. Barmouth marks the start of the Three Peaks International Yacht Race, where daft competitors interrupt sailing to Fort William by running up Snowdon, Scafell and Ben Nevis.

A couple of hours along the busy A496, with a pleasant detour on a minor road north of Harlech, which looks tiny (perhaps there was more we didn't see). Harlech Castle, now a spectacular ruin, was built in the 1280s as part of King Edward's determination to subdue the Welsh (again). Captured by Owain Glendower in 1404, it was soon retaken by the English. A familiar story.

Portmadog appears sooner than expected – perhaps I map-measured the hilly detours we ignored. We decide to give Portmerion a miss, as we're both tired by now. We pause for coffee and recover a little. Porthmadog was once prominent in the slate industry, when the Ffestiniog railway brought slate from Blaenau Ffestiniog to be exported. The final run from Portmadog to Pwllheli is very pleasant, with a pavement cycleway all along the A497, and our own wooded road for the last couple of miles. It's a remnant of the old road, complete with dead cat's eyes and rather overgrown, but still very welcome for cyclists.

Our accommodation in Pwllheli is called a hotel, but you need a text message and a door code to get in.

'I don't have any staff at present,' explains the manager on the phone. So why are you calling it a hotel? Only one set of towels between the two of us, and neither soap nor breakfast. I'm still tired and a bit groggy.

DAY 74   PWLLHELI TO LLANDUDNO   (58 MILES)

A slight change of route to reduce the mileage, so we miss out Nefyn as well as the Lleyn peninsula. I feel mean about this, but the Lleyn would have added at least one more day, and finding accommodation there was difficult. I'm feeling a little better this morning. Steve says it's a relief to wake up and find I'm still alive.

After an early breakfast in a convenient Costa, the way out of Pwllheli is of course the steep road leading up a long hill. The first walk of the day for me, but Steve is still in the saddle at the top. We're both a bit weary. A lengthy pull up to Llithfaen in glorious sunshine, but then a grand sweep down through the lanes to the A499 – where there's a good bike track all the way to Caernarfon. What a castle! Perhaps the most impressive of the ring of 13th-century fortresses Edward I built (to subdue the Welsh). He named his eldest son Prince of Wales here in 1301, a tradition continued today with Prince Charles invested here in 1969. We find a café in the walled town, and in comes a blind man with his guide dog. He's a Welsh speaker, and I wonder if the dog has to learn Welsh as well. You don't like to ask.

Out of Caernarfon and along a good cycle route next to the A487 and so into Bangor, where we accidentally skirt round the town, before turning round to search for the centre and lunch. Eventually we locate a coffee shops and sit outside chatting to two women cyclists from Edinburgh. Angie asks why I'm a vegetarian, and on learning I'm a Buddhist she says casually, 'Oh, I've met the Dalai Lama'. I shake her hand in respect. She starts quizzing me about Buddhism, and when I tell her my research on Buddhism in Britain has been published, she shakes *my* hand in respect!

We wriggle our way out of Bangor and along the NCN 5 towards Conwy. Steve checks his back wheel a couple of times, thinking the brake is catching – but no, he's got a puncture! His first one through all our trips, due to the super Schwalbe Marathon tyres. It would be the back wheel of course. We're away from the main road on a quiet track at Penmaenmwar. Steve hoicks the wheel off and swaps the inner tube, all in a few minutes. It would have taken me the rest of the afternoon.

Meanwhile I admire the massive sea-wall and avalanche shelters, built by Robert Stephenson to protect his railway from the coast and its wild weather. Penmaenmawr was Gladstone's favourite holiday spot, which I think shows a lack of imagination.

Then into Conwy with the wind behind us and the prospect of rain. Passing underneath the walls of the castle, we cross the River Conwy on the modern road bridge, with two nineteenth-century bridges on our right. Next to us is Thomas Telford's suspension bridge – one of the earliest anywhere in the world – built in the 1820s and designed in Gothic style to match the castle. Beyond this is Robert Stephenson's tubular box-girder railway bridge, crossing the river in a single span. Most through traffic now goes under the River Conwy by tunnel.

We turn left and ride up the coast path, which turns into half a mile of soft sand, with gorse and undergrowth either side. Notices tell us to be continually aware of flying golf balls, but my attention is flagging as we heave the bikes through deep sand. I'm not enjoying this. Eventually we find a way out of the golf course and back onto tarmac, where Steve (or his GPS) guides us expertly to our destination.

We choose not to cycle round the Great Orme, though obviously we should have done. The ancient copper mine here was once the world's largest. Archaeologists have discovered miles of tunnels and 'the largest prehistoric man-made chamber anywhere in the world', dating from the Bronze Age. I cannot remember being so tired. It's partly the *lurgy* (technical term for a heavy cold), but also the continual (continuous?) cycling. Even the gentlest hills have made me weary today.

As we're preparing to leave the hostel to look for a meal, Steve mislays his hearing aid, and after searching the room, he finds it in his underpants – the ones he's wearing! How did it get there? He said he didn't know how this happened, but at least he'll hear himself better while he's talking out of his arse. This would have been even funnier if we hadn't been so tired.

DAY 75   LLANDUDNO TO NEW BRIGHTON   (69 MILES)

I've had another bad night, with persistent sweating. I lay down on the bed at 8.00 on returning from the restaurant, and apart from getting undressed and a visit to the loo, I didn't move for 11 hours. I've never been this tired before. In the morning I feel a bit better, if rather sluggish. But Steve has caught the lurgy too, with an awful headache and feeling shivery. We retrieve our bikes and head off for a Costa, but Steve can barely deal with a croissant and a latte. We joked about taking the train home, but now he's really in a bad way, shivering with cold. Decisions are quickly made, and soon he's off to the station. I'm reasonably all right, so I'll carry on alone while I still can. But how will I find the route? What if I get a mechanical problem?

It's a fine morning, with high clouds and sunshine, and NCN 5 continues as a splendid coastal and promenade route – though it feels odd without Steve – along to Rhyl, where there's a Bike Hub Café. Emerging after my coffee and cake, another cyclist sitting outside points at my Raven and says, 'I'm suffering from bike envy!' This is not the first time my bike has been admired, and I launch into my explanation of Rohloff gears and the wonders of Thorn Cycles.

Rhyl is said to offer 'every kind of amusement and attraction, from bingo to windsurfing', with a five-mile promenade leading all the way to Prestatyn. What more could you ask? Out to sea there are hundreds of wind turbines, all going round and powering the country with no fossil fuels – except those used to make them. It's the morning for the Rhyl Half Marathon, and I'm soon weaving my way through groups of runners coming the other way. There are also quite a few joggers running *towards* them, so weaving in and out becomes more complicated. I'm twice accused of cheating by riding a bike.

After Prestatyn the NCN 5 goes inland and uphill, so I decide to risk the coastal A548 which is busy but flat. There's a pavement to ride on for almost all the way to Flint, albeit a bit bumpy and overgrown and in places. I'm passed by the bike-envy man and his friend, who are going quite a bit faster than me. 'Hello again!' they shout. It feels slightly odd to be greeted in a place where you don't know anyone.

I ride through Flint without realising it, and have to retrace my steps to find a Subway sandwich for lunch. Then down to Hawarden Bridge Station for a rendezvous with my distant cousins Paul and Alison, who lead me along NCN 568 – a wiggly route across marshland and urban estates – to Neston and Parkgate, where they have a favourite café. Coffee and cake and map-reading follows, with a few family stories as well. Before turning for home, they direct me onto the Wirral Circular Route, NCN 56, which takes me through Heswall and Hoylake, home of the famous golf course. I miss a turn and have to wiggle through minor roads inland, before emerging onto the North Wirral Coastal Path, which looks a bit rough. So inland again to Moreton briefly, then out to the coast again for a final concrete sea front ride into New Brighton. Steve emails to say he's safe at home – but has tested positive for Covid! So that's what the lurgy is.

DAY 76   NEW BRIGHTON TO LYTHAM ST ANNE'S (64 MILES)

Circumstances conspire against me this morning. I'm up and ready to go by 8.00 and feeling fine – but my bike's locked in the bar area and I can't get at it until 9.00 when the cleaners turn up with the keys. First hour wasted.

Soon I'm cycling down the coast on Route 56 with a fine view of the Liverpool skyline – the Liver Building (with the largest clock in Britain and the famous Liver Birds), the monstrous Anglican cathedral, and newer skyscrapers too. The main ferry terminal is fenced off for a major refurbishment. How to cross the Mersey? I ride round the docks to another ferry terminal. The only possible crossing includes a 30-minute river tour, and it doesn't go for another 40 minutes. Second and third hour wasted. But there's an educational commentary on board about the history of Liverpool – and the ferry has Sir Peter Blake's jazzy paintwork.

In the eighteenth and nineteenth centuries, Liverpool was one of the world's largest ports, with seven miles of docks by 1880. The city centre was substantially rebuilt in recent years with new accommodation, shops, restaurants and cinemas. But for everyone outside Liverpool (and anyone my age) it's mainly famous for the Beatles, all born here in the 1940s. The huge Albert Dock area includes the fabulous Beatles Story exhibition, which Caroline and I visited a few years ago, to celebrate my 64th birthday. A real magical history tour!

It's a struggle to get out of the city, with a strong headwind and a succession of grotty industrial areas. But my reward comes at Crosby, where NCN 810 leads along the coast for a fine view of Antony Gormley's *Another Place* – the famous 'iron men' in the sand, staring out to sea. A spectacular installation. But then it's just sand dunes, as far as I can see, so I head inland and ride through

Little Crosby, where it's trying to rain. I find my way back to the railway and follow from Hightown through most of Formby to Freshfield – where I *cannot* find the right way.

Here's my guardian angel again, this time a white-bearded cyclist. I ask for the way to Southport, and he offers to take me there, since it's where he's going. He leads me out of Freshfield, through some pleasant woodland and onto the NCN 62 Trans Pennine Trail, which brings us both into Southport. We chat about bikes and the Sea-to-Sea route, which he's going to tackle next week. He's a bit apprehensive about the hills, not without cause.

It's 2.00 before I'm sitting down in an Italian café in Southport, with 29 miles done instead of 25 as planned. Do these count as Bluck miles if Steve's not here? I do hope he's OK. Southport is a mixture of 'modern holiday attractions' and 'the style and atmosphere of a Victorian or Edwardian watering-place.' Also, the British Lawnmower Museum is here, should you wish to visit.

A summer afternoon, and an easy ride along the coast north of Southport on a traffic-free path. After a few miles, it curves round eastwards to reveal a very pleasant surprise. I was dreading the main road from here to Preston, but there's a traffic-free route all the way. There are some slightly lumpy pavements, but a great deal better than the dual carriageway.

The NCN 62 wiggles its way into Preston, where we got properly lost on LEJOG. But if you follow the signs, the path leads down to a quiet river crossing and a left turn onto the Preston Wheel. My bearded friend told me *just turn left*, and I follow his wise advice. The NCN 622 leads along the north bank of the River Ribble. Even the road works he warned me about are silent on a Sunday, with a bike route all the way through. Preston is the second oldest borough in England, with an MP since the 13th century. It's also the birthplace of Richard Arkwright (1732-92), inventor of the spinning frame, and the town was a centre for cotton spinning for many years.

Thence to Freckleton, some of the way using a dangerous cycle lane *on the dual carriageway* – madness! Finally I arrive in Lytham. The promenade round to St Anne's seems to take a long time, and it's 6.00 before I'm approaching the hotel. I've been tiring quite a bit this afternoon, with a push to make up for time wasted this morning with the fiasco of delays.

Lytham is almost entirely surrounded by golf courses, including the famous Royal Lytham and St Anne's. The promenade stretches right round to St Anne's. Bill Bryson called Lytham the best small town in the north, but I have a sneaking regard for another place, which I won't name, in case everyone flocks there and it is ruined by tourism. Lytham has a Lifeboat Museum, which I had kept as a lovely surprise for Steve, but he's not here and anyway it's closed.

DAY 77   LYTHAM ST ANNE'S TO LANCASTER (AND HOME) (42 MILES)

I'm woken at 3.00 am by people ending their party rather noisily. The words of *Get Off My Cloud* are going round in my head before I drift off to sleep again. By 5.30 a series of heavy lorries start up and are driven away. For a moment I imagine the revellers and the drivers are the same people, but this is unlikely.

The Blackpool promenade gives a wonderful ride along a sculptural waving route, though the stuff inland looks scruffy. The piers and surroundings are crammed with fish and chip shops, fun palaces, and people enjoying themselves. A Rastafarian cycles past with music blaring out from large speakers. Further along the promenade, beyond the famous and impressive tower, there's a long-dead Cypriot café with the title still visible on the concrete frontage: 'Blackpool Halloumi Nations.'

It's easy to be snooty about Blackpool. But six million people makes sixteen million visits here each year to have fun and buy the famous Blackpool rock. Well over a thousand tons of the stuff were sold here in the 1980s, enough to rot the teeth of all Britain's children (other tooth-rotting confectionery is widely available). The new promenade is wonderful – as well it might be for £100 million – but the town is badly run down, with empty hotels and shops. It's been called the unhealthiest place in Britain, with alcohol-related deaths and a shorter life expectancy for men. In 2014 the *Guardian* declared the New Kimberley Hotel, in a prominent position facing the sea, 'the worst hotel in Britain', though I can suggest a serious rival further north.

Cleveleys comes next, its elegant new Jubilee Beach promenade leading all the way along to their public toilet building. Possible rivalry with Blackpool? There's a gentle sunny promenade ride all the way round to the Fleetwood Ferry by 11.00, but the next crossing isn't until 2.15. The ferry itself is resting on a mudbank and likely to sit there for some time. An interesting conundrum – wait three hours for the ferry, which might make me late for the train home, or cycle round. How far is it? I need a pause in the Ferry Café to sort this out.

I reckon it's only about 13 miles, so it's an easy decision. Quite a pleasant flat ride south on minor roads through a built-up Thornton, and then I turn north, cross the River Wyre – clearly tidal at this point, though quite a bit further inland – and head out on the A588, which is not too busy. Through Hambleton and Stalmine on a good flat road, riding steadily and averaging a reasonable 11 mph. And so on to Cockerham and Condor green, on a lovely sunny afternoon. Here I join NCN 6, the Lancashire Coastal Way, along the east bank of the River Lune, round the corner and into Lancaster.

Lancaster Castle's Well Tower was used for prisoners awaiting trial or execution, including the ten Lancashire witches hanged in 1612. As recently as 1811 criminals had 'M' for Malefactor branded on their arm. Behave yourself in Lancaster! More recently, Anna Hughes had a new rear tyre and rear wheel repairs here, after a mere thousand miles on the old one. I think mine lasted at least five thousand before needing repairs, so perhaps it's made of sterner stuff.

The plan was to include a loop out to Morecambe at this point, but there's a national train strike tomorrow, so I head for the station to check on the situation. A helpful customer adviser suggests I take what I can get, so I jump on the next train for Carlisle. There's a whole compartment with room for *eight* cyclists and their bikes, and I have it all to myself. By now the Fleetwood Ferry would only be setting off on the first crossing after low tide, so I'm feeling rather pleased with myself, albeit sorry to miss Morecambe. I seem to have gained a couple of hours and had a nice bike ride I wasn't expecting.

Thence safely home – only to find that I too test positive for Covid! We divide up the house between us so that Caroline can keep out of my way, and I sleep in the spare room for a week. Unpacking the panniers, I realise I've been carting round four maps which relate to the final lap rather than this one. What an idiot! Let's hope that Steve and I are both fit again for the last lap – which starts in another fortnight.

This trip has been 677 miles – rather less for Steve – with a daily average of only 56, and the grand total is 4503 so far. I don't think there are 497 miles left now to bring this up to 5000. Who cares?

12

THE LAST LAP – LANCASTER TO CARLISLE

*DAY 78   LANCASTER TO BARROW-IN-FURNESS
(67 MILES)*

Two weeks later we're both feeling a good bit better. Our early train to Carlisle is delayed by half an hour due to a 'passenger disturbance'. Rioting in Wylam? No, it's a man who won't pay and won't leave the train, so they have to wait for the police. That's the second time. We miss the connection at Carlisle, but the next train gets us to Lancaster by 10.00 and we should be fine.

A good flat ride along the NCN 69 on a disused railway line to Morecambe, and onto the promenade, where the magnificent old station remains, now transformed into a 'popular entertainment venue'. The fashionable Midlands Hotel on Marine Road helped Morecambe become known in the 1930s as 'the Naples of the North', with famous figures such as Noel Coward and Coco Chanel staying here. (I'm guessing nobody calls Naples 'the Morecambe of the South'.)

We glide along the prom past the Eric Morecambe statue, thinking what a genuinely funny man he was. Cycling along to Hest Bank, we pretend to consider riding across Morecambe Bay. With 120 square miles of sand and mudflats, the tide comes in faster than you can run, and there are random spots of quicksand, known as *melgraves*, where you can sink up to your knees in seconds. The tide will drown you unless you're winched out. The sands have swallowed both horse-drawn carts and modern 4x4s, and 23 Chinese immigrant cockle-pickers were drowned here in 2004. There's an ancient low-tide route across from Hest Bank to Kents Bank, but it's an eight-mile walk and you need an experienced guide. Let's stick to the road.

Neither of us are fully fit after our encounters with Covid. We're both wheezing a little, with lungs not yet clear, and we tire easily. It's not just our age, though that doesn't help – you recover more slowly as the years wear on. This affects our route choices as we approach Carnforth. We intended to ride north on NCN 6, as we did on LEJOG nine years ago. But it looks bit hilly, so we opt for the coastal route on NCN 700 which looks flatter. Although we're both down to a single pannier for this short last lap, even modest hills take it out of us. So we ride slowly through Silverdale and on to Arnside. There's that single swift again, I'm sure it's the same one. Tired *and* delusional now.

The mud flats here are famous for sea-birds now, but in the nineteenth century Arnside was well-known as a boat-building centre. We pause here for an early lunch, with an excellent falafel and tomato chutney panini for me – yummy! It's tempting to catch the train across the Kent Channel from Arnside to Grange-over-Sands, which would save us 16 miles – obviously cheating, but there's a train in 30 minutes.... No, onwards, be big and brave, cough cough.

The NCN 700 runs through pleasant flat country, and on up into Levens, where we turn west into a strong and rather chilly wind. The cycle route is close to the busy A590, but on a minor road and much more peaceful. We ride down into Grange-over-Sands, where we pause for coffee on a terrace overlooking the sea. My chocolate brownie is so large and chocolatey that I'm struggling to manage it all – but I need to keep my strength up.

We leave the NCN route for a few miles for a more direct route through Flookburgh and past Holker Hall, through woodland on the B5278 and up towards Haverthwaite. Here we turn off along the River Leven, re-joining NCN 70 past a sign marked *Private Road: No Unauthorised Vehicles.* This is a lovely quiet route with no traffic at all, and we turn left onto a dismantled railway which is very special for me. It's the remains of the Furness to Newby Bridge line, where my great-uncle Bill was an engine driver! It's odd to cycle along a track bed where Grandpa's elder brother drove a train. Enthusiasts have restored three miles of track to run steam trains from Haverthwaite to Lakeside on Windermere, so I should come back and ride along the line itself.

There's quite a drag uphill beyond Greendod, and we really notice it. As we're thankfully plunging down again, we somehow miss a turn and come onto the very busy

A590. Damn! After a few hundred scary yards, we cross over and wiggle round minor roads to avoid the traffic, by which time we're almost into Ulverston, somehow seeming to ride *round* the town rather than actually through it.

South of Ulverston we cycle past Conishead Priory, originally founded in the twelfth century. The present house is a gothic revival building from the 1820s which bankrupted the owner. It's now owned by the enthusiastic (some say controversial) New Kadampa Buddhists. I stayed here during my research on Buddhism in Britain, interviewing members about their teachings and practice.

Then we're off on the A5087 with cars rushing past, for the last few miles into Barrow. There are some gentle hills to tire us out still further. Outside Newbiggin we pause on a bench to eat some Twixes and look out across Morecambe Bay. Beyond Morecambe the Heysham nuclear power station is glinting in the sun, with wind turbines beyond. Solar and wind power freely available, I'm just saying… Steve looks out to sea and wonders if we can see the Isle of Man. (No, it's much further round to the west.)

Finally we come down to Rampside and almost take the dead-end turn to Roa Island, before locating the odd wiggle onto the off-road tarmac NCN 700. This leads us gently into Barrow-in-Furness round the Piel Channel, past the massively ugly gas terminals and through the dock area into the centre. Barrow is now rather run-down and forgotten, but in 1870 its steelworks were the largest in the world, and it was a major port. In the 1880s my grandfather worked here as a teenager, before escaping to become a Methodist minister and open the way for middle-class offspring. Bill Bryson described the centre as a bleak place where dangerous-looking men with tattoos hung around as if it was a prison yard.

It wasn't at all bad where we stayed, though there was music blaring up from the bar while we were trying to get to sleep. We're both so tired – my quads didn't want to work at all as we walked a few streets down to a restaurant.

Some of today passed in a bit of a blur. There was no rain, it was cloudy and windy, there was some lovely countryside with fine distant views of the Lakeland peaks. But also a little of what we might call 'post-Covid brain fog', where we were slightly on autopilot, focusing on turning the pedals over and not falling off on the hills, rather than looking around us at the wonderful scenery.

DAY 79   BARROW-IN-FURNESS TO WHITEHAVEN (66 MILES)

We amble down to the Brewer's Fayre for an early and filling breakfast, next to the Dock Museum, which of course we ignore. There's far too much cycling on main roads in prospect today, but we have little alternative. We ride out of Barrow on the busy A590, then onto the equally busy A595 into Askham in Furness (which has bravely abandoned hyphens). There are hills and wind, and we're not really enjoying ourselves. We take a detour into Kirkby-in-Furness to avoid the main road for a couple of miles, and foolishly pass a café where we should have stopped.

Somehow we miss a turn which would have taken us

across to Foxfield, and so we have to ride another three miles to get there on the increasingly unpleasant A595. At Duddon Bridge we turn into the wind and up a really long hill, with traffic going fast in both directions. At least we're both wearing bright yellow tops, so the drivers can see us struggling.

We arrive in Millom hoping for a good lunch stop, cycling round in circles looking for a café, but winding up in a bleak pub where huge plates of fish and chips are on offer. We settle for coffee and cheesecake. A notice reads: *Please abide by our rules or you will be asked to vacate the premises.* Millom was a mining town in the nineteenth century, with seven pits extracting haematite near the seashore at Hodbarrow, the largest operation of its kind in Britain. The Hodbarrow Mines and Millom Ironworks were closed in 1968, and the town's population halved in the next few years. It's still quite a large place not to have a decent café.

We keep on the A595 again for another seven or eight miles, with the wind behind us at last, but still traffic and hills to negotiate. By the time we get to Bootle we're both grateful to turn off on a quiet road leading down towards the coast – and it's flat! We pass warning notices about an MOD firing range, and start having a little grumble about the amount of land the military own, where nothing seems to happen. A young man with long curly hair and a beard flags us down, listening to instructions on an old-fashioned walkie-talkie. Would we wait a few minutes while the gun is fired? Several motorists are waved to a halt and we're wondering how long this is going to take…. *BANG!* A hell of a noise, but no whistling shell or explosion.

The hippie gets the go-ahead and waves us on. He's probably a local civilian with his truck, drafted in on firing days to stop the traffic. Or have the haircut rules been relaxed for the Queen's Own Peace and Love Brigade?

After this excitement we ride round to Lane End – where the lane ends – and we're back onto the A595 for another few miles. Then we're gliding down a sweeping curve and onto the turn for Ravenglass and the beginning of NCN 72 Hadrian's Cycleway, which should see us home. The Ravenglass and Eskdale Railway was the first narrow-gauge railway in England, built in 1875 to carry iron ore down to the coast for transfer towards Barrow. There's also a railway museum here… and more importantly a café, where we linger for a while. We're in no hurry to proceed, and Steve is particularly tired.

The beginning of the NCN72 is a weird little path across the mouth of the River Mite and round a stony coastline to Saltcoats, where we're pleased to see tarmac again. Soon we're past Drigg on a good road, but Steve calls a halt with a flat front tyre. He pumps it up, but it's no good, and as we enter Seascale he has to replace the inner tube. At least it's much easier than the back wheel.

We're only a mile or so from Sellafield. In 1956 it was known as Windscale, Britain's first nuclear power station. A reactor fire the following year severely dented the image of the nuclear industry, and the plant pumped untreated nuclear waste into the Irish Sea. Cleaning up the waste at Sellafield will take until 2120 and cost £121 *billion* (I'm not making this up). We're spending three years of the entire defence budget at Sellafield, with no permanent solution for nuclear waste. The Visitors Centre here was once the most popular attraction in the Lake District (due to being out of the rain). There were 200,000 visitors a year in the 1990s, but numbers fell and the centre was closed in 2012 and later demolished.

There's a sign saying the NCN72 stops here, and resumes north of Sellafield. What? As Steve attends to the front wheel, I ask a cyclist who's resting on a nearby bench if we can still get along the coast path, even if the notice says we can't. He says it's a bit tricky in places, but it can be done. His advice is spot-on. The path leads over rubbery grid-mesh along the dunes, a fine sunny afternoon ride with the sea close in on our left, a little adventure all on its own. After a mile or so we have to hop off and push the bikes under a railway bridge where the path has collapsed. We sneak through feeling pleased with ourselves for having outwitted officialdom.

Riding past the hideous and heavily fenced-off remains of Sellafield, we reach a delightful section of the NCN72, lanes and tarmac paths through woodland, and round the edges of some rather scruffy villages, which Bill Bryson describes as 'little fragments of Barrow-in-Furness that have somehow drifted off and washed ashore.'

We miss out St Bees, which marks the start of the Coast-to-Coast Walk from the Irish sea to the North Sea, and has some wonderful views of the Lakeland mountains. Finally we glide down into Whitehaven, where we find a really good B&B and a fine meal in the local Italian restaurant. Another ancient fishing village, by the eighteenth century it had become a major port. In 1778, during the American War of Independence, the Scots-born captain of George

Washington's navy, John Paul Jones, mounted a raid on Whitehaven. When his men found their way into the local alehouses, the attack was easily repulsed. Jones is seen as a rebel or traitor here, but a hero in America – which may explain a lot.

At the B&B we find that Chancellor Rishi Sunak and Health Secretary Sajid Javid have both resigned to unseat Boris Johnson. How long can he last? Neither of us are fully fit, and we're really tired again by the end of the day. Steve lies down and falls asleep with his clothes on and I haven't the heart to wake him up. Perhaps he undressed in his sleep, as he's wearing pyjamas in the morning.

DAY 80   WHITEHAVEN TO CARLISLE   (61 MILES)

After another good breakfast, we head off on the NCN72 again along the promenade, with the wind behind us at last. It's a good route on minor roads and traffic-free sections, until we take a wrong turn round an industrial plant and accidently ride down to the coast at Haddington rather than Workington. We have to cycle back up the hill to link up with the NCN72 again, after which it's an easy run into Workington and a café stop. Tired already!

Workington was another port where coal was shipped out to other areas in England, and Maryport, which we reach next, was the same. The docks and harbour were built in the eighteenth century, with a million tons of cargo shipped out each year at the peak. The town still looks impressive in places, with a gridiron plan of historic houses. On the edge of the harbour is the Maritime Museum…

Beyond Maryport the B5300 is really busy, and by the time we get to Allonby we're fed up with it. Allonby was apparently used to receive whisky smuggled across the Solway from Scotland, which doesn't make any sense to me, as it's ten times further than the crossing at Bowness. Maybe the excise men were on the lookout further north.

We planned to continue along the coast, but instead we turn off and follow the NCN72, which wisely takes us off the main road. This is probably four miles further, but it's all on minor roads with the wind behind us and we're flying along. We arrive in Silloth, whose name derived from the 'sea laths' or granaries belonging to the Cistercian monks who grew grain and made salt here. What we need now is a lunch stop, and we enter a busy café at the same time as two women cyclists from Carlisle. The café owner assumes we're all friends and gives us a table together, so we have a pleasant lunch chatting about local cycle routes and our coastal challenge, while demolishing some excellent paninis with salad.

The route leads on through Abbey Town – taking its name from a Cistercian abbey founded here in 1150 – and through Newton Arlosh, which has an unusual medieval church, with five-foot thick walls in its defensive tower, designed to protect local people against border raiders from Scotland.

At Kirkbride we cut across to Glasson on the north Solway coast, rather than riding right round the coast via Bowness-on-Solway, which marks the western end of Hadrian's Wall. Today this saves us eight or nine miles but isn't cheating, as we've been right round the coastal route already on an epic journey. We caught the train to Whitehaven, stayed overnight and then cycled back home, which is exactly one hundred miles, to prove we could do it. I'm not sure we could repeat this now.

Just west of Bowness is Herdhill Scar, which marks the remains of the railway viaduct which once ran a mile and more across the Solway Firth to Scotland. It was opened in 1869 and trains ran across until the 1920s, despite the need for repeated repairs due to ice cracking the supporting pillars. It was only demolished in 1935, much to the dismay of local walkers, especially Scots who could no longer visit an English pub on the sabbath. We passed the other end of this former viaduct on Day One, so we must be very nearly home by now. The end is almost in sight.

Sure enough, at Glasson there's a very welcome sign saying Carlisle 10 miles, and this is the start of a gentle flat run along the marshes. At Burgh by Sands we pass an impressive statue of Edward I, covered in armour and holding a massive helmet in his hand. While fighting the Scots (as opposed to the Welsh) in 1307, Edward I died on the nearby Burgh Marshes. The road follows the old Roman Vallum, where there was once a barrier against the sea, but now the high tides can flood right across the road, sometimes catching out unwary motorists.

We're both exhausted by the time we reach Carlisle. Mutual congratulations, back-slapping and handshakes, though there's no brass band to mark the fact that we've *cycled round Britain*. We hop on a train and then head for home and a hot bath. We promise not to get back on a bike for a few days, or perhaps even longer.

The weather report comes on the TV after the news, and the map of mainland Britain still looks very wiggly. It seems somehow impossible that we've both cycled all the way round here. (Steve promises to go back to Llandudno and complete the three days round to Lancaster, and later he and Julie do exactly that, so we have both completed the journey.) For this final trip we have ridden 194 miles with an average of 65 miles each day, and our total is now 4697 miles with an overall average of 60 miles each day. That's not counting all the train journey days to and from Fort William, Thurso, Sunderland, Hull, Southampton, Cardiff and Lancaster. Apart from a couple of punctures each, the bikes have been wonderful, with all repairs done safely during their annual service, rather than having a wheel collapse on us in the middle of nowhere. This bike ride begins to feel like quite an achievement.

So we've ridden almost 5000 miles in 80 cycling days. I know that 4697 isn't exactly 5000 miles as claimed, but before you ask for your money back, how about adding our 252 miles for the Outer Hebrides trip? And I've also cycled 274 miles on Shetland and 96 on Orkney on my own, which I think we can fairly count as being around Britain's coast. Don't tell me about Northern Ireland.

So we can add 622 for the islands to the mainland 4697 above, making a grand total of 5319 expedition miles. Steve and I have cycled this distance again (and probably more) in what we laughingly called training. At least 40 miles a week for say 26 weeks each year for five years, which adds up to 5200 miles. We're almost certain to have cycled at least 10,000 miles together in all. No wonder I'm still feeling tired.

* * *

When we explain to people that we won't be at home for the next fortnight, because we're cycling round the coast of mainland Britain, they often ask if we're doing it for charity. We tell them it's just for fun, and our friends and neighbours think we're completely crazy. I've thought that myself at least once on each trip. Some of it hasn't been fun at all. Riding into horizontal rain on the Applecross Pass, struggling through brambles on the flooded railway track near Hartlepool, and being turned away from a fully-booked B&B in Felixstowe – none of that was any fun at all.

These low points are relatively few, compared with all those sunny days riding through towns and villages I'd never seen before, whole counties I knew little about, and places which reminded me of childhood holidays by the seaside. I'm left with a great sense of achievement, riding all the way round the coast of the island we live on – albeit not quite to the end of every road.

I've often thought there's something more here than simple enjoyment and new places and a final sense of satisfaction. There seems to be another reason in the background for all this coastal cycling, but it's taken me a long time to find it. At first I thought it was Bradley Wiggins, inspiring us to get back on our bikes by winning both the Tour de France and the London Olympics Time Trial in 2012. That's what led us to tackle LEJOG the following summer. We stayed overnight in Bradley's home village of Eccleston, and stored our bikes overnight in the very garage where his bike had once been locked up. The next day we were off to Kendal, a sensible 64 miles, and learned this was Bradley's regular training ride. He usually rode there and back – in the morning!

Each time Steve and I came back from a fortnight's cycling, Chris Froome or Geraint Thomas would win the Tour de France a few weeks later. Caroline and I would be glued to the telly, watching the Tour highlights for most of July.

Thinking about these three British riders – Wiggins, Froome and Thomas – brought to mind a famous name from the past. Reg Harris is all but forgotten now, but was once as well-known as Stirling Moss or Stanley Matthews, who were the Lewis Hamilton and David Beckham of their day. Harris was the World Amateur Sprint Champion in 1947 – the year I was born – and won two silver medals in the 1948 London Olympics. He'd surely have won gold if he hadn't crashed in training. Harris was strong enough to bend the rear triangles of his bike frame, and so had them rebuilt with *solid* chain stays and seat stays. Asked if the added weight would slow him down, Harris famously replied: 'They all go if you push 'em'.

Reg Harris's career was followed with enthusiasm by my father, a keen cyclist himself as a young man in the 1930s. He would cycle regularly from Hull to Oldham – eighty miles across the Pennines – on a fixed-gear bike to see his parents at the weekend. There was less traffic then, and cyclists would wait at the bottom of long hills to grab the tailgate of a slow lorry for a free lift.

My father's bike was an elderly F.W.Evans with Reynolds 531 steel tubing and a Sturmey Archer three-speed hub gear. His holiday snaps show that he rode it round Scotland in 1933 and he was still riding it to the shops in 1969. He worked in a bank all his life, and was careful with money.

This bike lived in the coal shed at home for twenty years. I hadn't given it a thought since my father died, but I remember it very well. It's a surprise to compare my Thorn Raven with his old Evans. Both bikes have matt black frames, hand-built from Reynolds steel tubing, built for comfort rather than speed, as my father would say. Both have flat bars with bar-end grips, wide tyres and a Brooks saddle. And both bikes have hub gears, though my Rohloff gives a much wider range, with fourteen gears compared to the Sturmey Archer's basic Low, Middle and Top. Both bikes even have the same 40-tooth chainwheels and 17-tooth rear sprockets!

My father would recognise the Raven as a much-updated version of his old F.W.Evans. How he'd love to ride a bicycle with fourteen gears! Have I copied his bike purely by accident? I had no conscious intention of doing so as I was choosing equipment for my Thorn. I remember walking into the upstairs showroom at St John Street Cycles and thinking immediately that these were the machines I wanted. Could it be that I recognised something of my father's bike?

Steve and I were half-way round our coastal journey, with three fortnights done and three still to go, before I remembered the stories my father told me about his cycling days. Eighty miles and back across the Pennines on a fixed gear for the weekend? That's a very fit young man! The next story was the cycling holiday he took in his early twenties. He rode from Yorkshire to Ullapool – in two days he said – to spend ten days walking and camping in the mountains, before cycling back in two days. This sounds impossible – it's nearly four hundred miles! But remember the young man we met in Brampton, cycling 200 miles from Thirsk to Edinburgh in a day. So if you're a fit young cyclist, setting out at 7.00 am and averaging say 15 mph including stops – you'll cover 200 miles by about 9.30 pm. Put like that I suppose it's just possible. My father was not usually given to exaggeration. If you're camping, you can cycle throughout the hours of daylight – and in the north in midsummer there's light for eighteen hours a day.

As a junior bank clerk with limited annual leave, he could never set off on a ride which would take longer than a fortnight. The final story was of a marathon journey he always wanted to do, but never had the chance. How could I have forgotten? He told me several times how he had always wanted to cycle *round the coast of Britain*. He would have had to do it exactly as we have. In these six fortnights, I've been riding round my father's dream.

When I cycled the Taunton to Bridgwater Canal again – on my own this time, after a week at a Buddhist retreat near Glastonbury – I rode past Pluto again. Not through meditating on a higher spiritual plane, but by following the Somerset Space Walk along the canal towpath from Taunton. I leaned the Raven against the plinth in Bridgewater and took a picture, with Pluto framed by my bike frame. Pluto was discovered in 1930, just before my father set off to ride from Yorkshire to Ullapool and back. Perhaps I've been cycling to Pluto in time as well as space, cycling back in time to understand more about the man who taught me how to ride a bike.

Like lots of men my age, when I look in the mirror now, I sometimes see my father's face. As I pull along a country road in Northumberland, I often think how much he'd enjoy doing exactly this, bowling along in the sunshine, without a care in the world. Fifty years and more after his death, I can still see him pedalling off into the distance, pushing slowly up another hill, and freewheeling down the other side.

APPENDIX

HELPFUL RULES FOR COASTAL CYCLING

Our original three rules gradually became ten. Then Steve drafted some further rules. Sometimes one of us was following a rule the other didn't recognise. But all was resolved amicably, and here are our Official Rules, combining the best from both lists, and omitting only the silly ones, which were mostly Steve's anyway. If you find any of all of these helpful on your own long-distance cycling trips, so much the better.

Rule One: Keep to the coast. Not the sandy beaches and the rocky cliffs, obviously. The tarmac will be fine. But some of the roads closest to the coast are dangerous dual carriageways. So we have:

Rule Two: Keep safe – avoid major roads. Be prepared to ignore Rule One to preserve life and limb, though a short stretch of trunk road sometimes saves a huge inland detour. What about the tiny roads leading only to a farm? These might double the distance you need to ride. So we arrive at:

Rule Three: Ignore dead-end roads. But looking at the map of Scotland, there are places we just had to visit – Ardnamurchan, Dunnet Head and Cape Wrath – all of them down dead-end roads. There might be more. So we have to add:

Rule Four: Visit interesting places. We have to get close to the furthest points on the mainland, so let's not waste the chance to see some nice places, even if those on dead-end roads. What about ferries? No that would be cheating, obviously. So:

Rule Five: No ferries! But on Scotland's west coast Mallaig and Kyle of Lochalsh are 20 miles apart as the crow flies, but 110 miles distant by road. The Armadale ferry to Skye avoids this two-day detour inland. We need a ferry to Cape Wrath anyway, and some estuaries would take a whole day to cycle round. So instead we have:

Rule Six: Avoid detours inland. Taking a ferry is sometimes a sensible short-cut. What about islands? Orkney and Shetland and the Scilly Isles? Each of them would add another week to the overall plan. Let's be reasonable:

Rule Seven: Visit islands as appropriate. Short cuts across Mull and Skye allow us to stay close to the mainland coast, upholding Rule One in spirit. No lounging around on islands! Meanwhile, the excellent Sustrans maps show national cycle trails and other recommended quiet roads. This seems the way to go, so we decided on:

Rule Eight: Keep to the Sustrans routes. The National Cycle Network covers many miles of coastal roads, and the maps often show alternative routes to avoid main roads. But from Aberdeen right round to Liverpool, lots of cities are on the coast. Neither of us enjoy urban cycling, so we decided to add:

Rule Nine: Avoid big places where possible. At least we might skirt round some of them, or sneak into them on cycle routes – like the canal towpath in the middle of Gloucester. But each trip means travelling to and from home, so we need:

Rule Ten: Start and finish each stage at a railway station. The advance booking and purchase of tickets for us and our bicycles is a story in itself. But away from big places and railway stations, we need to remind ourselves about the coast. So:

Rule Eleven: We have to see the sea every day. Otherwise it doesn't count. What's the point of cycling round the coast if you don't see it? We can't hug the coast all the time, but we need to keep it in mind. Of course coastal cycling is hard work, burning up calories, which need to be replaced to keep going. This leads us onto:

Rule Twelve: Look out for the next café. We need regular resting and refuelling stops. We need to look after ourselves. And it's not just cafés. When the weather turns nasty, you don't need to be big and brave. The next rule allows you to hide:

Rule Thirteen: Don't pass a bus shelter if it's raining. Time is not of the essence, so let's hide from the rain when we can. Bus shelters, bridges, and big trees can keep you dry sometimes. But when the rain stops, you may sometimes have different ideas about how to proceed. This could lead to disaster, so we need:

Rule Fourteen: Don't ignore each other, even if you know you're right. Should you disagree and head off in different directions, be ready to compromise, so that your paths cross again in the near future and you arrive at the same B&B. Meanwhile:

Rule Fifteen: Use pavements to avoid main roads. You shouldn't ride on the pavement in urban areas – it's bad manners, dangerous and illegal. (If only we could persuade car drivers that *parking* on the pavement is bad manners, dangerous and illegal!) But there are miles of rural pavements which save you getting mixed up with the traffic. Even a rough track is usually better than a main road. And finally:

Rule Sixteen: Rules are Made to Be Broken. Any or all of the above rules may be stretched, circumvented or ignored by mutual agreement. Especially if you're tired, hungry, bored, scared of traffic, or if you see something more interesting. Or if your bike has a mechanical failure. Or if your loved ones fall ill. Or for another reason you haven't thought of yet.

ACKNOWLEDGEMENTS AND BIBLIOGRAPHY

Many people contributed to these journeys. My cycling pal Steve has been a good friend, a source of constant amusement and moral support, and an excellent navigator and mechanic. Our long-suffering wives Caroline and Julie have tolerated our absences, welcomed us back home, and put up with us for decades. Steve and Caroline have read drafts of the text and added helpful comments and corrections.

My thanks to everyone who welcomed us into their B&B, guest house, pub or hotel, often showing great kindness to a pair of scruffy guests. Even the few who were grumpy, mean-spirited or drunk have added to the flavour of the book. Thanks also to the café and restaurant and pub staff who kept us fed and watered throughout, with coffee and scones and carrot cake, and some excellent evening meals and local beers.

Guardian angels appeared when we were lost or confused. A lorry driver showed us a quiet route away from a dangerous dual carriageway. Women walking their dogs pointed us towards the next village or café – or back onto the road we should have been on. A Taunton man guided us onto the towpath. Megan and Sophie from Sustrans led us to the Avonmouth Bridge. A white-bearded cyclist rode with me into Southport. A cyclist sitting on a bench at Seascale explained the easy way through to Sellafield. If any of you read this – thank you!

A special thank-you to the staff at St John Street Cycles in Bridgewater, who measured us for our wonderful Ravens, built the bikes up for us, and delivered all the spare parts we could possibly need. Our Ravens have been incredibly reliable and always a joy to ride. Further thanks to Palace Cycles in Carlisle and Aragon Cycles in Penrith for efficient servicing to keep us on the road.

Helpful information about places we visited were provided by: *The AA Illustrated Guide to Britain's Coast* – outdated now but still full of interesting detail; Sue Clifford and Angela King, *England in Particular* – crammed with quirky stuff about this unusual country; Nicholas Crane, *Great British Journeys* – with helpful historical background; Neil Oliver, *The Story of the British Isles in 100 Places* – an inspiring account of key sites in our island history; and Bill Bryson, *The Road to Little Dribbling* – a very funny sideways look at Britain and some of its inhabitants.

We were guided round constantly by the wonderful series of Sustrans maps, full of helpful information about hills, alternative routes and street plans. It wasn't their fault we got lost once or twice. *Traffic-Free Cycle Rides* (Sustrans, 2015) also gave us some useful route-finding tips. Final thanks to Anna Hughes, *Eat Sleep Cycle* (Summersdale, 2015) and Mike Carter, *One Man and His Bike* (Ebury

Press, 2012). Anna's athletic account convinced us that we were much too old to do this all at once.

ABOUT THE AUTHOR

Robert Bluck is a Zen practitioner, meditation teacher and cyclist. After retiring as an Open University lecturer, he rode from Cornwall to Shetland (including the Outer Hebrides), and then completed a 5,000-mile journey round the coast of mainland Britain. When not cycling, he is the Buddhist Chaplain at Durham University.

This book is printed on paper from sustainable sources managed under the Forest Stewardship Council (FSC) scheme.

It has been printed in the UK to reduce transportation miles and their impact upon the environment.

For every new title that Troubador publishes, we plant a tree to offset CO_2, partnering with the More Trees scheme.

For more about how Troubador offsets its environmental impact, see www.troubador.co.uk/sustainability-and-community